Volume
1

BiG as LiFE
The Everyday Inclusive Curriculum

by
Stacey York

Cover Illustration by Athena Hampton
Interior Illustrations by Susan Avishai

 **Redleaf Press**

BOWLING GREEN STATE UNIVERSITY
DISCARDED
LIBRARY

BOWLING GREEN STATE
UNIVERSITY LIBRARIES

P9-ASJ-439

©1998 Stacey York
All rights reserved.

Book design by MacLean & Tuminelly
Interior illustrations by Susan Avishai
Cover illustration by Athena Hampton

Published by: Redleaf Press
                  a division of Resources for Child Caring
                  450 N. Syndicate, Suite 5
                  St. Paul, MN 55104

Distributed by: Gryphon House
                  Mailing Address:
                  P.O. Box 207
                  Beltsville, MD 20704-0207

Library of Congress Cataloging-in-Publication Data

York, Stacey, 1957–
    Big as life : the everyday inclusive curriculum / by Stacey York.
        p.   cm.
    Includes bibliographical references and index.
    ISBN 1-884834-39-6 (v. 1). — ISBN 1-884834-51-5 (v. 2)
        1. Multicultural education—United States—Curricula.   2. Early
childhood education—United States—Curricula.   3. Curriculum
planning—United States.   4. Social values—Study and teaching
(Early childhood)—United States.   5. Early childhood education–
–Activity programs—United States.
    LC1099.3.Y67   1998
    370.117'0973—dc21   98-17429
                                                              CIP

DISCARDED
LIBRARY

CURR
371.9
Y636
V.1

Information and ideas in previous publications were instrumental to writing this book. The following acknowledges these sources and lists the activities they apply to in *Big As Life*:

Bittinger, Gayle. *Learning and Caring About Our World* (Everett, WA: Totline, 1990): Tree Snacks, Windup Toys. Brick, Peggy, et al. *Bodies, Birth, and Babies: Sexuality Education in Early Childhood Programs* (Hackensack, NJ: The Center for Family Life Education Planned Parenthood of Bergen County, 1989): Baby Bodies, Girl and Boy Bodies, Our Private Parts. Carlson, Laurie. *Kids Create!* (Charlotte, VT: Williamson, 1990): Pinwheels. Cutting, Beth J., and Ann Lovrien. *Parenting with a Global Perspective* (St. Paul: Vocational Consumer and Family Education Network, Minnesota State Board of Vocational Technical Education, 1986): Ecosystems. Edwards, Carolyn Pope. *Social and Moral Development in Young Children* (New York: Teachers College, 1986): Baby, Child, or Adult; Find a Way, Love and Affection, Size and Age, What Is the Right Name? Who Would You Ask? Green, Moira D. *474 Science Activities for Young Children* (Albany, NY: Delmar, 1996): Can You Balance Your Body? Models and Fashion Dolls, Name Reflections, Reflection Pictures, Surprise! Super Sound Conductors. Jenkins, Peggy. *The Joyful Child: A Sourcebook of Activities and Ideas for Releasing Children's Natural Joy* (Tucson, AZ: Harbinger, 1989): Affirmation Jar, Crayon Scribbles, Quality Cards, Simon Says. Judson, Stephanie, ed. *A Manual on Nonviolence and Children* (Gabriola Island, Canada: New Society, 1977): Playground Problem Solving. Kohl, MaryAnn, and Cindy Gainer. *Good Earth Art: Environmental Art for Kids* (Bellingham, WA: Bright Ring, 1991): Candles. Kohl, MaryAnn, and Jean Potter. *Science Arts: Discovering Science Through Art Experiences* (Bellingham, WA: Bright Ring, 1993): Volcano. Kohl, MaryAnn. *Scribble Cookies* (Bellingham, WA: Bright Ring, 1985): Batik Printing, Individual Weavings. Kubat, Patricia, et al. *Teaching Young Children About African-Americans* (Minneapolis: Greater Minneapolis Day Care Association, 1990): Rock School. Kissinger, Katie. *All the Colors We Are* (St. Paul: Redleaf, 1994): Skin Color. Lewis, Barbara A. *The Kid's Guide to Service Projects* (Minneapolis: Free Spirit, 1995): Accessibility Check, Book Drive, Clean Air Please, Playground Request, School-Age Program. Moll, Patricia Buerke. *Children and Books I: African American Story Books and Activities for All Children* (Tampa: Hampton Mae Institute, 1991): I've Got the Blues. Nichols, Wendy, and Kim Nichols. *Wonderscience: A Developmentally Appropriate Guide to Hands On Science for Young Children* (Albuquerque: Learning Expo, 1990): Tele-phones. Oppenheim, Carol. *Science Is Fun! For Families and Classroom Groups* (St. Louis: Cracom, 1993): Thunder and Lightning. Orlick, Terry. *The Cooperative Sports & Games Book* (New York: Pantheon, 1978): Find a Place for Everyone. Orlick, Terry. *The Second Cooperative Sports & Games Book* (New York: Pantheon, 1982): Rock-a-Bye Baby. Prutzman, Priscilla, et al. *The Friendly Classroom for a Small Planet* (Gabriola Island, Canada: New Society, 1988): Breathing Exercise, Family Roots, Story Dancers. Rockwell, Robert E., et al. *Everybody Has a Body* (Beltsville, MD: Gryphon, 1992): Glasses, Grab This, Hands That Help, Muscle Testing, Put Your Hands Together For…, Tooth Decay. Slaby, Ronald G., et al. *Early Violence Prevention Tools for Teachers of Young Children* (Washington, DC: NAEYC, 1995): I'm Mad! Smith, Charles A. *The Peaceful Classroom* (Beltsville, MD: Gryphon, 1993): Babies! Class Banner, Classroom Tree, Disabilities, Feelings Drawings, Hand Talk, Hand Words, Learn Our Names, Our Bodies Show How We Feel, Our Class Mobile, Part of the Picture, Picture Yourself, Red Rover, What Are Feelings? Smith, Charles A. *Promoting the Social Development of Young Children: Strategies and Activities* (Palo Alto, CA: Mayfield, 1982): I Like My Body. Sunal, Cynthia. *Early Childhood Social Studies* (Columbus, OH: Merrill, 1990): What a Wonderful Person You Are. Williams, Robert A., et al. *Mudpies to Magnets: A Preschool Science Curriculum* (Beltsville, MD: Gryphon, 1987): Are You Wound Up? Mud Houses. York, Stacey. *Roots and Wings: Affirming Culture in Early Childhood Programs* (St. Paul: Redleaf, 1991): Baby Pictures, Boy and Girl Paper Dolls, Boy and Girl Picture Cards, Body Picture Cards, Carving, Children at School Picture Cards, Classmates Paper Dolls, Classroom Scrapbook, Communication Picture Cards, Cultural Diversity Picture Cards, Daily Life and Celebrations, Discovering My Body, Environment Picture Cards, Face Puzzles, Family Photos, Family Picture Cards, Feelings Picture Cards, Felt Families, Felt Friends, Finger Paint Mix-Up, Folktales, Group Tree, Hair, Homes, How Do You Feel About Color? How Would You Feel If…? Just Like Me/Just Like You, Line Up, Match-Ups, My Voice, Patterns, Photo Masks, Pottery, Real and Pretend, Similar To Me, Skin Color Match-Ups, Skin-Colored Playdough, Smelling Jars, Sock Puppets, Sound Choice, Thumbprints, Touching Game, True or False, Washing, Weaving, We're All Human, Where Does My Family Comes From? Who Is Missing?

To all early childhood teachers
whose "good works" make a difference in children's lives each day
and who live without receiving appreciation, adoration,
or a worthy wage.

CONTENTS

ACKNOWLEDGMENTS

It has taken me almost five years to get *Big As Life* into your hands. The book may bear one name, but many people helped along the way. First and foremost, I want to thank God for the vision, inspiration, and perseverance. This book is not about me.

I'd like to thank Jane Toleno for helping me brainstorm the first drafts of the curriculum webs. Thanks to Eileen Nelson and Redleaf Press for their willingness to publish it. I'd like to thank Ruth Fahlman, Ann Griffin, Theresa Lenear, and Fran Mattson for reviewing the first draft. Special thanks to Mary Pat Martin for her careful reading and wonderful suggestions, and to Joan Bibeau for her careful review of the first draft. Her stories and ideas about how she would use *Big As Life* in her classroom were so affirming.

Thanks to Beth Wallace, Rosemary Wallner, and Mary Steiner Whelan, who edited and shaped *Big As Life*. Thanks to Sharon Cronin, Louise Derman-Sparks, Sharon Henry, and Cirecie Olatunji for providing support, encouragement, and the most incredible environment for thinking through anti-bias issues.

I'm always grateful for my women's spirituality group—Ann, Barbara, Denise, Mary Jo, Michele, and Nancy. For eleven years you've given me a safe place to be and grow.

A big hug and kiss to my husband, Dennis, who says my writing *Big As Life* meant him suffering so others could benefit. Thanks to my family, who kept asking, "Aren't you done with that yet?" They showed me that I could live among them *and* write, be it on the floor, couch, or bed. Writing seated cross-legged on the living room floor while hosting a Super Bowl party was my greatest accomplishment.

I couldn't have kept my family happy and finished *Big As Life* without my trusty Macintosh PowerBook, which got hit by lightning and didn't skip a beat. Whoever said soda pop, crumbs, drool, dog hair, wet tennis balls, and computers don't mix?

And finally, an "Atta dog!" to Biko and Dakotah, my two faithful writing companions.

PREFACE

Developing curriculum is a fun and creative process. Like many teachers, I have curriculum materials all over the place. Activity books with dog-eared and high-lighted pages fill my bookshelves. Open any drawer in my home or office and you are likely to find unintelligible notes about curriculum ideas scribbled on scrap paper, napkins, and the back of deposit slips. Down in the basement, banker's boxes full of old curriculum materials fill a storage closet. And of course there are my old reliable and beloved curriculum activity files that I compiled in college.

Even with all of these resources, curriculum planning was often frustrating. I knew I had good ideas, I just couldn't find them. Suddenly I had a compelling feeling to pull together all of my curriculum resources—and the organizing, writing, and rewriting began. Now many of my favorite resources are all in one place. I am excited to share them with you.

I have wanted to write a curriculum book for a long time. *Big As Life* is as much for me as it is for you. I would like to know how you used this book and found it helpful in planning your curriculum. You can write to me in care of the publisher, Redleaf Press. I also encourage you to share your ideas with others. Through sharing ideas, resources, and successes and failures, we can all make our curriculum even better!

When I first completed the unit webs and outlines, I laid them out on the floor. It was amazing to see them all at once. For the first time I knew how possible it is to weave multicultural/anti-bias education into the curriculum. Immediately upon seeing the webs, I knew that this curriculum was very do-able. It's not beyond us. It's within our reach. It just takes some time and energy to think it through. It takes a conscious effort to transform the curriculum from the ground up. The end result is a curriculum that is simple, straightforward, and practical.

At the same moment, I also realized that this was big. I kept telling people, "This is big. This is really big." After all, here were sixteen units that intentionally addressed emotions, social skills, culture, diversity, critical thinking, and social action. In a new and deeper way, I realized how multicultural/anti-bias education could change our lives. I knew with every bone in my body that early childhood educators could make a positive difference.

I relived this experience four years later, when I completed the first draft of the manuscript. It was late at night. Everyone else in my family had gone to bed. I sat staring at this huge stack of over 600 pages. My only thought was, "This is big." I walked around the house in amazement, mumbling to myself, "This is big. This is really big." And then a voice inside me said, "Stacey, *life* is big."

It's true. Life is big. What better gift to give children than to give them life, to give them big lives? Life alone is worthy of being the center of education. A curriculum of life gives each of us a sense of belonging, meaning, fullness, conviction, and commitment. This curriculum invites each of us—children, parents, and teachers—to embrace life.

This curriculum makes me laugh. Whenever I think about it, I smile, shrug my shoulders, and shake my head in amazement. Life is good. Life is to be lived. Life is big. Here before us is a curriculum that's as big as life.

Stacey York
September 1997

INTRODUCTION

Integrating Multicultural/Anti-Bias Education into the Curriculum

Big As Life is an answer to a question that has challenged me for the past seven years: How can you integrate multicultural/anti-bias education into the curriculum so that it is a natural part of the day?

During the past few years, I have witnessed significant changes in a large portion of the early childhood community's approach to multicultural education. When I first began training teachers, they asked me dozens of questions about the relevancy of multicultural education, including, "Do we really need this?" "Is multicultural education developmentally appropriate for young children?" and "Why should I do multicultural education when all of my children are the same?" These questions reflected our profession's ignorance about the role of culture in our lives, the impact of racism on children's development, and children's development of prejudice.

The questions have changed over the past few years. Today teachers rarely ask me if multicultural education is important. Most teachers I work with have purchased multicultural materials for their classrooms. They have posters, dolls, children's books, and art materials that represent all the different colors of skin. They implement activities like tasting breads from many cultures, and they talk with children about similarities and differences. These teachers are convinced that this work is important. They know it is relevant to children's life experiences and their level of development. Now they are searching for ways to go beyond what they have begun. They ask me more advanced questions like the following:

How can I make multicultural education a natural part of the day?

How can I integrate multicultural education into the curriculum?

I feel like I'm not doing enough. There's got to be more, but I'm not sure what it is. Can you give me some ideas?

We're serving a different population than we used to, and our curriculum isn't relevant—it just doesn't seem to be effective. How can I make the curriculum relevant to the children in my class?

I want to explore diversity with the children in a deeper way, but I don't want to make any of the children feel "different"—you know, put on the spot and ashamed. What can I do?

Teach to the Whole Child

Whether we are early childhood educators, child care workers, parents, or administrators, we need a curriculum that truly fosters the development of the whole child. We cannot forget that all areas of development are interwoven. The development of self-identity, emotional health, and social skills are foundational elements of a multicultural/anti-bias curriculum. As a field, we have made great strides in improving the cognitive and language components of the early childhood curriculum. We must continue to support children's physical and creative development.

Use A Relevant Curriculum

We live in a society that is changing quickly. Young children today are much different from young children five years ago. The issues that early childhood educators face are much more complex and challenging than anything faced by classroom teachers in the seventies and eighties. In many cases, the curriculum has not kept up with these changes. We need a curriculum that helps children deal with and make sense out of their lives. We need a curriculum that instills hope, pride, and self-confidence in children while empowering them to take positive action on behalf of themselves and others.

The Purpose of This Book

1. To offer a curriculum planning process that incorporates the children and their families' lives.
2. To offer a curriculum that integrates multicultural and anti-bias education.
3. To offer a curriculum that fosters the development of the whole child, with equal emphasis on self-identity, cognitive, language, physical, creative, emotional, and social development.
4. To offer a curriculum that reflects and honors the lives of children and their families.

Big As Life is a follow-up to my earlier book *Roots and Wings: Affirming Culture in Early Childhood Programs*. It is my attempt to integrate multicultural/anti-bias education into early childhood curriculum. I want this book and its information to excite you, inspire you, and empower you to create and implement a curriculum that reflects and honors the lives of children, families, and communities.

How to Use This Book

This book is divided into two parts. Part 1 outlines the elements of a transformative curriculum, including its relevant goals and objectives. This information is a summary of my experience as well as that of other professionals. At the end of part 1 is a list of recommended resources for further information on a transformative curriculum.

The eight curriculum units presented in part 2 put the information in part 1 into practice. Within these units you will find everything you need to conceptualize, plan, and present a curriculum unit.

At the beginning of each unit is a description of how young children might approach the topic. A web and unit outline help you visualize the content and flow. The section entitled "Teaching Through the Interest Areas," suggests materials to add to each interest area to support the curriculum unit. The areas are presented alphabetically: Art, Blocks, Dramatic Play, Literacy, Manipulatives, Music, Science, and Sensory.

"Investigating the Theme," the largest section of each unit, contains activity ideas to support the development of the whole child. Math, critical thinking, and science activities support children's cognitive development. Creative development is addressed by activities that focus on art and music. Also included are activities that focus on emotional, social, and language development. Physical development and health, safety, and nutrition activities can also be found within this section.

"Affirming Ourselves and One Another" contains activities that focus on cultural identity, diversity, bias and stereotypes, human rights, social action, and community service.

"Opening the Door" is the final activities section of each unit. In this section, suggestions to support parent involvement, parent education, classroom visitors, and field trips encourage parent and community involvement.

"Classroom Resources" contains a list of commercial resources that support the unit, including visual displays, children's books, videos, music, computer software, organizations, and teaching kits. At the beginning of each unit you will find a materials list for each classroom interest area. You will find more information, including company information and print materials, in the "Resources and References" section at the back of the book.

When using this curriculum, keep the following points in mind:

The Author's Perspective. I am a European American woman. I live with my family in a middle-class suburb in the Midwest. I teach child development at a community college located in downtown Minneapolis. This multicultural/anti-bias curriculum comes from a European American perspective—it makes sense to me given my life experience. This curriculum was not developed by a multicultural collective. It does not move the center of focus from European Americans to the experiences of people of color.

With that in mind, I ask you to examine the curriculum from your perspective. Please read this book with a critical eye, stay true to your center, and do not veer from what you know in your heart to be right for the children, families, and community.

A Work in Progress. This book is a work in progress. Some of the ideas have been tested in a variety of early childhood programs. Some have not. Please make this curriculum your own. Web your own units. Adapt the activities. Add your own ideas.

Recognize the Developmental Level. This curriculum is written for children four through eight years old. Some of the activities may not fit the children in your program. They may not be developmentally appropriate. They may be too simple or too advanced. Some of the fine-motor or art activities, for example, may be beyond the developmental level of four year olds. Some of the math and critical thinking activities may be too simple for seven and eight year olds. Adjust the curriculum to match the developmental level of your class.

Reflect Your Context. The activities may not reflect the context of your program. You may need to revise and adapt them to fit the cultures and daily lives of the children and their families. For example, many classrooms are made up of children who speak many different home languages. It is not uncommon for classrooms to have three to five languages represented among the students. Each unit in this curriculum includes some simple suggestions of ways to incorporate children's home languages. Even if all the children in your classroom speak the same language, you can introduce them to other languages by singing songs, reading books, learning words, and presenting activities in another language.

Take What Fits and Leave the Rest. Each unit contains lots of activity ideas—this is to show you the possibilities and spark your creativity. Please don't feel that you have to present every activity. Half-day programs and programs that meet fewer than five days a week have particular time constraints. It would not be wise, or even feasible, to incorporate so many activities into the curriculum. On the other hand, if you teach in a full-day program that meets five days a week, you will likely find that having so many ideas at your fingertips is helpful.

Respect But Don't Burden Children. This curriculum addresses a wide variety of social realities. It incorporates self-identity, human diversity, housing, violence, and environmental pollution. Teachers must help children be competent within their lives and yet not burden children by overexposing them to all the injustices in the world. Too often, though, teachers and adults underestimate children's awareness of social issues.

We need to respect children's ability to see and make sense of what is going on in the world around them. For example, I recently had the opportunity to work with preschoolers who experienced a flood. They clearly understood that the river over-flowed its banks and the water filled up their homes and their toys floated away and now they had to live in a motel.

Other instances can be used to empower and teach children. For example, this year a large portion of the trees in the wooded area where I live were cut down to build townhouses. As a result, the five deer that lived in the area are gone. We no longer see them walking down the street or eating the grass in our yards. When we get together with neighbors, we talk about the loss of the deer. For young children in our area, this experience is an introduction to the wants and needs of animals and endangered species.

In both instances, children can be empowered by helping them analyze, make decisions, and take action about the injustices in their daily experiences. And we can introduce them to adults who are working to solve community problems, helping those in need, or fighting injustice.

PART 1

A Vision For Education

The Purpose of Education: Transform Individuals and Society

I believe that the purpose of education is personal empowerment and social change. Education empowers individuals when it helps them understand how their lives are touched by the prevailing social forces. We need to learn how to recognize the ways in which our identities are influenced by society. We are empowered when we understand how ethnocentrism, racism, sexism, classism, ableism, and homophobia impact our lives.

We live in a democracy. The strength of a democracy comes from the active participation of its citizens. Education should prepare children to participate actively and positively in their neighborhoods and communities. Education should also seek to prepare children to challenge parts of society that are hurtful, biased, or destructive. Education can help children learn to work together to transform society so that it better serves the interests of all groups of people. This approach to education is called "transformative education" because, ultimately, it seeks to transform both the child and society.

This way of thinking about education calls for a dynamic curriculum that changes and adapts to different classrooms and communities. We need a curriculum that connects children and teachers to our neighborhoods and communities. We need a curriculum that empowers children to become positive active forces in their communities. To support the goals of transformative education, we need a transformative curriculum.

What Is Curriculum?

Curriculum is everything we do with children. It is a road map, a blueprint for learning. It provides guidance and direction. It helps you translate child development into educational practice. Therefore, it is a core component of an early childhood education program.

There are many approaches to curriculum in use today. Some of the best known are Bank Street, Reggio Emilia, High/Scope, emergent curriculum, Montessori, and the Creative Curriculum. A transformative curriculum is compatible with many other approaches. While each of these approaches differs from the others, they share the following basic elements.

Philosophy. Every approach to curriculum is based on underlying beliefs about how children learn, what children should learn, and the role of education in our society. Many curriculum models have a philosophy statement that makes these beliefs explicit. The section above entitled "The Purpose of Education" could be considered part of a philosophy statement for a transformative curriculum.

Goals and Objectives. Goals and objectives are the bridge between child development theory and the curriculum. Early childhood education goals and objectives should be based on our knowledge of child development. Goals are the general statements that describe what we hope will happen as a result of participating in an educational program. Objectives are the specific outcomes or indicators that we use to monitor our progress in reaching the curriculum goals. The curriculum is the journey we take with the children. The goals are the roads we take to reach our journey's end, and the objectives are the signposts that keep us on track along the way.

Teaching Methods. The teaching methods used in early childhood education are fairly consistent across the different curriculum models. Most contain free-choice play, small-group time, and large-group time.

Free-choice play is a child-directed teaching method in which the classroom is arranged into interest areas. Materials are set out on low open shelves and rotated regularly. Children choose where they want to play and spend a significant amount of time, usually at least 45 to 60 minutes, actively engaged in free-choice play. The teacher prepares the learning environment, helps children make choices, and facilitates and extends their play. Teachers also offer planned activities for individual and small groups of children in the various interest areas. For example, a special collage activity might be offered in the art area, a cooking activity in the science area, and a story writing activity in the book area.

Small-group time is a teacher-directed learning experience. Usually the class is divided into small groups of children. Each adult takes a small group and facilitates a planned activity designed to foster one of the curriculum goals.

Large-group time is a teacher-directed learning experience in which the entire class comes together. It is often conducted on the floor, where children sit cross-legged in a circle. Large-group times may consist of music, movement, singing, storytelling, creative dramatics, role-playing, and discussions.

Educational Content. Some early childhood programs emphasize social development, while others emphasize cognitive development. The content of an early childhood curriculum should be comprehensive. It should foster the development of the whole child. Its goals, objectives, and learning experiences should address all areas of development: physical, cognitive, language, social, emotional, self-identity, and creative.

Elements of a Transformative Curriculum

A transformative curriculum has seven key elements that make it different from traditional early childhood curriculum.

1. The curriculum is *contextually relevant*. It accurately reflects the cultural, social, political, and geographic context of the children and families.

2. The curriculum *accommodates the changing nature of knowledge* and supports children in making meaning out of their lives and the world around them.

3. Adults and children are *co-learners and co-teachers*, investigating the curriculum content together and learning from one another.

4. The curriculum is *child-centered*, reflecting the children's daily lives, questions, and passions.

5. The curriculum is *inquiry-based*. Children learn to think for themselves through open-ended questioning, problem posing, analyzing, reflecting, and problem solving.

6. The curriculum is *integrated* and addresses all areas of development. Traditional subject areas like reading and math are taught through the exploration of the content, which is the children's lives.

7. The curriculum results in *empowerment through taking reflective action*. Children learn to stand up for themselves and others.

This means that we need a curriculum that

    Focuses on people rather than objects
    Uses a discovery or inquiry approach
    Reflects children's real lives and real experiences
    Fully integrates diversity
    Helps children connect their experiences to educational content
    Helps children value human life
    Promotes appreciation for community
    Provides children with an opportunity to experience democratic living
    Promotes depth of learning

Teaching "In Context"

Education should be grounded in the present and contextually relevant. It must be relevant to the context of the children's lives. The word *context* refers to the social environment in which the children live. It is the cultural, historical, social, and political makeup of the community. Children's extended families, neighborhoods, communities, geographic regions, and home cultures make up the context in which learning takes place.

The curriculum should reflect the geographic region. A program in Alaska or in the southern United States should look different from one in the Northern Plains. The curriculum used in a rural school should differ from those in urban and suburban schools. The curriculum should also reflect the culture of the children and families. More specifically, the curriculum in a Native American Head Start program in the Northern Plains should differ from the curriculum in a Native American Head Start program in the Southwest. A Baptist preschool located in a suburb of a major city should have a curriculum that is different from the one used by a downtown child care center. Creating curriculum from the context of our lives means there are no simple and fast recipes. Cookie-cutter curriculum cannot possibly take into consideration and reflect the context in which children and families live.

Knowledge Is Constructed and Reconstructed

Knowledge is always in process and constantly undergoing transformation. Knowledge changes as we try to make meaning out of our life experiences. For example, our understanding of family changes with our life experiences. A marriage, a divorce, the death of a parent, or the birth of a child all cause us to rethink and create a new meaning of family. We need a curriculum model that accommodates the changing nature of knowledge and encourages children to make meaning out of their lives and the world around them. This kind of curriculum fosters self-awareness by focusing children and teachers on the process of exploration, discovery, and constructing knowledge ("making meaning"), as well as on the products created.

Co-Learning and Co-Teaching

In transformative education, teachers and children learn together. A teacher cannot come into a community or a classroom assuming to know more about the children and families than they know about themselves. Nor can a teacher enter a community expecting to fix the children and families. Teachers do not have the right to teach their life experiences as though they were models for humanity. The teacher's role is to draw the life experiences and knowledge out of the students and then help them make their own sense out of it. Teachers are not all-knowing, pouring information into the children as though they were empty pots. Teachers become investigators, asking questions and looking for answers with the children. You learn from, as well as teach, the children and families. Together you share responsibility for the learning process. As a result, the children and parents also become teacher-learners.

Child-Centered

Often education treats children as objects. They are objects to be trained, objects to receive information from the all-knowing teacher, and objects to be filled with knowledge.

Transformative education views children as the subject of the curriculum. Teachers study the children's lives, their passions, and their questions. A transformative curriculum empowers children by helping children see themselves as the primary actors in their own lives, to see themselves as important in and of themselves.

Inquiry-Based

In a transformative curriculum, learning is a dialogue. Teachers present the curriculum content as a question for others to answer, or as a problem for others to solve. Teachers and children pass the questions back and forth. Everyone shares, expands, analyzes, and challenges life experiences, ideas, thoughts, and feelings. Teachers provide experiences to help children reflect on their lives, broaden their understanding of their lives, and create meaning in their lives. Presenting problems to solve changes the teacher's role. The teacher now asks questions, guides children through the discovery process, and helps children find answers to questions by connecting them to a variety of resources.

Integrated Learning

Traditional curricula focus on subject areas such as language arts, math, science, and social studies. Teachers teach each subject in distinct sections separate from other subject areas. This organization results in a specific "math time," to be followed by "reading time," and so on. Although teachers cover all areas of the curriculum, the subjects are unrelated to one another, and skills are taught apart from a unifying context that would make them meaningful to children.

A transformative curriculum teaches to the whole child. It fosters development on all levels. Subjects like reading or math and developmental areas like language or cognitive development are integrated into the study of a unifying content area, or theme. Teachers integrate into the curriculum learning experiences designed to foster specific areas of development or, often, several specific areas of development at the same time. For example, children might develop language (or study reading, for older children) by telling or writing stories, doing research, writing letters, looking at books, having conversations, and so forth, *about* a topic that interests them, like families. An integrated curriculum is like a tapestry. The children's lives are interwoven with carefully planned learning experiences you design to foster the total development of the child.

Empowerment Through Taking Action

Knowledge alone is not power. Nothing is more disempowering than becoming fully aware of a situation and not having any ideas of what to do. A curriculum that helps children understand bias or violence but does not help them take action toward change ultimately breeds a sense of being overwhelmed and feelings of hopelessness.

A transformative curriculum empowers individuals and fosters social change. Empowered children can think for themselves and act on their own behalf. The dialogical learning process helps children break free from limiting socially prescribed roles and identities. The teacher helps children to think about their options and the consequences of their behavior and learn to take reflective action rather than simply react.

There are different types of action. Reaction is a mindless, purely emotional response to a given situation—as when a child hits another child in anger. Inaction is when we do nothing, even though we know better or may desire to do something but don't have the courage. Reflective action is a thoughtful response to a situation. Reflective action can be individual (one child acting alone), or it can be a group response (a number of children acting together). Reflective action can be on behalf of ourselves and our own best interest, or it can be on behalf of the well-being of others.

Teachers must be very thoughtful when encouraging children to take action. There is a fine line between an adult giving children the opportunity and support to stand against injustice and an adult using children to take a personal stand against injustice. I think of tired, cranky children being "forced" to walk a picket line or march with adults on an issue that only the adults are passionate about. This type of action does not empower a child.

We must also keep in mind the social and political context of taking action. Are children of color being put in potentially dangerous situations when they are taught and encouraged to take action against social injustice? How do teachers help children decide when, where, and how to take action? When is standing silently or turning and walking away the most powerful response?

The Goals of a Transformative Curriculum

Early childhood multicultural education/anti-bias is now in its toddlerhood. Through working with others, I have come to believe that having a knowledgeable and positive cultural identity and providing culturally relevant education are the most important things that we as early childhood educators can do in the name of multicultural education.

I have identified nine goals of a transformative curriculum. The first four have been adapted from the four goals of an anti-bias curriculum that were originally developed by Louise Derman-Sparks and the ABC Task Force in *Anti-Bias Curriculum: Tools for Empowering Young Children,* and then further refined by Carol Brunson Phillips. The last five address specific areas of child development.

The nine goals of a transformative curriculum are

1. To foster each child's construction of a positive, knowledgeable self-identity within a cultural context.

2. To foster each child's comfortable, empathetic interaction with diversity among people.

3. To foster each child's critical thinking about bias.

4. To foster each child's ability to stand up for himself or herself and others in the face of bias.

5. To foster each child's social and emotional development.

6. To foster each child's cognitive development.

7. To foster each child's language development.

8. To foster each child's creative development.

9. To foster each child's physical development.

Because the first four may be less familiar, I have discussed them at length in the following section.

A Positive, Knowledgeable Self-Identity

The first goal addresses the child's self-identity within a cultural context. The goal encompasses two parts of identity—*self-identity* and *group identity*.

SELF-IDENTITY

A Vision for
Education

A POSITIVE,
KNOWLEDGEABLE
SELF-IDENTITY

Self-identity is a more current term for *self-concept*. Self-concept is what a person thinks about himself or herself. To have a positive self-identity you have to know who you are.

According to Louise Derman-Sparks, self-identity also includes self-esteem, self-confidence, and self-evaluation (Derman-Sparks, 1989). In other words, self-identity not only involves knowing who you are, but it also involves how you feel about who you are. The goal of a multicultural curriculum is to help children recognize and become knowledgeable about themselves and develop positive feelings about their identities.

Children's sense of self can be strengthened or weakened by the people around them. Adults give children a sense of who they are and their place in the world. Children must experience acceptance, acknowledgment, respect, and pride in who they are. Otherwise, they may become confused about themselves, reject their identity, and try to be like somebody else. If an adult rejects or denies children's true identities, it can also cause them to feel abnormal and deficient.

As you foster children's self-identity, however, it is very important to involve the families. Different geographic regions, cultural communities, families, and individuals have differing views on this topic, and you will need the families' guidance.

Self-identity can be a particularly tender topic for biracial families and individuals. Some biracial people may feel that they fit comfortably into either world. But a biracial family or child may also struggle with a sense of alienation ("I don't belong in either world—it's like I'm suspended between the two"). Some parents may tell their biracial children that they are one identity or the other. A child in this situation may become confused if the family and school differ in their definition of who the child is. Involving families as you foster children's self-identity will help avoid this unnecessary confusion.

GROUP IDENTITY

The term *self-concept* became limiting because it viewed identity from a purely individual basis. Children form their self-identities based upon society's expectations of them. Our society teaches children that skin color, gender, home language, culture, social class, religion, sexual orientation, and whether or not a person has a disability matters. Recently, we have begun to better understand how society impacts the formation of self- identities. As a result, the definition has been expanded to include group identity.

Group identity includes awareness and pride of one's physical features, culture, home language, gender, age, physical ability, social class, religion, and family structure. Group identity can be multilayered and complex. For example, a Latina girl who is hearing impaired or an African American man who is gay identify with more than one group. In these instances, the individual's family and extended family play a large role in helping the person learn who they are.

Children begin to form their group identity in the early years. For example, it is common for two year olds to introduce themselves by holding up two fingers or announcing, "I'm two." At this stage of life, age is a core aspect of the child's self-identities. By age three or four, many children of color identify themselves in terms of their ethnicity. At age three, Jamaica introduced herself by announcing all in one breath, "I'm-Jamaica-I'm-African-American!"

Unfortunately, children grow up in a biased society. In mainstream United States society, light skin is preferred over dark skin, boys are preferred over girls, youth is preferred over maturity, people who are able-bodied are preferred over people with disabilities, European cultural patterns are preferred over African, Asian, Native American, or Latino cultural traditions.

Children's development of a group identity is harmed by society's mixed messages and double standards. By the age of five, most children prefer the mainstream values and have begun internalizing the negative value given to women, people of color, the elderly, people of different sexual orientations, and the physically challenged. It's not uncommon to hear a preschool girl say, "I wish I could be a boy because boys can be doctors." A four-year-old girl who is Deaf signed to her parents that she would be able to hear like her friends when she grew up. A six-year-old Hmong boy refused to look at the classroom display of Hmong quilts and handicrafts. He shook his head and walked away saying, "Hmong, yuck!"

The child's internalization of society's biases often results in denying and rejecting a part of one's own self to feel acceptable to mainstream society. This is a concern because a strong group identity and orientation help children of color, children with disabilities, and girls cope with and challenge the potentially damaging impact of societal bias against them.

On the other hand, children who are European American, male, or able-bodied risk internalizing society's false messages of superiority. As members of the groups with social power, they are being socialized into internalized entitlement. At four and five we hear comments from these children like "White girls go first" and "I don't have to listen to you, Black teacher." A challenge to teachers is how to help European American children, boys, able-bodied children, and wealthy children maintain high self-esteem without having them feel like they are better than everyone else.

Providing a culturally relevant learning environment is the best way to foster children's self-identities. It is within a cultural context that children learn who they are and how to behave. It is the strong, positive, knowledgeable cultural identity that will give the child the drive to succeed and the personal strength to endure bias.

A positive self-identity within a cultural context is the focus of the first goal of a transformative curriculum because it lays the foundation for getting along with others. Once children have an accurate understanding of who they are, it is much easier for them to differentiate themselves from others and accept others for who they are. With a positive and accurate self-identity, children are likely to develop empathy for those who are different. They are able to feel what others might feel. Children with a strong self-identity have a higher degree of self-awareness which, in turn, allows them to become aware of others. It's also the development of a strong sense of self that allows us to stand up for ourselves.

Comfortable Interaction with Diversity

Diversity is all around us and in every aspect of our lives. Given the diversity in American society, we need to raise future generations who are not limited by stereotypic thinking and prejudices. The second goal of a transformative curriculum focuses on helping children to appreciate, live side-by-side, and work cooperatively with many different kinds of people. The bottom line of this goal is treating each other well—treating each other with respect and dignity. That's how we will know if we have really achieved comfortable interaction with people who are different from us.

Acknowledging different ways of being prepares children for living in a diverse society. It teaches them to accept the range of human diversity and to not feel threatened when they see or are around people who are different from them. Once children have an accurate understanding of who they are, it is much easier for them to differentiate themselves from those who are different from themselves. The ability to accept and comfortably interact with people who are different from us is an essential tool for living in a diverse society.

Children become aware of human characteristics at a very early age. Infants as young as six months notice skin color. By age two, children are aware of physical features, gender differences, and obvious physical disabilities. They often show their interest in others by staring, pointing, or touching another child's hair or skin. Three year olds notice language differences. They begin to ask questions about the characteristics they notice. Fours and fives become increasingly aware of and interested in cultural practices. They are curious about how people eat, speak, dress, move, work, and carry out family roles.

Between the ages of two and seven, children form beliefs, preferences, and attitudes about human diversity. Children take the messages they receive from friends, family, the community, and the media and organize them in their own way. They form ideas about the meaning of physical features, culture, age, gender, money, and disabilities. They begin to construct their own (often inaccurate) beliefs about why people are different and where they fit in. Young children also begin to develop strong positive or negative feelings about how they look.

Young children make many errors in their thinking as they begin to construct their social beliefs. They are often confused about which parts of themselves will stay the same and which parts of themselves will change as they grow up. A young European American child says to her Asian American playmate, "I'm gonna have eyes like yours when I grow up." Children are also easily confused by subtle differences, such as why two people with different skin tones consider themselves part of the same racial group. Young children's errors can take the form of false associations and over-generalizations. They tend to assume that height is an indicator of age. They think children who are taller are older than children who are shorter. A four-year-old boy may be afraid to try the Spanish rice his classmates made because he thinks it will make him speak Spanish. A five year old may announce that her teacher cannot be a mom because she is visually impaired.

STEREOTYPIC THINKING

During the early years, children begin to base their thinking on stereotypes. "That's a girl toy!" "She can't be my friend. She has icky clothes." "We hate handicaps." "You got a boy haircut." These statements by preschoolers show that they have begun to internalize the prevailing social attitudes within their community.

PREJUDICE

Prejudice is a learned behavior defined as a preconceived judgment of a person or group of people made without really knowing them. Preconceived ideas housed in the subconscious are at the root of prejudice. These subliminal thoughts are actually stereotypes, which can trigger feelings such as fear or anger. The combination of stereotypic thinking and the accompanying emotions result in prejudicial behavior.

Prejudice or discriminatory behavior emerges around age three and is fully formed by age twelve. Children often acquire bias through parents, family members, friends, neighbors, schoolmates, teachers, the curriculum, and the media (most often television). Children mimic attitudes and prevailing beliefs of the adults with whom they have contact. Prejudice is therefore the direct result of the society in which they live.

Prejudice can be passive or aggressive. Silence is the most common form of passive prejudice; however, it can also include ignoring, avoiding, and distancing. Aggressive forms of prejudice include name-calling, teasing, taunting, rejecting, threatening, or beating. Passive prejudice is demonstrated when a child avoids a classroom aide who speaks with a strong accent by refusing to talk to her, or when an able-bodied child distances herself from a child who has cerebral palsy by refusing to hold hands with him on a field trip. Aggressive prejudice is demonstrated when a European American child calls a Native American child "redskin" or when a group of boys playing in the block area shout, "No girls allowed!" and refuse to let them play too. It is important to remember that anyone can be prejudiced toward any aspect of human diversity.

Critical and Creative Thinking About Bias

The third goal of a transformative curriculum focuses on fostering children's critical thinking skills. Critical thinking involves identifying the problem, gathering and analyzing information, and drawing conclusions. This process will help young children recognize bias when it occurs. They can learn to identify stereotypes and analyze a situation of bias in terms of fairness ("Is this fair or unfair?").

Creative thinking is related to critical thinking. Creative thinking involves using information to create new and original solutions to problems created by bias.

We can begin working with children around these issues by providing children with simple explanations. For example, try to define *stereotype* and *prejudice* to young children. You might say something like the following:

A Vision for
Education
___

STANDING UP FOR
ONESELF AND
OTHERS IN THE
FACE OF BIAS

Stereotype is a word you might not know. A stereotype can be a picture or an idea. Stereotypes make us think that all people from a group are the same. Stereotypes are not true. Stereotypes confuse us. When you hear people say *all* or *never* about a group of people, that's a signal that they are lumping all people together.

Prejudice is when someone doesn't like you, and they don't really know you. Prejudice is judging people by the way that they look, or disliking people because they are different from you. Prejudice is not treating people fairly or equally. Prejudice is not playing with someone, not sitting by someone, name-calling, teasing, or laughing at someone because you don't like how they look. Prejudice makes people feel hurt, left out, and lonely. We are all alike as well as different. Differences are good. We can like and play with people who are different from us.

Here's an example of how critical and creative thinking about bias work together. A teacher reads a library book to the children and together they recognize that the author is portraying one of the Native American characters stereotypically. He points the stereotyping out to the class, and leads the children in a discussion of the consequences of these types of illustrations and characters. He asks questions like, "What kind of false ideas about Native Americans might this picture give you? Do you think all Native Americans wear feathers today? How might this illustration of a cartoon bear wearing a headdress make Native Americans feel?" With older children, he may also invite them to look at the impact of the words that are used to describe Native Americans, like "savage," "buck," "squaw," or "primitive." All of this is the teacher modeling critical thinking for children and encouraging them to think critically. Next, the teacher may use creative thinking to generate a response to the bias in the book by asking the children to rewrite the story and draw new illustrations, for example.

Learning how to think critically about bias does not happen on its own. Children cannot learn these skills from the environment through free play and multicultural materials set out in the classroom. This goal can only be achieved through thoughtful learning experiences and discussions that adults plan and lead.

Standing Up for Oneself and Others in the Face of Bias

The fourth goal of a transformative curriculum addresses social and democratic skills and builds on all the previous goals. When children have a positive self-identity, are comfortable with diversity and have developed their critical thinking about bias, they can learn to stand up for themselves in the face of bias. Standing up for yourself involves being empowered, not victimized. It's the ability to protect yourself. A child who stands up for himself when called a name is able to say, "That's not my name. I don't like it when you call me that."

Through this goal children learn to take personal responsibility for their actions in the face of bias—either their own discomfort with another's difference or someone else's prejudice directed toward them. Standing up to bias also involves acts of true friendship—for example, standing up for others when they are experiencing name-calling, teasing, or rejection. This also helps children learn that working as a group more effectively challenges unfair situations.

Curriculum Objectives

In any curriculum, the goals reflect the ideals. The goals are broad statements of what we would like to accomplish. Goal statements, like the nine goals of a transformative curriculum, are made more concrete through the use of objectives. Objectives are much narrower in focus and are written in behavioral terms. Objectives are useful in planning and designing activities or learning experiences. Here is a complete list of the goals and objectives of a transformative curriculum.

Goal 1

Foster each child's positive, knowledgeable, and confident self-identity within a cultural context.

Objectives

- recognize and celebrate own physical features
- recognize and celebrate own home language
- recognize and celebrate own dress
- recognize and celebrate own diet and style of eating
- recognize and celebrate own family
- recognize and celebrate own name
- identify the meaning of one's name
- identify own culture
- identify own cultural traditions and customs
- appreciate own cultural heritage
- recognize the concept of homelands
- recognize and use one's home language
- experience self-worth
- believe in one's strengths and abilities
- recognize one's beauty
- experience dignity and pride
- set high expectations for oneself
- feel special and unique
- accept one's cultural identity
- use positive, descriptive language to describe one's physical features
- identify with one's culture
- recognize own family's celebrations
- share own family's celebrations with others
- share own cultural experiences with others
- learn about role models within one's culture
- believe in oneself
- feel valued
- experience an opportunity to contribute to classroom life

GOAL 2

Foster each child's comfortable, empathetic interaction with diversity among people.

OBJECTIVES

- appreciate the beauty and value of others
- accept others
- appreciate physical characteristics of others
- learn about similarities and differences
- appreciate people who are different
- experience positive, respectful interactions with people who are different from oneself
- recognize that people have the same basic needs
- recognize that people have different lifestyles
- develop positive attitudes toward human differences
- understand that all people are similar to and different from one another
- recognize that people do things in different ways
- recognize that human differences make people unique and special
- recognize that our community is made up of many different types of people
- name some of the cultural groups that make up the United States
- recognize own culture within the United States
- understand that all people deserve respect
- show respect to all people
- feel empathy for others
- learn about the cultures of the other children in the class
- notice another's point of view
- recognize ways people grow and change
- increase ability to cope with change
- develop an open, flexible attitude toward change
- develop openness to new experiences
- learn the names of their classmates
- pronounce the names of their classmates correctly
- experience human diversity
- increase comfort with human diversity
- learn about leaders from diverse cultural groups
- recognize the contributions from all cultural groups

Goal 3

Foster each child's critical thinking about bias.

Objectives

- learn about stereotypes
- begin to recognize stereotypes
- compare real and pretend
- learn about the concept of prejudice
- recognize that some people are afraid of others
- recognize that some people have misconceptions about others
- recognize that some people treat others unfairly because of differences
- understand that unfair treatment because of differences is wrong
- compare respectful and disrespectful behavior
- learn about the concept of fair and unfair behavior
- recognize unfair behavior when it occurs
- compare fair and unfair
- recognize that name-calling hurts others
- resist name-calling
- recognize that teasing others hurts
- resist teasing
- recognize who is left out and who is included
- recognize that rejecting others hurts
- explore why people are discriminated against
- think of ways to respond to discrimination
- resist rejecting others
- put self in other person's situation
- learn to think before acting
- learn about human rights
- show a concern about people's well-being
- show concern for people in our community
- learn about the importance of doing something about discrimination
- recognize one's misconceptions about human diversity
- learn simple, truthful information about human diversity
- recognize importance of not making judgments based on appearance
- recognize that people within a group are not all alike
- think for oneself
- practice distinguishing right from wrong

GOAL 4

Foster each child's ability to stand up for himself or herself and others in the face of bias.

OBJECTIVES

- stand up for self
- stand up for another person
- positively contribute to the classroom
- positively contribute to the community
- recognize that people can work together to help one another
- develop conflict resolution skills
- develop a sense of personal social responsibility
- cooperate with others
- relate values and principles to action
- develop a sense of responsibility to oneself
- develop a sense of responsibility to one's family
- develop a sense of responsibility to one's culture
- develop a sense of responsibility to one's community
- seek protection from harm
- seek adult assistance in case of mistreatment
- take action against bias
- participate as a group member
- participate in group decision making
- generate solutions to problems
- experience nonviolent conflict resolution
- experience working cooperatively with others
- coordinate actions with others to accomplish a shared goal
- recognize human rights

GOAL 5

Foster each child's healthy social and emotional development.

OBJECTIVES

- recognize emotions
- describe own emotions
- express emotions appropriately
- show sensitivity to the emotions of others
- initiate friendships
- maintain friendship
- attract and hold the attention of others
- lead and follow peers
- cooperate with others
- offer, accept, and request generosity
- offer, accept, and request help
- offer, accept, and request sharing
- offer, accept, and request affirmation
- differentiate between an accident and "on purpose"
- differentiate between right and wrong
- respect authority
- recognize rules
- respect rules
- know appropriate ways to protest rules
- participate as a group member
- set high expectations for oneself
- try new things
- believe in oneself
- demonstrate trust
- demonstrate initiative
- demonstrate honesty
- experience joy
- take turns
- identify classmates by name
- greet and welcome others
- invite others into play
- cope with frustration and disappointment
- share with others

GOAL 6

Foster children's cognitive development.

OBJECTIVES

- be aware of numbers
- count by rote
- count logically
- measure people and objects
- match
- classify
- sequence and order objects and events
- recognize shapes
- describe spatial relationships
- observe changes over time
- estimate
- use graphs
- participate in problem solving
- use all one's senses to learn about the world
- experience situations from different points of view
- observe changes and transformations
- recognize cause and effect
- evaluate the result of cause and effect
- predict possible outcomes
- examine alternatives
- think about consequences
- make choices
- use all senses to learn about the world
- observe natural materials
- describe the property of objects
- explore the natural world
- relate to animals
- care for animals
- care for plants
- care for the environment

GOAL 7

Foster children's language development.

OBJECTIVES

- listen to others
- experience being listened to
- recognize voices
- notice differences in language
- learn new words
- label people, objects, and feelings
- use words to describe similarities and differences
- use words to acknowledge unfairness
- express self through words
- give and receive information
- participate in a conversation
- ask who, what, where, when, how, why, and how much questions
- answer questions with words
- explore printed materials
- listen to a story
- follow the sequence of a story
- retell a story
- recognize one's written name
- explore writing materials
- see one's words in writing

GOAL 8

Foster children's creative development.

OBJECTIVES

- express and develop creativity
- express self through art
- express self through music
- listen to instrumental music
- listen to songs
- sing songs
- create songs
- move body to music
- respond to rhythm with body
- recognize rhythmic patterns
- create rhythmic patterns
- explore simple instruments
- express self through movement
- express self through drama
- use imagination
- appreciate beauty
- explore and experiment with art media
- dance to music
- participate in pretend play

GOAL 9

Foster children's physical development.

OBJECTIVES

- be aware of body in space
- develop kinesthetic awareness
- identify body parts
- discriminate left from right
- balance body
- develop and improve coordination
- move body in a variety of ways
- walk up and down steps
- climb on equipment
- run
- jump
- hop on one foot
- gallop/skip
- catch a ball
- throw a ball
- kick a ball
- pedal a tricycle
- put things together and take things apart
- manipulate objects and tools
- eye-hand coordination
- understand need for healthy bodies
- develop skill in caring for one's body
- identify health helpers
- learn how to keep oneself safe
- use tools and equipment safely
- practice safety procedures

Organizing the Curriculum

There are as many ways to organize curriculum as there are approaches to planning it. Historically, early childhood programs like nursery schools and child care centers have organized their curriculum content around the developmental areas mentioned earlier. Public school programs like prekindergarten, kindergarten, and primary grade classrooms have organized curriculum around subject areas. Traditionally, subject areas include physical education, health, math, science, English, social studies, art, music, drama, and dance. Both organizing systems can achieve a comprehensive curriculum, and a transformative curriculum can find a home in either.

Two recent trends are changing the organization of early childhood curricula. First, there is greater overlap of early childhood and primary curriculum models. More school districts are adopting an early childhood model for their kindergarten and primary grades, but they continue to organize their educational goals and curriculum by subject area. Second, many early childhood educators are recognizing that much early childhood curriculum lacks meaningful content and intellectual integrity. They are looking for a more systematic way of structuring curricula. *Big As Life* capitalizes on these trends and uses the strengths of both methods.

For instance, I broke the classic early childhood category of cognitive development into three distinct curricular areas (math, critical thinking, and science) because too often cognitive activities are limited to numbers, colors, and shapes. I wanted to encourage teachers to explore a wider range of activities to support this critical developmental area. On the other hand, I used language development as a curricular area covering speaking, reading, writing, listening, and home language activities, feeling that "language" was the simplest and most inclusive term for these closely related subject areas. I used the traditional developmental areas of social, emotional, and creative development because they best describe the types of learning experiences children need to develop a rich inner life and positive social skills, and they are too often left out of a curriculum organized around subject areas.

Big As Life also intentionally incorporates the basic elements of a multicultural/anti-bias curriculum. Curricular areas including diversity, bias and stereotypes, and cultural identity were included to support the four goals of anti-bias education. Anti-bias activities are also woven through each curricular area.

If all of these different ways to classify activities are confusing, here's a chart to show how they match up!

Common Curriculum Areas		
Big As Life	**Developmental**	**Kindergarten Primary**
Math Critical Thinking Science	Cognitive Development	Math Science
Language Home Language	Language Development	Reading Writing
Cultural Identity Emotional Development	Emotional Development	
Social Development Diversity Bias and Stereotypes Social Action Community Service Human Rights	Social Development	Social Studies
Music Creative Development	Creative Development	Art Music Drama
Physical Development Health, Safety, and Nutrition	Physical Development	Physical Education Health

Review the above list of curricular areas in light of a transformative curriculum. Can you imagine how activities in the categories of math, science, language development, emotional development, social development, physical development, and health and safety could help children understand themselves and their experience? Can you see how home language and cultural identity activities could connect children to their families, neighborhoods, and cultural communities? Can you see how activities about diversity, critical thinking, bias and stereotypes could help children develop a simple and accurate understanding of human diversity and bias? Can you see how social action, community service, and human rights activities can help children become positive forces in their communities? I've chosen curricular areas which I believe have the potential to transform both children and society.

Planning a Transformative Curriculum— A Summary

Planning a curriculum is often referred to as both a science and an art. There is precision and reason in making sure that there is a logical progression to the curriculum, but it is also an opportunity for you to express yourself. You use your creativity as you revise and adapt activities, figure out new ways of using existing materials, and write new verses to familiar songs. Through the process of planning curriculum, you individualize it, put your own unique perspective on it, and make it your own.

Good curriculum is the result of following a curriculum planning process. I use a nine-step process that is the result of trial and error. I have been using this process for the past five years and teaching it to others for the past year, with great results. Following is a summary of this process. You can find a more in-depth explanation, complete with examples and illustrations, in the companion volume to this book.

The Nine-Step Planning Process

STEP 1   CREATE A COLLABORATIVE CLIMATE

Designing curriculum takes a lot of thought and creativity. I believe that curriculum is best developed by a group of people because then you can tap as many resources as possible. The first drafts of the curriculum webs found in part 2 were created by teachers sipping coffee around a kitchen table on a Saturday morning. Some of the unit webs have since been refined by groups of twenty or more.

In order for people to work together as a group, you need to create a collaborative climate. Set the stage for collaboration. Set aside time for curriculum planning away from the classroom, create a relaxed and casual atmosphere, encourage everyone to contribute, and facilitate dialogue.

STEP 2   LEARN ABOUT THE CONTEXT

A transformative curriculum is based on inquiry and problem posing. Development of a transformative curriculum begins with a genuine inquiry into the real lives of the children and families in your classroom. Learning about the context involves getting to know the individual children, getting to know the children's families, learning about the cultures represented in your classroom, identifying the prevailing biases and stereotypes, uncovering the community issues that impact families, and recognizing the regional history that continues to shape people's lives.

STEP 3   **IDENTIFY THE THEMES**

As you get to know the children, families, and community, some themes will begin to emerge. Examine the information you have uncovered. Ask yourself, "What are the children interested in?" "What do they care passionately about?" and "What do their parents want them to know?" Identify the key issues that keep coming up again and again. The themes in part 2 represent very broad, simple topics that are interesting to many young children and families.

What Is "Webbing"?

Webbing is a brainstorming method many people use to quickly generate ideas. The term *webbing* refers to the final result, which resembles a spider web.

Webbing is a bit different from traditional brainstorming, which results in a list of ideas. This listing, which has been described as a linear form of thinking, is a style of processing information most often used by European American males. Women and people from other cultures, on the other hand, are more likely to use a circular style of thinking. Webbing depicts this circular style of thinking and shows the connections and relationships between ideas.

Webbing allows you to branch many ideas from one idea. It helps you see all the directions in which you could go—that's why some people call it *mind mapping*. Webbing also provides you with a one-page record of all your ideas, which is very helpful for people who are visual learners or like to see the whole picture at a glance.

STEP 4   **WEB THE UNIT**

Once you select a theme, you need to develop it. A quick and easy way to develop the unit is to use a brainstorming technique called *webbing*. Keep the curriculum inquiry-based and child-centered by identifying questions that the children would ask about the topic. For example, think of the questions the children would ask about the topic "Family." What do they know about families? What do they want to know about families?

In addition, include a series of questions that move from inquiry to action and questions that reflect the goals of a multicultural/anti-bias curriculum. For example, "What are all the different kinds of families?" "How are families alike and different?" "How do families change and stay the same?" "What are the stereotypes about families?" "How can we challenge the stereotypes?" "What do families want and need?" and "How can we work together to help families?"

STEP 5   **OUTLINE THE WEB**

The web provides a rough sketch of the curriculum unit. A quick glance is all that is needed to see what is involved in the unit. Most teachers look at the web they have created and immediately begin thinking of possible activities. I suggest, however, that you take the questions on the web and list them in the order that the children, parents, and teacher will examine them—from simple to complex, most familiar to the children to least familiar. Look at the list and determine how many weeks of curriculum you have and how you might cluster the content into weekly subthemes. Once you know the content, the length, and the order of the curriculum unit, you are ready to plan activities.

STEP 6   **IDENTIFY MATERIALS TO ADD TO THE LEARNING ENVIRONMENT**

This is a straightforward step in the curriculum planning processes. Early childhood teachers recognize the important role of the classroom environment to children's learning. Most rotate classroom materials on a regular basis. Simply review the web and outline. Then select and add teaching materials, learning games, prop boxes, toys, books, and music to the classroom interest areas that support the theme.

STEP 7   **SELECT AND PLAN LEARNING EXPERIENCES**

Learning through play is enhanced by planned, hands-on learning experiences. Review the curriculum goals and objectives, unit web, and outline. Select and plan activities to represent all the developmental areas. (See page 34 for a sample curriculum planning form.) Use the web as a source for creating original learning experiences. You may have your own tried and true activities that fit the unit or ones you can easily adapt. You can also look to activity books for ideas.

STEP 8   **IDENTIFY CURRICULUM RESOURCES**

There are many resources available to support a transformative curriculum. Curriculum resources include materials for the interest areas, posters, children's books, children's music, videos, computer software, and organizations. Locate home-made and commercial materials that support your curriculum.

STEP 9   **TRANSFER THE INFORMATION TO LESSON PLANS**

Scheduling the daily and weekly learning experiences is the last step in the curriculum planning process. Lesson plans provide you with a detailed guide for the week. Most teachers write out their daily activities on a weekly lesson plan form and share them with supervisors, teaching assistants, and parents. Select a lesson plan form or design your own. Review the unit outline, interest area materials, and learning experiences. Keep two things in mind as you fill in the lesson plans. First, pay attention to the sequence of activities. Make sure they progress from simple to complex and familiar to unfamiliar. Second, make sure each week reflects a variety of activities, so that you address all areas of development.

Curriculum Planning Form

Theme _____

Week _____

	Monday	Tuesday	Wednesday	Thursday	Friday
Large Group					
Free Choice					
Small Group					
Large Group					
Art Area		Dramatic Play Area		Manipulatives	
Block Area		Sensory Table		Science	

Enhancing the Environment

Adding multicultural materials to the classroom is often the first step to diversifying curriculum. Multiethnic dolls, posters, children's books, instruments, and art materials are some of the multicultural materials commonly used in early childhood education. It's not always easy to find classroom materials that are both age-appropriate and nonstereotypic. Teachers who live in major metropolitan areas find that they can purchase skin-colored markers and multiethnic dolls at local discount department stores. This isn't the case for teachers who live in many suburban or rural areas. Other teachers get their materials at local, regional, and national conferences. They make a visit to the exhibit hall a priority, but many teachers aren't able to attend conferences. Another popular way to purchase materials is mail order. All teachers can request and receive catalogs as a way to keep up to date on the best and newest commercial early childhood teaching materials.

Big As Life will help you identify multicultural, disability-aware, and gender-fair teaching materials. There is a complete list of some of my favorite suppliers in the back of the book. Each curriculum unit contains a list of materials that you could add to the classroom interest areas to support learning through the environment. These lists are very detailed and long. Please don't assume that you should have all of the materials listed in order to implement a curriculum unit. I tried to list a wide variety of materials with the hope that you already have some of the materials in a storage closet and reading the list will jog your memory and help you think about using materials in a new way. The lists may also be used as guidelines for future purchases if you find that your program lacks some core materials needed to support a specific curriculum unit or interest area or an inclusive curriculum in general.

Just to get you started thinking about classroom materials, here is a very basic list of some of my favorite core materials for implementing an inclusive curriculum. I would keep these in the classroom year round, regardless of the curriculum unit.

Art Materials

Basic art materials to have on hand include skin-colored markers, crayons, tempera, craft paper, and felt. People Colors art materials are the best of what is currently available. They have the widest range of colors, and the most realistic. Children who are very light-skinned and children who are very dark complected are able to find and mix a shade that matches the color of their skin.

Block Play Figures

Block Play People by Lakeshore are made of a hard rubber that is durable and easy to clean. They fit well in the palm of a child's hand and proportionately complement the unit blocks. The people are dressed in street clothes and have very realistic features, including facial expressions. People of every age, body size, and physical ability are represented. Some of the female figures wear skirts or dresses, while others wear pants. All of the major ethnic groups that make up American society are represented.

Other sets of block play figures that are available include Special Needs Children Wooden Figures, Differently Challenged Children, and Wooden Stand-Up

Figures (Constructive Playthings); Wedgie Families with Mobility-Impaired Boy (Edvantage); Inclusive Play People (Educational Equity Concepts); Our Helpers Play People (Nasco); and Dinkytown Day Care Kids Play Set and School Bus and Little People (Beckley-Cardy).

Dolls

Dolls continue to be a source of frustration. While there are many multiethnic doll sets to choose from, none of them realistically capture children's facial features or expressions. This is a source of frustration to may teachers and parents. Lakeshore's multiethnic school dolls are some of the best child-like dolls available. They are plastic with movable arms and legs and rooted hair. A boy and girl from each of the major ethnic groups is available. They look like young children and come dressed in non-stereotypic play clothes. Lakeshore also sells a doll with a prosthesis and adaptive equipment, such as wheelchairs, protective helmets, dog guides and harnesses, leg braces and crutches, walkers, hearing aids, and eyeglasses. These dolls can be used in the dramatic play area and as persona dolls.

Baby dolls (which look like babies rather than children) are available through most of the major catalog suppliers, often called "feels real" or "just born" baby dolls. Environments' twenty-inch newborn dolls are particularly realistic in both size and facial expression. Look for dolls that are a softer vinyl and anatomically correct.

Cloth dolls are also a wonderful addition to a classroom, either as accessories in the dramatic play area or as persona dolls. People of Every Stripe makes a variety of cloth dolls (one of the benefits of cloth is that it offers a wider range of skin colors). Their dolls have hand-painted faces and realistic hair. Send them a photo and they'll make a doll to match your specifications. Their dolls really meet the needs of biracial children and children from under-represented ethnic groups.

Play Food and Cooking Utensils

Many of the catalog companies carry similar sets of ethnic play food. Constructive Playthings sells the most complete and the most varied food sets, including the international bread set and Hispanic, Asian, Middle Eastern, Dim Sum, Taco, and Italian food sets. They also have European American meal sets and produce. Lakeshore has Chinese and Japanese food sets and sells the most complete pretend cooking sets. Their Asian and Hispanic cooking sets include real cooking utensils that can be used for either dramatic play or classroom cooking experiences.

Dramatic Play Furniture

All of the early childhood school supply companies sell dramatic play furniture. Look for high-quality hardwood pieces that come with a warranty. A basic set often includes a stove, sink, refrigerator, unbreakable full-length mirror, table, and chairs. Consider adding a hutch, child-sized doll bed, doll highchair, doll buggy, vinyl-covered couch and easy chair, washer and dryer, dishwasher, microwave, ironing board and iron, and housecleaning set. These items can be rotated into and out of the dramatic play area over time to maintain children's interest in it and to support the various units.

Literacy

Often the literacy area is limited to a book corner with a library shelf unit and a selection of books. The whole-language movement has helped to expand our thinking about children's development of reading and writing. Every literacy area should contain materials that foster the basic skills of listening, speaking, reading, and writing. Include a flannel board and flannel board sets, puppets, magnetic boards, tape player and cassettes, and writing and book-making supplies.

For More Information

Over the years, I have read and recommended many excellent resources, and the writing of other educators has certainly shaped my previous books *Roots and Wings: Affirming Culture in Early Childhood Programs* (St. Paul: Redleaf, 1991) and *Developing Roots and Wings: A Trainer's Guide to Affirming Culture in Early Childhood Programs* (St. Paul: Redleaf, 1992). Here's a list of some of the books that have greatly influenced my teaching practice.

Arnold, Rick, and Bev Burke. *A Popular Education Handbook* (Toronto: CUSO/Ontario Institute for Studies in Education, 1983).

Bredekamp, Sue, and Teresa Rosegrant, eds. *Reaching Potentials: Appropriate Curriculum and Assessment for Young Children, Volume 1*, (Washington, DC: NAEYC, 1992).

Derman-Sparks, Louise, and the ABC Task Force. *Anti-Bias Curriculum: Tools for Empowering Young Children* (Washington, DC: NAEYC, 1989).

Freire, Paulo. *Education for Critical Consciousness* (New York: Continuum, 1973).

Freire, Paulo, and Ira Shor. *A Pedagogy for Liberation* (South Hadley: Bergin and Garvey, 1987).

Freire, Paulo. *Pedagogy of the Oppressed* (New York: Continuum, 1970).

———. *The Politics of Education* (South Hadley: Bergin and Garvey, 1985).

Horton, Miles, and Paulo Freire. *We Make the Road by Walking* (Philadelphia: Temple University Press, 1990).

Shor, Ira. *Critical Teaching and Everyday Life*. 2nd ed. (Chicago: University of Chicago Press, 1987).

Shor, Ira, ed. *Freire for the Classroom* (Portsmouth, NH: Boynton/Cook, 1987).

PART 2

The Curriculum Units

BODIES

Young children love their bodies, from the first discoveries of fingers and toes to delighting in belly buttons. They enjoy learning to name their body parts and drawing pictures of their bodies. Children seem to especially delight in gaining control of their bodies. Swinging, jumping rope, skipping, and climbing to the top of the jungle gym are accompanied by shouts of "Teacher, Teacher! Look at me! Look at me!" If the children seem interested in bodies—how they work, how they move, and how they grow—give them the opportunity to learn.

UNIT 1:

BODIES

Look for this symbol
to find activities you
can use for circle time.

WEB

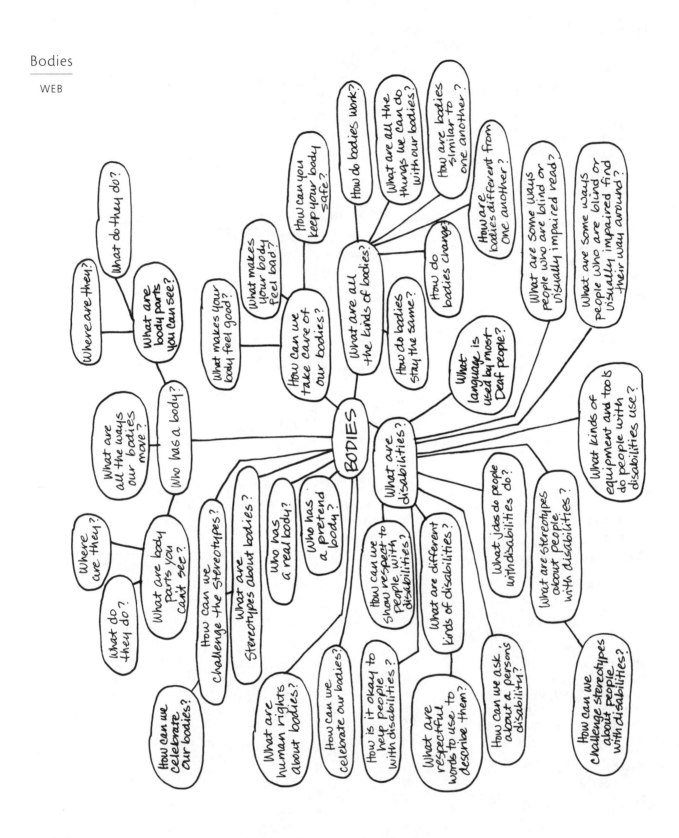

Where are they?

What do they do?

What are body parts you can see?

How can you keep your body safe?

What makes your body feel bad?

What makes your body feel good?

How do bodies work?

What are all the things we can do with our bodies?

How are bodies similar to one another?

How are bodies different from one another?

What are some ways people who are blind or visually impaired read?

What are some ways people who are blind or visually impaired find their way around?

How can we take care of our bodies?

What are all the kinds of bodies?

How do bodies stay the same?

How do bodies change?

What are the ways our bodies move?

Who has a body?

What language is used by most Deaf people?

What kinds of equipment and tools do people with disabilities use?

BODIES

What are disabilities?

Where are they?

What do they do?

What are body parts you can't see?

How can we challenge the stereotypes?

What are stereotypes about bodies?

Who has a real body?

Who has a pretend body?

How can we show respect to people with disabilities?

What are different kinds of disabilities?

What jobs do people with disabilities do?

What are stereotypes about people with disabilities?

How can we celebrate our bodies?

What are human rights about bodies?

How can we celebrate our bodies?

How is it okay to help people with disabilities?

What are respectful words to use to describe them?

How can we ask about a person's disability?

How can we challenge stereotypes about people with disabilities?

OUTLINE

I. Who has a body?
    A. What are body parts you can see?
        1. Where are they?
        2. What do these body parts do?
    B. What are body parts you can't see?
        1. Where are they?
        2. What do these body parts do?
    C. What are all the ways our bodies move?

II. How can we take care of our bodies?
    A. What makes your body feel good?
    B. What makes your body feel bad?
    C. How can you keep your body safe?

III. What are all the kinds of bodies?
    A. How do bodies work?
    B. What are all the things we can do with our bodies?
    C. How are bodies similar to one another?
    D. How are bodies different from one another?
    E. How do bodies stay the same?
    F. How do bodies change?

IV. What are disabilities?
    A. What are different kinds of disabilities? What are respectful words to use to describe them?
    B. How can we ask about a person's disability?
    C. What kinds of equipment and tools do people with disabilities use?
    D. What language is used by most Deaf people?
    E. What are some ways people who are blind or visually impaired read?
    F. What are some ways people who are blind or visually impaired find their way around?
    G. What jobs do people with disabilities do?
    H. What are stereotypes about people with disabilities?
    I. How can we challenge stereotypes about people with disabilities?
    J. How can we show respect to people with disabilities?
    K. How is it okay to help people with disabilities?

V. Who has a pretend body?

VI. Who has a real body?

VII. What are stereotypes about bodies?

VIII. How can we challenge the stereotypes about bodies?

IX. What are our human rights about bodies?

X. How can we celebrate our bodies?

MATERIALS LIST

ART

skin-colored paints, crayons, markers, felt, and craft paper

butcher paper roll

hand mirrors

sponge people shapes for sponge painting (for example, Active Kids Sponges, *Kaplan*; Sponge People and Hands Set, *Constructive Playthings*)

people stencils (available from *Lakeshore* and *Constructive Playthings*, among others)

BLOCKS

a variety of multicultural people figures, including figures of people with disabilities

people figures of medical workers

toy ambulance

medical block accessories (for example, Operating Room, *Beckley-Cardy*; Playmobil Hospital Room, *Constructive Playthings*)

DRAMATIC PLAY

multicultural cooking sets

multicultural play food sets

multiethnic baby dolls

multiethnic preschooler dolls

adaptive equipment for dolls with disabilities (available from *Lakeshore*)

medical costumes (available from *Lakeshore*)

play medical kits (available from *Constructive Playthings* or *Sandy and Son*)

doctor's office: white shirts or surgical scrubs, face masks, stethoscopes, bandages, cotton balls, cots, pillows, sheets, baby scale, tongue depressors, flashlight, plastic syringes, prescription pad and pencil, eye chart, appointment book, calendar, medical charts, health care pamphlets, sign with the international hospital or medical care logo, name tags, chairs and magazines for the waiting room

hair salon or barber shop: hand mirrors, table, chairs, capes, blow-dryers, curling irons, clippers, crimping tools, curlers, barrettes, shaving materials, empty hair care product containers and written directions, hairstyle magazines, pretend cosmetology licenses, appointment books, receipt pads and pencils

LARGE MOTOR

equipment to foster body awareness (for example, Look and Do Movement Activity Kit, The Movement Maze, Two-Way Balance Beam, *Lakeshore*; Twister Game, *Nasco*)

LITERACY

children's books: fiction, nonfiction, and bilingual books about bodies (see resource list at the end of the unit)

cassette player and theme-related storybook cassettes

body flannel board or magnetic sets (for example, Human Body Parts Flannel Aid, *Nasco*; My Body Magnetic Board, *Lakeshore*; Everybody's Beautiful People Cut-Outs, *ABC School Supply*)

multicultural hand puppets of people, including health care workers

American Sign Language rubber stamps and stamp pads

MANIPULATIVES

multicultural puzzles about people and bodies (for example, Boy Puzzle, Doctor, Nurse, Dentist Puzzles, Girl Puzzle, Good Habits Puzzles, My Head and Body Parts Puzzles, Step-Up Healthcare Puzzles, *Constructive Playthings*; Feet Puzzle, Jason Body Parts Puzzle, Left and Right Hand Puzzles, *Edvantage*; Face and Body Puzzles, Sequence Puzzles, Special Needs Kids Puzzles, *Sandy and Son*; Body Puzzle, Environments; Children with Special Needs Puzzles, *Kaplan*; Our Body Puzzle, *Animal Town*)

games to do with bodies, personal safety, and health (for example, Body Bingo, *Lakeshore*; Ha-Choo Game, *Beckley-Cardy*; Footloose: A Physically Active Game for Kids, *Sandy and Son*; Funny Face Board Game, *Animal Town*; Sesame Street Feeling Fit Game, *Nasco*)

other theme-related manipulatives (for example, Mystery Box, *Lakeshore*; Footsteps to Numbers Tactile Mat Counting Feet, *Edvantage*)

sequencing cards and matching cards about bodies (for example, Body Parts Cards, *Beckley-Cardy*)

SCIENCE

anatomically correct baby dolls

charts or models of the human body (for example, Hands-On Anatomy! Human Body, *Beckley-Cardy*; Human Ear, Human Tooth, Mouth and Brush, *ABC School Supply*; Take-Apart Human Body, *Lakeshore*)

body reference books

magnifying glasses (for example, Magnifiers, available from *Lakeshore*)

X rays of body parts

stethoscopes (available from *Beckley-Cardy*, among others)

floor scale

SENSORY

sensory table or dish tubs

anatomically correct baby dolls

soap and washcloths

TEACHING THROUGH THE INTEREST AREAS

Art

Set out skin-colored crayons and paints, a large roll of craft paper or brown butcher paper, and hand mirrors.

Blocks

Encourage hospital play by providing figures of medical workers, medical doll furniture, an ambulance or emergency medical play vehicle, and materials for making signs.

Dramatic Play

Set up a doctor's office, medical clinic, or hospital in the dramatic play area by providing the following items: white shirts or surgical scrubs, face masks, stethoscopes, bandages, cotton balls, cots, pillows, sheets, baby scale, tongue depressors, flashlight, plastic syringes, doctor's kits, baby dolls, prescription pad and pencil, eye chart, appointment book, calendar, medical charts, health care pamphlets, a sign with the international hospital or medical care logo, name tags, chairs and magazines for the waiting room.

Set up a hair salon or barber shop in the dramatic play area by providing the following items: dolls, hand mirrors, table, chairs, capes, blow dryers, curling irons, clippers, crimping tools, curlers, barrettes, shaving materials, empty hair care products containers and written directions, hairstyle magazines, pretend cosmetology licenses, appointment books, receipt pads and pencils.

Encourage children to wash and style the dolls' hair. Because of outbreaks of head lice, you may not be able to allow children to comb and style one another's hair.

Literacy

Set out a collection of fiction, nonfiction, and bilingual books on bodies; tape recorder and tape recordings of children's books on bodies in different languages; body flannel board sets; hand puppets of health care workers and people; writing and bookmaking materials; and American Sign Language rubber stamps and stamp pads.

Manipulatives

Set out body puzzles, body part matching games, body-related board games, Lego building blocks with figures of health care workers, and bodily care sequence cards.

Music

Set out collections of lullabies from many cultures, cassettes with songs for and about people with disabilities, and exercise and movement cassettes.

Science

Set out a floor scale, height chart, models or charts of the human body, magnifying glasses, X rays of body parts, and reference books on bodies.

Sensory

Wet the sand in the sensory table and add hand and foot molds or simply encourage children to make handprints in the damp sand.

Fill the sensory table with soapy water. Set out washcloths and dolls from the dramatic play corner and encourage the children to wash the dolls.

ACTIVITIES: INVESTIGATING THE THEME

Creative Development

Body Painting. Invite children to paint a picture without using their hands. Ask them, "What other body part could you use to hold a brush? What other body part could you paint with?"

Body Tracings. Trace children's bodies on large sheets of butcher paper and encourage them to color in the outlines of their bodies. Help them cut out the outlines of their bodies and display them on the wall. With older children, place the child's body tracing on top of a second piece of butcher paper and cut along the outline, making two identical body shapes at the same time. Staple the two body shapes together along the edges. Leave an opening so the children can stuff the doll with crumpled newspapers. Once the body tracings are stuffed, staple the opening closed.

Face Puzzles. Help children discover that, despite having similar features, each person's face is unique. Take a close-up photo of each child's face. Use a color photocopier to make enlargements of the photos. Glue the photocopies to pieces of oaktag or poster board and cut into puzzle pieces. Older children can make and put together their own puzzles.

Feet Painting. Roll out a 5-foot length of butcher paper. Set out shallow trays of skin-colored paint at one end and dish tubs of water at the other end of the paper. Invite children to take off their shoes and socks, step into the pan of paint that is most like their skin color, walk across the paper, step into the pans of water, and then wipe off their feet with a towel. You can display the foot mural in the classroom or hallway.

Handprint Mural. Set out pans of skin-colored paint. Invite children to dip their hands in a pan of paint that best matches their skin color and then press their hands down on paper.

Hands and Feet Certificate. Invite the children to make certificates that include prints of their hands and feet to give to their families. Invite children to press their hands into a shallow dish of paint and then onto a 12-by-18-inch piece of construction paper. Let the handprints dry. Invite children to step into a dish tub with a small amount of paint and then step onto the construction paper, making footprints directly below their handprints. Write the child's name and age in the center of the certificate and copy the following saying below the name and age:

> My footprint's unique
> My handprint is too
> And they are just as special
> As all that I do.
>
> (*Everybody Has a Body*, Robert E. Rockwell, Robert A. Williams, and Elizabeth A. Sherwood. Beltsville, MD: Gryphon House, 1992; p. 204. Used with permission.)

Healthy Bodies Mural. Set out magazines, scissors, crayons, and markers. Secure a large sheet of butcher paper to the top of a table. Invite children to make a mural illustrating all the things we can do to take care of our bodies and keep our bodies healthy.

Moving Bodies. Invite children to make a collage of moving bodies. Children can cut pictures from magazines of people moving and using their bodies and glue them to a piece of construction paper. Make sure to include pictures of people of all sizes and shapes, as well as people with disabilities.

My Body Is an Instrument. Introduce children to the idea that they can make a variety of sounds with their bodies. Invite the children to make a sound by clapping their hands together. Then ask them to find other ways of making sounds with their bodies. As a child discovers a different sound, ask the rest of the children to look at the child and try to make the same sound. Some possibilities are whistling, humming, smacking lips, stamping feet, snapping fingers, clicking tongues, speaking, singing, slapping thighs, and sucking in air.

Paper Sack Heads. Invite children to stuff a lunch sack or medium-sized grocery bag with crumpled newspaper. Tie the end closed with a piece of yarn or string. Set out a variety of face parts made from construction paper, fabric scraps, or craft foam. Include eyebrows, eyelashes, eyes, noses, mouths, and ears. In addition, set out yarn, glue, and roving for hair. Encourage the children to look at themselves in the mirror and then choose face parts to make a face that looks like themselves.

Self-Portraits. Invite children to paint a picture of themselves. Help them get started by standing with them in front of a full length mirror and noticing all of their body parts. Set out mirrors in the art area and encourage children to draw or paint a picture of their face. If you are lucky enough to have a Plexiglas easel, simply duct tape a mirror to the back of the easel. Make a print of the child's portrait before washing the easel clean.

Stethoscopes. Cut out the individual cups from egg cartons. Cover the outside of the egg carton cup with aluminum foil. Poke a hole in the bottom and put a piece of yarn through the hole. Invite children to use their stethoscopes in the dramatic play area.

Weaving. Talk with the children about how some people use fabric to tell stories about their lives. Some people make quilts, some dye their fabric in bright colors and patterns, some embroider pictures on fabric, and still others weave rugs and wall hangings. Show children samples of weaving, needlework, and quilting.

Make a simple loom by cutting notches a half inch apart on the top and bottom of a piece of cardboard. Wrap a thin piece of yarn around the cardboard from top to bottom, wrapping it over and over so that the yarn is in each of the slits. Secure by tying the ends. You should have vertical lines of yarn a half inch apart. Begin weaving by threading a plastic needle with another piece of yarn in and out of the vertical lines. Weave 2 inches at the top to form a secure edge. Set out the loom and demonstrate how to weave the yarn between the threads on the loom. Let the children try to follow the in and out sequence. Leave the materials out for a week or two so that children can add to the weaving. When finished, display the weaving along with other samples of weaving and stitchery.

Critical Thinking

Age and Actions. Young children are beginning to form ideas about what is appropriate and expected behavior of people at different ages. Help children identify different age groups: babies, young children, older children, teenagers, adults, and the elderly. Once they've identified each age group, ask them how old they think babies are, how old they think young children are, and so on. Then ask them what kinds of things each age group does. Follow up with, "How do you know?"

Size and Age. Young children often associate bigger body size with being older and smaller body size with being younger. Show the children a picture of two children that differ in height and look similar in age. Or set out two figures of children cut from felt that are different in size. Ask the children if they think the two children in the picture are the same age. If not, who do they think is older? Tell them the two children are the same age, but that one child is taller and one child is shorter. Ask them why they think that there is a difference. Talk with the children about how people grow at different rates.

Emotional Development

Control Your Body. Young children need to learn self-control. Invite them to take the self-control challenge. Challenge children to see if they can successfully complete a variety of tasks that require self-control. For example:

Can you sit next to your friend at circle time without touching her?

Can you stand in line without pushing?

Can you sit down at the snack table and wait for everyone to be seated and served before you start to eat?

Can you listen quietly to others without interrupting?

Invite children to contribute their ideas of how they can control their bodies in the classroom. Write down the children's ideas and the ways you would like children to control themselves, and post this in the classroom.

How Do You Feel When You're Sick? Help the children reflect on how they feel when their bodies get sick. Ask them open-ended questions:

How do you feel when you have an earache?

How do you feel when you have a sore throat?

How do you feel when you have a stomachache?

Who takes care of you when you are sick?

What do they do to help make you feel better?

Set out some dolls, blankets, medical supplies, a washcloth, and a cup. Invite children to show how they would help someone who is sick to feel better.

I Can Move My Body. Foster children's self-esteem and self-confidence in their bodies. At circle time, ask each child to show the class something she can do with her body.

I Like My Body. Foster children's acceptance and appreciation for their bodies. Bring pictures of body parts to circle time. Show the pictures to the children one at a time. Ask children to identify the body part. Invite children to say why they like that particular body part. For example, "I like my (_body part_) because (_reason_)." Set out art materials and invite children to draw pictures of their bodies and dictate to you what they like about their bodies.

Our Bodies Show How We Feel. Give children a chance to relate physical gestures and body language to feelings. Tell the children you want to show them some ways people use their bodies to show others how they are feeling. Role-play stomping your feet, shaking your fist, waving your index finger, placing your hands on your hips, and clapping your hands. Invite children to take a turn acting out a feeling with their bodies and seeing if the rest of the class can guess the feeling.

With each feeling, ask the children what they could do instead. For example, if a child chose to stomp his feet to show the feeling of anger, follow up by asking the children, "What can you do instead of stomping around when you are angry?"

Compare children's movements to the American Sign Language (ASL) signs for feelings. ASL uses facial expressions and hand, arm, and body motions to communicate feelings.

Part of the Picture. Collect a variety of magazine photographs of people expressing different feelings. Include feelings like tired, sad, mad, afraid, happy, surprised, or excited. Try to use photographs in which people are expressing emotions with their entire bodies. Invite children to look at these pictures of people who are showing their feelings through their bodies and faces.

Cut a slit across a large sheet of construction paper or poster board that is large enough for the photographs to slide through. Ask the children, "Let's see if you can tell how the person is feeling by looking at part of the picture." Put the picture behind the slit paper and push the picture through the slit, exposing only a portion of the person. If the children cannot correctly guess, expose more of the picture. Show children the whole picture after they have correctly guessed the emotion. Continue with other pictures.

Health, Safety, and Nutrition

Dental Health. Talk with children about the importance of eating healthy foods and brushing our teeth after meals to keep our teeth healthy. Demonstrate how to correctly brush your teeth.

 Fire Safety. Invite a local firefighter or fire safety specialist to visit the classroom and talk with the children about preventing burns and what to do if their clothes catch on fire. Children can learn basic fire safety concepts like don't touch the top of the stove, don't pull a pot off the stove, don't play with matches or cigarette lighters, and "stop, drop, and roll" if your clothes catch on fire.

 Relax. Invite children to get in a comfortable position. Tell them to close their eyes and breathe slowly. Talk them through deep breathing, saying something like "Slowly breathe the air in through your nose and send the air down to your tummy. Slowly breathe the air out of your nose." Repeat at least three times. Ask the children if they can feel their bodies relax. Tell them that sometimes relaxing feels like your body gets soft and quiet. Play an instrumental cassette tape and invite the children to lie down, close their eyes, and breathe deeply as they listen to the music. Conclude the activity by talking about how relaxing helps keep our bodies healthy, and everyone needs time to relax their bodies.

Respect Yourself. Make a simple board game that will help children identify ways to keep their bodies healthy and strong. Use small figures of people as game markers. Write a respectful or disrespectful behavior in some of the squares on the game board. For example, "Go to bed on time, move three squares," "Eat candy bars and soda pop, move back two squares," "Brush your teeth after lunch, move ahead one square," "Wear your mittens, boots, scarf, and hat on cold days, move ahead three squares," "Wash your hands before you eat, move ahead three squares."

Wash My Hands. Use the following song to teach children about the importance of washing their hands.

WASH MY HANDS

by Frances A. Ferguson
Tune: *Shake, Shake, Shake My Sillies Out*

Gotta wash, wash, wash my hands clean,
Wash, wash, wash my hands clean,
Wash, wash, wash my hands clean,
And I wash my hands today.

Gotta soap, soap, soap my sudsies up,
Soap, soap, soap my sudsies up,
Soap, soap, soap my sudsies up,
And wash my hands today.

Gotta scrub, scrub, scrub my dirt away,
Scrub, scrub, scrub my dirt away,
scrub, scrub, scrub my dirt away,
And wash my hands today.

Gotta dry, dry, dry my water away,
Dry, dry, dry my water away,
Dry, dry, dry my water away,
And wash my hands today.

Gotta wash, wash, wash my hands clean,
Wash, wash, wash my hands clean,
Wash, wash, wash my hands clean,
And wash my hands today.

(*The Giant Encyclopedia of Circle Time and Group Activities for Children 3 to 6*, Kathy Charner, editor. Beltsville, MD: Gryphon House, 1996; pp. 214 and 215. Used with permission.)

Washing Hands. Teach children that the easiest way to prevent illness is to wash their hands. Make a rebus chart of the hand washing steps. Demonstrate how to wash your hands and give the children a chance to show you how they wash their hands. Put the following steps on your chart: (1) Wet your hands. (2) Soap your hands. (3) Scrub your hands. (4) Rinse your hands. (5) Turn off the water. (6) Dry your hands with one paper towel. (7) Throw the paper towel in the trash can.

Language Development

Home Language. *Learn the words for body parts in American Sign Language and the home languages of the children in your classroom.*

Bodies

LANGUAGE
DEVELOPMENT

Body Picture Cards. Glue a set of body picture cards onto construction paper. Body picture cards can be made by cutting out large magazine pictures of people that represent a variety of body shapes, sizes, and abilities.

Hold up one picture at a time and ask open-ended questions:

Who can tell me about this picture?

What do you see?

How would you describe this person's body?

What is this person doing with her body?

What else do you think she can do with her body?

How is this body like yours?

How is it different from yours?

What else can you tell me about this person's body?

Counter stereotypes that may emerge from the discussion by asking, "Why do you think so?" or "How can you tell?" and then offer simple and accurate information.

Body Picture Stories. Sit down with a small group of children and some pictures of people using their bodies. Include pictures of people with disabilities in active roles. Show the children one picture at a time. Ask the children what they see in the pictures. Encourage the children to make up stories about the people using their bodies in the pictures. If possible, write down the children's stories.

My Body. Here's a simple finger play to help young children identify body parts.

A mouth to speak kind words each day *(point to mouth)*
Two ears to listen to what others say *(cup hands around ears)*
Two feet that help me run and play *(move feet as if running)*
Two hands to put the toys away *(pretend to pick up toys)*
Two eyes to see nice things to do *(point to eyes)*
Two lips to smile the whole day through *(point to lips and smile)*
A body that helps when there's work to be done *(point to self)*
Makes a happy day for everyone *(clap hands or pat self on back)*

(*Busy Fingers Growing Minds: Finger Plays, Verses and Activities for Whole Language Learning*, Rhoda Redleaf. St. Paul: Redleaf Press, 1993; p. 34. Used with permission.)

One Really Big Body. Talk about the basic parts of the human body. Unroll a large piece of butcher paper. Talk about where the body parts should go if you make a person whose body fills up the entire sheet of paper. As a group, decide on the identity of this person. Will it be a boy or a girl? What skin color should it have? What facial features should be included?

Ask one or two children to paint a head and face, another couple of children to paint the arms and hands, another couple of children to paint the chest and stomach, and a few to paint the legs and feet.

Similar to Me. Ask children to look at one another's bodies and then see if they can name all of the ways their bodies are similar to one another. Tape a large piece of paper to the wall and write the children's observations of their bodies on the paper.

Ten Little Fingers. Here's a simple rhyme to teach children to foster appreciation for their bodies.

> I have ten little fingers and ten little toes. Two little arms and one
> little nose.
> One little mouth and two little ears.
> Two little eyes for smiles and tears.
> One little head and two little feet.
> One little chin, that makes (*child's name*) complete.
>
> (*Creative Resources for the Early Childhood Classroom*, second edition, Judy Herr and
> Libby Yvonne. Albany, NY: Delmar Publishers, 1995; p. 404. Used with permission.)

Math

Body Match. Make four or more sets of body matching cards. Find duplicate photos in magazines, use a color photocopier to duplicate body photos, or use stencils of people. Place the cards in a basket and encourage the children to find the matching sets. You could also make matching cards by tracing children's hands and feet. Cut matching sets of hands and feet out of various shades of skin-colored felt.

Body Shapers. Review basic geometric shapes with children. Then challenge them to make shapes with their bodies. Encourage children to look at one another's body shapes and to think of other shapes they can make with their bodies.

Body Sort. Collect pictures of a variety of people or small (realistic) people figures. Make sure the collection represents the diversity of races, cultures, genders, ages, and abilities present in society. Place the figures of people or the pictures in a basket. Set out the basket along with a sorting tray. Invite the children to classify the people any way they like. Be prepared to counter stereotypes or prejudices that emerge from the children's conversation while sorting.

Discovering My Body. Help children learn about their bodies and compare their height, weight, skin color, hair, and facial features to others. Place mirrors, magnifying glasses, a scale, and a tape measure on a table for the children to explore. Encourage the children to measure one another's bodies. Chart the height and weight of all the children in the class. Take measurements throughout the year to help the children become aware of changes in their bodies.

Hand to Hand. Make plaster molds of hands and feet. Fill a plastic dish tub with wet sand. Have the children press their hands and feet in the sand. Fill the prints with plaster and let it harden (about 10 minutes). The children can compare their actual hands and feet to the plaster representations of them.

Hands and Feet. Trace children's hands and feet on poster board or oaktag. Encourage the children to use the hands and feet to measure objects in the classroom.

Line Up. Tape butcher paper to a wall or fence. Have the entire class line up side by side with their backs to the paper. Trace the outlines of each child's body with a felt-tip pen. When you are finished, encourage the children to look at the mural and see if they can recognize each person's outline. What characteristics do they use to match an outline to a child? Give the children an opportunity to color their own body outlines.

Problem Solving. Invite children to problem-solve around assistive technology. If you have children with disabilities in your classroom, it may be possible to have the children solve a real problem. For example, if Maria uses a wheelchair and can't maneuver in the playground through the deep sand, what could the children invent to make the playground accessible to Maria? If you don't have children with disabilities in the classroom, consider posing a hypothetical situation involving either you or one of the children. For example, ask them, "What if I had a car accident and then I needed to use crutches to get around the classroom? Do you think I could climb up the ladder to get into the loft? What do you think we could do to make it possible for me to get up there?" Be careful not to phrase the question in terms of helping someone who is dependent, but in terms of fairness and working together to solve a common problem.

Skin Color Match. Make four or more sets of people matching cards. Use a body shape stencil or gingerbread cookie cutter to trace a simple human body shape. Use skin-colored crayons, markers, or paints to color pairs of bodies the same skin color. Place the cards in a basket and encourage the children to find the matching sets.

 Sort Ourselves. Make some large circles on the floor with yarn or masking tape. Invite the children to put themselves into groups according to physical characteristics. Show them the circles on the floor. Begin by sorting the children into two groups (for example, children with brown eyes in one circle and children with blue eyes in another circle). Ask the children if they can think of other ways to sort themselves.

Music

 Move Those Parts. Sing and move to songs like "Head, Shoulders, Knees, and Toes" or "The Hokey Pokey" to help children recognize body parts. Substitute the names of a variety of body parts. Sing the songs in Spanish or another language.

Smiles Are Funny Things. Here's a song about smiles to sing with children. It's sung to the familiar tune of "Auld Lang Syne."

> A smile is quite a funny thing,
> It wrinkles up your face;
> And when it's gone you never find
> Its secret hiding place.
> But far more wonderful it is
> To see what smiles can do;
> You smile at one, he smiles at you
> And so one smile makes two.

He smiles at someone, since you smiled
And then that one smiles back;
And that one smiles until, in truth
You fail in keeping track!
And since a smile can do great good
By cheering hearts of care,
Let's smile and smile and not forget
That smiles go ev'rywhere.

(*The Joyful Child: A Sourcebook of Activities and Ideas for Releasing Children's Natural Joy*, Peggy Jenkins. Tucson, AZ: Harbinger House, 1989; p. 99. Used with permission.)

Physical Development

Baby Moves. Have children pretend they are babies and take them through the first year of life. Start with having children lie on the floor, then they learn to roll over, sit up, creep, crawl, stand up, walk, run.

Body Puzzle Parts. Trace children's bodies with a felt tip marker onto large sheets of poster board, oaktag, or cardboard. Cut the body tracing into large pieces to make a floor puzzle. Encourage the children to try to put their body puzzles together.

Can You Balance Your Body? Set out the balance beam and invite children to try to walk across the beam without falling off. Set out a variety of light and heavy objects that children can carry as they walk across the beam. For example, give the children an empty bucket and ask them if they think it will be easy or hard to walk across the beam carrying the bucket. Put some rocks or blocks in the bucket so that it is heavy. Ask children if it was easier or harder to walk across the beam carrying the bucket. Give children a yardstick or a 3-foot length of bamboo. Invite children to hold the stick across their bodies with both hands and try to walk across the beam.

Find the Parts. Point to body parts on yourself and see if children can find the body parts on their own bodies. Start with the head and facial features like face, hair, eyes, nose, mouth, ears, and teeth. Later, move down the body to include neck, shoulders, back, arms, hands, fingers, hips, legs, feet, toes. Gradually add more difficult body parts like waist, thigh, knee, ankles, chest, stomach, elbow, wrist.

Foot Ball. Divide the class into two teams. Have the children take off their shoes and sit in two rows facing each other and just far enough apart from one another so that their toes barely touch. Place a lightweight ball on top of the children's feet at one end of the line and challenge them to work together to pass the ball up and down the row using only their feet.

Obstacle Course. Set up an obstacle course that encourages children to move their bodies in a variety of ways. Children can walk on the balance beam, jump over a stack of blocks, crawl through a tunnel, and hop to the wall.

Par Course. Make a par course with five to ten different physical exercises for children to do with their bodies. For example, touch your toes one time, do two jumping jacks, hop on one foot three times, hop on the other foot four times, take five steps on the balance beam, take six steps backward, toss the beanbag into the basket seven times, jump up and down eight times, walk like a crab for nine steps, and take ten deep breaths.

Touching Game. Play a group game about finding and touching body parts. Invite the children to stand up. First ask them to find and touch different body parts on their own body. Then ask them to use their hands to touch a friend. Then ask children to touch various body parts on their friend. You can then ask children to touch physical features related to race (hair, eyes, nose, mouth, skin).

Walking, Running, Hopping. Ask the children if they can walk fast, slow, like a giant, and like they are "light as a feather." Repeat with other body movements like running, crawling, hopping, jumping, galloping, skipping.

Science

Heartbeats. Ask the children if they have hearts in their bodies. Ask the children to point to their hearts. If they do not know where the heart is located, show them. Invite them to put the palms of their hands against their chests to see if they can feel it beating. Set out some stethoscopes and invite children to listen to their own hearts and their classmates' hearts. Clean off the ear pieces by wiping them with rubbing alcohol.

Hidden Parts. Introduce children to some of the major body parts that they cannot see because they are under our skin. Tell them that these body parts are called organs. You might want to use a model, chart, or book to introduce children to the brain, heart, lungs, stomach, intestines, blood, bones, and muscles.

Muscle Testing. This activity helps children recognize that muscles help our bodies work. It is because of strong muscles that we can push and pull, lift and carry things. Set out three buckets filled with sand or rocks. Invite children to see how long they can hold one of the heavy buckets. Show them how to stand with their arms extended out in front of them. One at a time, place a bucket in each child's hand and use a watch to measure how long they can hold the bucket. Ask children how it feels when their muscles are working hard and when their muscles get tired.

Thumbprints. Help children discover that all people have physical characteristics that make them unique and different from everyone else. Encourage children to make prints of their thumbs by pressing their thumbs onto an ink pad and then onto a piece of paper. Label each print with the child's name. Compare and contrast the prints. Make two sets of each child's print, mix up all of the fingerprint cards, and see if the children can find the matching pairs.

Tooth Decay. Ask the children if they ever drink soda pop. Have they ever thought about what is in the drink—and if it's good or bad for them? Set up an experiment to see what happens to teeth if a person drinks too much soda pop.

Show the children a bottle of cola and a baby tooth. Tell the children, "Let's see what will happen if we put the tooth in the cola." Drop the tooth into the cola, write the date on the bottle, and set it in the science area. As a group, observe the tooth once a week and write down the children's observations.

Social Development

Disabilities. Introduce children to the idea that some people's bodies work differently than others, or don't work the way we expect them to.

Use correct terminology: *Deaf* for people who use sign language; *hearing impaired* or *hard-of-hearing* for people who use hearing aids and verbal English; *blind* for people who don't see at all; *visually impaired* for people who have some vision; *mobility-impaired* for people who use wheelchairs, crutches, or braces (it's also okay to refer to "people who use wheelchairs" specifically); and *developmentally disabled* for people with developmental disabilities (a more current and respectful term for retardation).

Ask the children if they know anyone

who's Deaf and uses American Sign Language?

who's blind and uses a dog guide or a cane to navigate?

who uses a wheelchair, braces, or crutches?

who has a developmental disability like Down's syndrome?

who uses a tape recorder to read books, or a magnifying glass to read the newspaper?

who uses hearing aids to hear what people are saying?

Continue the discussion by asking the following questions:

What do you know about this person?

Where does she live?

What work does she do?

Who is in her family?

How did she become disabled?

Try to elicit as full a picture as possible of the person's life. Depending on the disability, you may want to ask how she gets around, if she uses any assistive devices, if she drives a car, and how she communicates with her family.

Be prepared with some examples of your own in case the children don't come up with any. You may want to prepare persona doll stories or bring in photos. You could tell the story of a real person in your life (perhaps even someone who could visit the classroom) or make up the stories. Be sure that most of the people you present in this way are shown as independent, active adults with homes, families, jobs—people who meet their own needs and function in the world.

If you don't know anyone personally who is willing to visit your classroom, every state has at least one Center for Independent Living and a statewide Independent Living Council who can help you find someone.

Gentle Touch. Ask children if they can think of examples of gentle touches. Ask them if anyone ever rubs their backs to help them relax and go to sleep. Take out some hand lotion and show the children how to gently massage a hand. Invite children to find a partner and ask them to take turns massaging each other's hands. Put a small amount of lotion in the children's hands.

Hands That Help. Invite children to think of all the helpful things their hands can do. Write down all their ideas. Ask children to take turns acting out ways to have helping hands. Encourage the rest of the children to guess what each child is doing.

How Would It Be? Ask children if they can imagine how it would be if their hands didn't work the way they do now. Follow-up with open-ended questions designed to further the discussion:

> How might you play your favorite game?
>
> How might you eat?
>
> How might you draw?
>
> How might you dress yourself?

Set out some Ace bandages and invite the children to experiment with what it might be like if their arms or hands didn't work. Help children explore alternative ways of meeting their needs. Have some adaptive equipment available for children to use, and be prepared to focus the conversation on creative problem solving rather than on the things children cannot do or the things that are difficult. You may also want to be ready to do additional research with the children to find out how people who are mobility impaired handle a given situation, if you don't know. Pay attention to stereotypes that emerge from the children's conversation.

You may also want to set out earplugs and blindfolds to allow children the opportunity to see what it would be like to have their hearing reduced or not to be able to see.

You might explain to children that some people with disabilities have other people called personal assistants who come in to help them with things they cannot do alone. Emphasize that these helpers don't make decisions for people with disabilities—they might help a person eat, for example, but not decide what she has for breakfast; or help her get dressed, but not decide what she wears. People with disabilities get to choose the kind of help they want, just like kids do. Sometimes kids need adults to help them with a task, but sometimes they can do it all by themselves. Children get to choose when they need help and when they want to try it alone, and so do people with disabilities.

I'm Sick. Help children learn how to help others who are sick. Ask the children, "Who helps you feel better when you are sick. How can we help people who are feeling sick to feel better?" Set out a pillow, a blanket, a bowl of water, a washcloth, and a cup. Invite children to role-play being sick and taking care of someone who is sick.

Photo Masks. Use a color photocopier to enlarge close-up photographs of a variety of people. Glue the photocopies of the faces to poster board. Punch eyeholes and holes near the edges to attach a string and make a mask. Encourage children to try on the different masks, look at themselves in the mirror, and engage in dramatic play.

Put Your Hands Together For...

Introduce the word *applause* by saying something like, "We make noise by clapping our hands together to show that we like someone or something. Applause is another word for clapping." You may want to introduce them to "Deaf applause"— with fingers spread, hold hands at about head level and rotate them back and forth slightly from the elbow (keep the wrist rigid).

Ask children to name times when people show their appreciation by clapping their hands. Ask children to think about times during the day when we could applaud one another. Give each child a chance to say something they know how to do and the class can applaud their skills and accomplishments.

Words Not Bodies. Teach children that it is not acceptable to use our bodies to express anger or to fight. Hitting, kicking, biting, and pinching hurt others. Ask the children, "How do you feel when someone hits or kicks you? How can we use our words instead of our bodies to express anger or solve our problems?"

ACTIVITIES: AFFIRMING OURSELVES AND ONE ANOTHER

Human Rights

Everyone has the right to healthy food, safe homes, and health care.

BARRIER: Sometimes these aren't available or they're too expensive.

Everyone has the right to go independently to public buildings and events in their community.

BARRIER: Some buildings aren't built so that people with mobility impairments can get in by themselves. Some buildings don't have bathrooms that are big enough for person in a wheelchair to use. Many public events are not interpreted for people who are Deaf. Many public buildings are not marked so that people who are blind are able to find the right room.

Everyone has the right to keep their bodies safe and not to be hurt by anyone else.

BARRIER: Sometimes people get angry and forget that it's not okay to hurt other people.

DISCUSSION QUESTIONS: Help children think about what their bodies need to be healthy. Ask them, "What things do our bodies need to live and be healthy? Why do you think some people don't get what they need to keep their bodies healthy? Do people have good food, safe homes, and health care in our community? Is our community accessible to people with disabilities? Are people safe in our community? What choices could people make to help keep their bodies healthy? How could we help people keep their bodies healthy? How can we work to make sure people have what they need in our community?"

Cultural Identity

Baby Pictures. Collect pictures of each child as a baby. Show the pictures one at a time and see if children can guess who it is. Collect current photos of each child. Put each picture in a resealable bag and see if children can match the baby picture with the current picture of each child. How did they know who it was? What part about their body is the same? What part about their body has changed? Adopted children or children in foster care may not have a baby picture. Check with parent(s) or guardians before presenting this activity.

Dance. Introduce children to the traditional dances of the cultures represented in your classroom. You might ask parents and older brothers and sisters to visit the classroom and demonstrate a traditional dance.

Lullabies. Invite parents to share lullabies from their cultures. Help children recognize that we use music and songs called lullabies to help us calm our bodies and go to sleep.

Ways We Get Well. Ask parents to share their culturally based practices of caring for their children when they are sick. Invite parents to visit the classroom and show the children some of the methods their family uses to heal their bodies.

Diversity

Assistive Devices. Collect a variety of assistive devices for people with physical disabilities. You could include crutches, a walker, cane, wheelchair, or braces. Ask the children, "Does anyone know what these things are? Why might someone use these?" Show children how people with physical disabilities might use the equipment. Talk about how this equipment helps people move their bodies. It takes a lot of practice to learn how to use this equipment. Set the devices in the dramatic play area and encourage children to incorporate them into dramatic play. Monitor children's play for stereotypes and be ready to respond to them; also be sure that children understand that adaptive equipment is not play equipment. This is especially important in situations where a child in the classroom uses adaptive equipment regularly.

Baby, Child, or Adult. Set out a collection of pictures or figures of people that represent the life span. Ask children to identify the babies, little children, big children, and adults.

Everybody Grows. Explore how our bodies both stay the same and change as we grow. Introduce children to the idea that our bodies grow and change through the song "Growing," by Hap Palmer, which children can sing and move to. Then show children pictures of people at different life stages. Ask them, "What can a baby do with her body? How would you describe a baby's body?" Then move to the next stage and ask the following questions:

How would you describe a toddler's body?

How is a toddler's body different from a baby's body?

What stayed the same as the baby grew?

What parts of the baby's body changed?

If you work in a program that serves infants and toddlers, take a walk down to their classroom and observe the infants and toddlers at play. Continue with questions about the remaining stages of life.

Finger Paint Mix-Up. Help children explore shades of skin color through finger painting. Put a small amount of black, brown, red, yellow, and white powdered tempera onto finger paint paper. Pour about 3 tablespoons of liquid starch on the paper. Invite children to mix the powdered tempera and starch by finger painting. Encourage them to make skin colors. They could even try to make the color of their own skin.

Glasses. Talk with the children about why people wear eyeglasses and how they work. Ask children if they know anyone who wears glasses. Why do people wear eyeglasses? Tell children that some people wear glasses because they cannot see objects that are far away. Other people wear glasses because they cannot clearly see objects that are near to them. Eyeglasses help people see things clearly. Set out a few pair of old eyeglasses. Invite the children to examine and try on the glasses. Ask the children such questions as, "How is your vision with the glasses on? Is it better or worse? How can we help our classmates who wear glasses care for their glasses?"

Grab This. Help children gain perspective on one another's experiences. Talk with children about how babies cannot move their fingers very well and that is why it is hard for them to play with toys the same way that preschooler and school age children do. Set out some gloves, mittens, and small manipulative toys like Lego building blocks, puzzles, and stringing beads. Invite children to put on a glove or mitten and try to use the manipulatives. Ask them if it is easier or harder with the gloves on. Talk with children about how sometimes people break their fingers or their fingers don't work. Encourage children to wonder what that would be like. Set out some craft sticks and first aid paper tape. Offer to put splints on children's fingers. Invite them to try to use the manipulatives. Ask them to think of other ways to use the toys.

Hands! Invite children to hold their hands up in front of them. Ask the children, "Does anyone see freckles on their hands? Does anyone have a cut on their hands? Does anyone have a scar on their hands?" Invite the children to look at the skin color on their hands, turn their hands over, and look at the color of their palms. Then invite them to look at one another's hands. Ask them, "How are our hands similar? How are our hands different?"

Just Like Me/Just Like You. Help children explore the concept of alike and different. Display pictures of people that represent different cultures and abilities. Set out a mirror so that children can look at themselves. Ask the children to pick out all the pictures of people who look like them. If a child seems unsure about selecting a particular picture, encourage her to look in the mirror. Talk about the common features between the people in the pictures and the child. For example, "Your hair is curly like this girl's, but your skin is like that boy's." To extend this activity, ask the children to find a friend and pick out all of the pictures of people who look like their friend.

Our Skin Has Color. Invite children to examine their skin. Teach children this simple rhyme:

> What color is your skin?
> Look and see.
> What color is your skin?
> Can you tell me?

Go around the circle and ask each child to name their skin color. Tell the children, "Find something in the classroom that's the same color as your skin. Finding something that's the same will end this game!"

Shapes and Sizes. Help children recognize that bodies come in many different shapes and sizes. Gather photographs of people from magazines to illustrate a variety of body shapes and sizes. Hold the photographs up one at a time and ask children to look at the photographs and describe the bodies they see. You may want to introduce words to help children name what they see. For example, you might introduce the words *tall, short, slender, muscular, large, small, thin,* and *fat.* With older children, you could introduce hourglass, apple, and pear as types of body shapes. Reinforce the idea that everyone has their own body shape and size.

Skin Color. Introduce children to how we get our skin color. Read the book *All The Colors We Are,* by Katie Kissinger. This children's book includes discussion questions and four skin-color activities. Gather skin-colored paint swatches and invite children to pick a paint chip that closely matches their own skin.

Skin Color Match-Ups. Set out a collection of knee-high stockings in shades of tan, white, black, yellow, and red. Encourage children to put the stockings on their hands to find a color that matches their skin color. Explore lighter and darker shades. Talk about how we are all shades of brown and that nobody's skin color is really white, red, or yellow.

Skin-Colored Playdough. Set out the ingredients so that children can make skin-colored playdough. Use skin-colored tempera paints to color the playdough, or have children mix white, black, brown, red, yellow, and blue playdough to make a ball of playdough that matches the color of their skin.

Washing. Help children discover that skin color is a physical feature that does not wash off. Encourage children to finger paint. Talk about the brown paint on the children's hands. Notice how it looks on different colors of skin. Ask, "What will happen to your skin when you wash your hands? Will you wash off your skin color? Does it make a difference if your skin is light or dark?" Talk about how skin color doesn't wash off and how it always stays the same.

Bias and Stereotypes

Accessibility Check. Take a walk through your building and see if it is accessible to children and adults with physical disabilities. You might want to do some research ahead of time with the children and make a checklist of things to look for. Talk about what you could do about any barriers that you find. Ask questions such as the following:

What might be hard to reach for a teacher who used a wheelchair?

How would someone who used a wheelchair wash dishes at our sink?

Would the wheelchair fit underneath the sink?

Are there any stairs, bumps, or steep hills that a wheelchair couldn't go up or over?

How would a Deaf person know if our phone was ringing?

How would a Deaf person know if our fire alarm went off?

How would a mom or dad who was blind know which room was which?

Don't Be a Sissy. Children may stereotype girls as unathletic, weak, and uncoordinated, and boys may be stereotyped as strong, athletic, and coordinated. In reality, there is very little difference between the large-motor abilities of preschool-age girls and boys. Remind children that calling someone a sissy or saying things like "You throw like a girl" is putting girls down. It is also a way of saying that boys are better than girls, and that is not true. Both girls and boys are strong and competent. Introduce children to both female and male athletes.

No Name-Calling. Children may make fun of people by calling them names. Help children recognize that name-calling hurts. Teach children that it's not okay to make fun of people's bodies. As a group, make a list of words that are used to make fun of people's bodies. Talk about how you can help one another avoid using these words.

Strengths and Abilities. Young children often assume that children with disabilities who cannot speak, or walk, or who wear diapers are "babies." Some young children may think that if they play with a child who has a disability, they too will become disabled. Help children recognize all the things that people with disabilities can do and understand that wearing diapers or using a wheelchair doesn't make a person a "baby." Help children realize that a disability isn't like a cold or the flu—you cannot catch it.

You might consider role-playing the situation with a puppet or persona doll, or telling a story ("I have a friend who was afraid that…"). You might also tell stories about people with disabilities who contributed to the world—Franklin Delano Roosevelt, Harriet Tubman, Ludwig van Beethoven, Ray Charles, Thomas Edison, Marlee Matlin, Shirley Chisholm. You might research and tell the story of the liberation struggle of Deaf people at Gallaudet University in Washington, DC, or tell stories about Deaf people who have active jobs, such as pro baseball players, firefighters, or paramedics (books are available from Gallaudet University Bookstore). Avoid presenting people with disabilities as brave or as "overcoming" their disability. You might have various people with disabilities visit the classroom to talk about their lives.

Community Service

Get Well Cards. Set out construction paper and a variety of art materials. Talk with the children about how it feels to be sick. Invite children to make get well cards for someone they know who is sick, or you could identify a short-term "pen pal," someone in the hospital that has a relationship to your program. If the children have experience with community service, they could make get well cards for sick children in a local hospital. Take a field trip to the hospital to hand deliver your get well cards.

Social Action Suggestions

Barrier-Free. Work together to draw attention to and remove any physical barriers that restrict or limit people with disabilities from full participation in your program.

Clean Air, Please. Learn about the effects of cigarette smoking on our bodies and campaign for a smoke-free child care center or school.

Skin-Colored Bandages. Invite children to examine skin-colored bandages and the container they come in. Compare the color of the bandages with your actual skin color and talk about the similarities and differences. Determine if the bandages really are a skin color. Read the description on the box. If the company is making claims that are not true, assist the children in writing a letter that challenges the advertising and requests a more appropriate alternative.

ACTIVITIES:
OPENING THE DOOR

Classroom Visitors

Ask local health care providers to visit the classroom and talk about how they help children and adults take care of their bodies.

Field Trips

Visit a local hospital or health care clinic.

Parent Involvement

Ask parents to come and share ways that they care for their bodies. For example, parents may share ways that they exercise, choose and prepare foods, care for and braid hair, or care for their skin and nails.

Parent Education

Invite a public health nurse, nutritionist, dentist, or other health care professional to present a parent workshop on preventative health care, lead poisoning, recognizing and treating common communicable diseases, home safety, or basic first aid. Invite a chemical dependency counselor to talk about the effects of alcohol and drug abuse on children and families.

CLASSROOM RESOURCES

Children's Books

All By Self: A Father's Story About A Differently Abled Child, Ronn Taylor (Birmingham, AL: Colonial, 1990).

All The Better To See You With, Margaret Wild. (Morton Grove, IL: Whitman, 1993).

All The Colors We Are: The Story Of How We Get Our Skin Color, Katie Kissinger (St. Paul: Redleaf, 1994).

Arthur's Eyes, Marc Tolon Brown (Boston: Little Brown, 1993).

Belinda's Bouquet, Leslea Newman (Boston: Alyson Wonderland, 1991).

The Best Face Of All, Wilesse Commissong (Chicago: African American Images/ Wilesse Commissong, 1991).

Black, White, Just Right! Marguerite Davol (Morton Grove, IL: Whitman, 1993).

Body Battles, Rita Golden Gelman (New York: Scholastic, 1992).

Bright Eyes, Brown Skin, Cheryl Willis Hudson and Bernette G. Ford (East Orange, NJ: Just Us, 1990).

Clap Your Hands, Lorinda Bryan Cauley (New York: Scholastic, 1992).

Come Sit By Me, Margaret Meerfiled (San Francisco: Down There, 1990).

Dancing Feet, Charlotte Agell (San Diego: Gulliver, 1994).

Don't Call Me Fatso, Barbara Philips (Chatham, NJ: Raintree/Steck-Vaughn, 1992).

Everyone Poops, Taro Gomi (Brooklyn, NY: Kane/Miller, 1993).

Faces, Shelly Rotner and Ken Kreister (New York: Macmillan, 1994).

The Family Visits The Doctor, Nayvin Gordon (Nashville: Winston-Derek, 1995).

The Gas We Pass: The Story Of Farts, Shinta Cho (Brooklyn, NY: Kane/Miller, 1994).

Handsigns: A Sign Language Alphabet, Kathleen Fain (San Francisco: Chronicle, 1993).

The Handstand, Barry Rudner (Louisville, KY: Tiny Thoughts, 1990).

Hats Off To Hair, Virginia Kroll (Watertown, MA: Charlesbridge, 1995).

Here Are My Hands, Bill Martin Jr. (New York: Holt, 1987).

HIV Positive, Bernard Wolk (New York: Dutton, 1997).

How Far Will I Fly? Sachi Oyama.

How Many Teeth? Paul Showers (New York: Scholastic, 1991).

Itchy, Itchy Chicken Pox, Grace Maccarone (New York: Scholastic, 1992).

Knock-Knock Knees And Funny Bones: Riddles For Every Body, Judith Matthews and Fay Robinson (Morton Grove, IL: Whitman, 1993).

Let's Find Out About Toothpaste, Kathy Barabas (New York: Scholastic, 1997).

My Body Belongs To Me, Kristin Baird and Marilyn Kile (Circle Pines, MN: American Guidance, 1986).

My Body Is Private, Linda Walvoord Girard (Morton Grove, IL: Whitman, 1987).

My Tooth Is About To Fall Out, Grace Maccarone (New York: Scholastic, 1995).

New Shoes For Silvia, Johanna Jurwitz (New York: Morrow, 1993).

Now I'm Big, Margaret Miller (New York: Greenwillow, 1996).

Outside And Inside You, Sandra Markle (New York: Simon, 1991).

Patrick Gets Hearing Aids, Maureen C. Riski and Nikolas Klakow (Naperville, IL: Phonak, 1994).

Skeletons! Skeletons! All About Bones, Katy Hall (New York: Platt, 1991).

Someone Special Just Like You, Tricia Brown (New York: Holt, 1991).

Stranger In The Mirror, Allen Say (Boston: Houghton, 1995).

Two Eyes, A Nose, And A Mouth: A Book Of Many Faces, Many Races, Roberta G. Intrater (New York: Cartwheel, 1995).

Wave Goodbye, Rob Reid (New York: Lee, 1996).

We Can Do It! Laura Dwight (New York: Checkerboard, 1992).

What Am I Made Of? David Bennet (New York: Aladdin, 1991).

What Is Beautiful? Maryjean Watson Avery (Berkeley, CA: Tricycle, 1995).

Who Shakes The Frame? Ricardo Alcántara.

Where Is Your Nose? Trisha Lee Shapple (New York: Scholastic, 1997).

Where There's Smoke, Janet Munsil (Toronto: Annick, 1993).

The Wonder Of Hands, Edith Baer (New York: Macmillan, 1992).

Your Bellybutton, Jun Nanao (Brooklyn, NY: Kane/Miller, 1995).

Your Skin And Mine, Paul Showers (New York: Harper, 1991).

Music

The Children of Selma. *Who Will Speak For The Children?* (Rounder, 1987).

"Black Is Beautiful"

Fink, Cathy, and Marcy Marxer. *Nobody Else Like Me* (A&M, 1994).

"Harry's Glasses"

"I See With My Hands"

"Kye Kye Kule"

"Walkin' On My Wheels"

Grammer, Red. *Hello World!* (Smilin' Atcha, 1995).

"Shining Eye"

"We're All In This Together"

———. *Teaching Peace* (Smilin' Atcha, 1986).

"Shake Your Brains"

Hartmann, Jack. *Make A Friend, Be A Friend* (Educational Activities, 1990).

"My Name Is Daniel"

Hunter, Tom. *Bits And Pieces* (Song Growing, 1990).

"Lines On Your Face"

Lefranc, Barbara. *I Can Be Anything I Want To Be* (Doubar, 1990).

"Touch A Rainbow"

Mad Cobra. *Positively Reggae* (Sony, 1994).

"Unity"

Pirtle, Sarah. *Two Hands Hold The Earth* (Gentle Wind, 1984).

"Two Hands Hold The Earth"

Rogers, Sally. *Peace By Peace* (Western, 1988).

"Don't Push Me Down"

"Hands"

Shih, Patricia. *Big Ideas!* (Glass, 1990).

"The Color Song"

Tune Into Kids. *Color The World* (Endeavor, 1992).

"Kick It"

"Move Your Bones"

Visual Displays

Constructive Playthings
Friends Together Posters
Health-Cleanliness Picture Packets
Safety Picture Packet

Nasco
Anatomical Chart Set For Children

Northern Sun Merchandising
Hello Babies Poster

Organization for Equal Education of the Sexes
Linda Bove Poster

Sandy and Son
Multicultural Growth Chart
My Body Poster
My Skeleton Poster

Syracuse Cultural Workers
Babies Poster

Videos

Eye And Ear Care (Educational Activities, 1985).

Fire And Rescue (Educational Record Center, 1993).

Fire Safety For Kids (Educational Record Center, 1995).

Germ Busters (Educational Record Center, 1996).

Going To The Doctor (Educational Record Center, 1994).

Going To The Doctor's (Constructive Play-things).

A Kid's Guide To Personal Hygiene (Kimbo Educational, 1989).

Skeleton: Eyewitness Natural World Videos (Educational Record Center, 1994).

We All Sing Together, CTW Sesame Songs Home Video (Random House, 1993).

Computer Software

The Human Body CD-ROM, Beckley-Cardy

What Is A Bellybutton? CD-ROM, Time Life

Additional Resources

The American Lung Association
National Office
1740 Broadway
New York, NY 10019
Offers excellent education materials like Octopuff in Kumquat.

Colgate-Palmolive Company
c/o JMH Communications
1133 Broadway, Suite 1123
New York, NY 10010
(800) 334-7734
Offers educational oral health materials like Bright Smiles, Bright Futures.

Gallaudet University Bookstore
800 Florida Avenue NE
Washington, DC 20002
(202) 651-5505
Gallaudet University is the only Deaf university in the United States. Its bookstore carries not only a selection of standard ASL texts and dictionaries, but also a wide variety of children's books with sign components, videos of children's stories and fairy stories told in ASL, videos of ASL literature, books about the Deaf liberation struggle, and the life stories of Deaf people. They have a catalog.

BOYS AND GIRLS

"Are you a boy?" "That's a girl doll cause it's got lipstick." "That's a boy toy!" "No girls can play, go away!" Usually sometime in the second year, children begin to notice gender. Certainly the diapering, toileting, and dressing that occur in child care settings gives children an opportunity to examine the physical differences between boys and girls. During the preschool years, they begin to develop ideas about what is and is not appropriate gender-related behavior. They also begin to develop attitudes about their own worth, capabilities, and place in the world based on their gender. And, of course, they begin to develop attitudes toward the opposite sex.

Exploring gender issues with children gives them an opportunity to form positive gender identities, examine stereotypes, clarify misinformation, and form positive attitudes about and interactions with children of both sexes.

BOYS AND GIRLS

 Look for this symbol to find activities you can use for circle time.

WEB

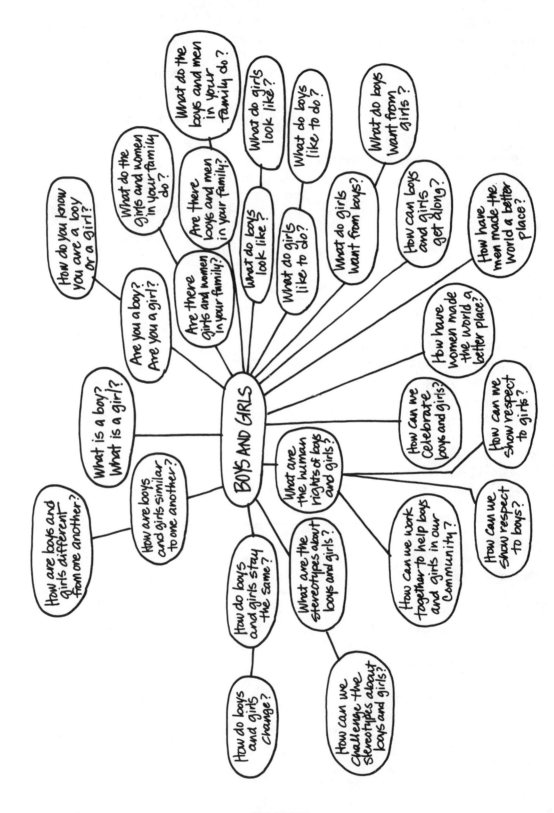

OUTLINE

I. Are you a boy? Are you a girl?

II. How do you know you are a boy or a girl?

III. Are there girls and women in your family?

IV. What do the girls and women in your family do?

V. Are there boys and men in your family?

VI. What do the boys and men in your family do?

VII. What is a boy? What is a girl?

    A. What do boys look like? What do girls look like?

    B. What do boys like to do? What do girls like to do?

    C. What do boys want from girls? What do girls want from boys?

    D. How can boys and girls get along?

VIII. How are girls and boys similar to one another?

IX. How are girls and boys different from one another?

X. How do boys and girls stay the same?

XI. How do boys and girls change?

XII. What are the stereotypes about boys and girls?

XIII. How can we challenge the stereotypes about boys and girls?

XIV. What are the human rights of girls and boys?

    A. How can we show respect to boys?

    B. How can we show respect to girls?

    C. How can we work together to help boys and girls in our community?

XV. How can we celebrate boys and girls?

XVI. How have women made our world a better place?

XVII. How have men made our world a better place?

MATERIALS LIST

ART

skin-colored paints, crayons, markers, felt, and craft paper

butcher paper roll

children's magazines

tracing templates of boys, girls, men, and women

BLOCKS

a variety of multicultural people figures, including figures of people with disabilities

green mats or carpet squares for grass

miniature playground equipment (for example, the Playmobil Playground from *Constructive Playthings*)

aluminum foil for making slides

paper and markers for making signs

DRAMATIC PLAY

multicultural anatomically correct baby dolls

multiethnic preschooler dolls (for example, Friends Dolls, Children with Hearing, Motor, and Visual Impairments Dolls, *People of Every Stripe*; Multi-Ethnic School Dolls, Lakeshore; Multi-Ethnic Dolls, *Constructive Playthings*)

doll furniture and housekeeping sets (available from *Constructive Playthings* and *Lakeshore*)

gym: tumbling mats, simple exercise equipment, water bottles, wristbands, sporting goods equipment, jogging suits, tennis shoes, exercise charts, gym sign, poster of rules for using the gym, logos of local gyms, weight scale, stopwatch, women's and men's sports magazines

baby care: cradles, baby carriers, strollers, baby buggies, receiving blankets, diapers, bottles, potty chairs, baby food containers, small board books to read to babies, books and pamphlets on baby care, baby care magazines, blank baby books for children to write in

LARGE MOTOR

equipment that encourages partner play and turn-taking (for example, Bowling Set, No Miss Mitts, Rimball, *Constructive Playthings*; Giant Hopscotch Mat, *Lakeshore*; Vinyl Practice Balls, *ABC School Supply*)

LITERACY

children's books: fiction, nonfiction, and bilingual books about boys and girls (see resource list at the end of the unit)

cassette player and theme-related storybook cassettes

flannel board or magnetic sets of playgrounds or boys and girls (for example, Boy and Girl Felt Friends, *Environments*)

multicultural hand puppets of boys, girls, men, and women (for example, Children of America Doll Puppets, *Lakeshore*)

MANIPULATIVES

multicultural puzzles of children and adults (for example, Children At Play Puzzles, Multicultural Children Puzzle, Non-Sexist Multi-Ethnic Career Puzzles, Play Scenes Jigsaw Puzzles, *Constructive Playthings*; Multi-Ethnic Kids Floor Puzzle Set, *Lakeshore*; Children with Special Needs Puzzles, *Kaplan*) card games and lotto games about boys and girls (for example, Old Bachelor Card Game, *Northern Sun Merchandising*; Play Scenes Lotto, *Educational Equity Concepts*)

boy and girl or playground counters (for example, Kid Counters and Sports Ball Counters, *Lakeshore*)

SENSORY

anatomically correct dolls

washcloths and soap

SCIENCE

charts of the human body

anatomically correct dolls

body reference books

materials to encourage the exploration of air (for example, hand pumps, a pinwheel, a hand fan, straws, and a whistle)

TEACHING THROUGH THE INTEREST AREAS

Art

Set out children's magazines, templates of boys, girls, women, and men

Blocks

Add green mats or carpet squares (for grass), pretend playground equipment, aluminum foil for slides, people figures of children and adults, paper and markers for making signs to encourage park or playground play.

Dramatic Play

Set out athletic and exercise equipment to replicate a gym. Add tumbling mats, simple exercise equipment, water bottles, wristbands, sporting goods equipment, jogging suits, tennis shoes, exercise charts, a gym sign, poster of rules for using the gym, logos of local gyms, a weight scale, a stop watch, and women's and men's sports magazines. Notice any stereotypes the magazines display and explore them with the children. For example, is the women's magazine focused on fashion and weight loss while the men's magazine focuses on building muscles? What is the difference between men's and women's clothing in the magazines—different colors, more or less flesh exposed? Are men and women models posed differently?

Set out baby care equipment and materials like cradles, baby carriers, strollers, baby buggies, receiving blankets, diapers, bottles, potty chairs, baby food containers, small board books to read to babies, books and pamphlets on baby care, baby care magazines, blank baby books for children to write in.

Large Motor

Set out rocking boats, teeter-totters, balls, jump ropes, basketball hoops and balls to encourage partner play and turn-taking.

Literacy

Set out children's magazines, writing and bookmaking materials, a collection of nonfiction and fiction books on girls and boys, playground flannel board sets, theme-related books on cassette, a tape player, and puppets of boys, girls, women, and men.

Manipulatives

Set out puzzles of boys, girls, and children, as well as the children at play lotto game.

Music

Set out cassettes with silly songs, play-related songs, and songs about boys and girls.

Science

Set out anatomically correct dolls, charts of the human body, and body reference books to encourage exploration of boys and girls bodies.

Set out materials to encourage the exploration of air. Include hand pumps, pinwheels, hand fans, straws, and whistles.

Sensory

Add anatomically correct dolls, washcloths, soap, and water to the sensory table.

ACTIVITIES: INVESTIGATING THE THEME

Creative Development

Girls and Boys Collage. Make a collage by cutting out pictures of boys and girls from magazines and gluing them onto butcher paper.

Pinwheels. Set out 8½-inch squares of construction paper, a pencil with an eraser, and straight pins and invite children to make pinwheels. Cut a straight line from each of the corners of the construction paper to the center, stopping an inch from the center. You will end up with four triangles. Fold the right corner of each triangle to the center. Place a pencil behind the center of the pinwheel. Push a pin through all the corners and into the pencil eraser to hold the pinwheel onto the pencil.

Portraits of Boys and Girls. Invite children to paint a picture of a boy, girl, or boys and girls playing together.

Sock Puppets. Set out felt scraps, fabric trim, yarn, buttons, glue, and a variety of socks in different shades of brown. Encourage children to make a sock puppet that looks like them.

Critical Thinking

When I Grow Up. Children form gender-related ideas about what they want to do when they grow up. Ask the children what their mothers or other women they know do each day. Ask them what their dads or other men they know do each day. Continue the discussion with open-ended questions:

> What are jobs women can do?
>
> What are jobs men can do?
>
> What would you like to do when you grow up and are a woman?
>
> What would you like to do when you grow up and are a man?

Be ready to counter any stereotyping that you hear, perhaps by adding to the children's thinking: for example, "I have a friend who wants to be a carpenter when she grows up," or, "I know a man who stays home to take care of his baby." Develop the stories as much as possible.

Emotional Development

I Am Caring and Strong. Nurture children's self-esteem and confidence in their personal strengths and ability to care for others. At circle time, ask the children to name or show the class something caring that they can do for others. Then ask the children to name or show a way in which they are strong.

You Can Cry. Some young children, especially boys, have difficulty accepting and showing feelings of sadness and pain. Ask children the following questions:

> Can boys cry?
>
> Can girls cry?
>
> Can daddies and men cry?
>
> Can mommies and women cry?
>
> When was a time that you cried?

The following poem by Dr. Charles Smith will teach children to accept and show their feelings:

> Poor little boy with sad eyes *(point to eyes)*
> See him now, how much he cries *(mimic crying, hands to eyes)*
> He tries to stop with all his might *(clench teeth, grimace)*
> He doesn't know *(shake head)*
> That tears are all right *(nod head while pointing to "tears")*
>
> (*The Peaceful Classroom*, Charles Smith. Beltsville, MD: Gryphon House, 1993; p. 71.
> Used with permission.)

Health, Safety, and Nutrition

Safe Play. Go through the playground and each of the classroom interest areas with the children. In each area, ask the children for safe ways that girls and boys could play in this area. Make a list of guidelines for safe play to post in each of the areas and review the guidelines periodically.

Toy Safety. Set out a bucket of different types of toys. Invite the children to examine the toys and decide which toys are safe and which toys could hurt someone. Talk about what makes toys safe or dangerous.

Language Development

> **Home Language.** *Learn the words for* boy, girl, man, *and* woman *in American Sign Language and the home languages spoken in your classroom.*

Boy and Girl Picture Cards. Use a commercial set of pictures of people or make your own set by cutting out large magazine pictures of boys, girls, men, and women and gluing them onto construction paper. Hold up one picture at a time and ask open-ended questions:

Who can tell me about this picture?

What do you see?

What kind of person is it?

How do you know?

What else can you tell me about this boy or girl?

How is this person like you?

How is this person different from you?

Notice and counter any stereotypes children come up with. For example, they may think a woman is a man because she has short hair, they may say a woman with short hair couldn't possibly be a mom, or they may say a fat person eats too much.

Boy and Girl Picture Stories. Sit down with a small group of children and some pictures of boys and girls. Show the children one picture at a time. Ask the children what they see in the picture. Encourage the children to make up a story about the boys and girls in the picture. If possible, write down the children's stories or invite the children to write their own stories and to read one another's writing.

My Book About Girls/My Book About Boys. Invite the children to make their own book about their gender. Ask them, "What is a boy? What is a girl?" Ask children what it means to be a girl or boy and what they like about being a boy or a girl.

Our Book About Boys and Girls. As a class, make a book about boys and girls. Emphasize all the things that boys and girls can be and do. Set out art materials to encourage children to illustrate their book. Notice any stereotypes that emerge from children's work, and be prepared to offer alternative ways of looking at the issues.

Math

Boy and Girl Sort. Collect a variety of pictures of boys and girls. Place the pictures in a basket. Make sure that the set reflects cultural diversity and includes girls and boys with disabilities. Set out the basket and a sorting tray. Invite children to classify the boy and girl pictures any way they like.

Estimate It! Put objects such as balls, marbles, or jacks in a pouch and pass the pouch around so that each child can feel it. Ask the children to guess the number of objects that are in the pouch.

Game Play. Challenge the children to make a board game that both boys and girls would enjoy. Set out oaktag or poster board, spinners, dice, poker chips, square chips for game cards, crayons, markers, and scissors. Point out any stereotypes that emerge. For example, children may use flowers, rainbows, hearts, or the color pink to make the game appealing to girls, and use bolder colors, superheroes, or action motifs to make the game enjoyable for boys. Ask the children, "Is it true that only girls like pink and flowers? Is it true that only boys like action?" Counter these kinds of assumptions with your experiences with your friends or with the children ("But my friend Jessie likes to run fast and play hard," "I remember Paul working on that rainbow painting the other day").

Girl and Boy Match. Make four or more sets of girl and boy matching cards. Find duplicate photos of girls and boys in magazines, use a color photocopier to make duplicates, or use stencils of boys and girls. Make sure that the set reflects cultural diversity and includes girls and boys with disabilities. If you use the stencils, use skin-colored crayons, markers, or paints to color in the girl and boy shapes. Place the cards in a basket and encourage children to find the matching pairs.

How Far? Set up opportunities for children to throw a ball or beanbag, kick a ball, or jump from a standing position. Measure the distance of each throw, kick, or jump. Make a chart.

How Many? Each day, count how many girls are present and how many boys are present. Chart the number of boys and girls present for a week.

Shape It. Set out a variety of shapes, construction paper, and glue. Invite the children to use the shapes to make a figure of a boy or a girl.

Toy Sort. Set out a basket containing a variety of small toys. Invite children to sort the toys. Make a list of all the different ways that the children sort the toys.

Your Shoes and My Shoes. Invite the children to take off their shoes and put them in a pile. Mix them up. Then see if the children can match the shoes. Can they match the shoes to the right person? Challenge them to make a pattern with the shoes. When they are done, use a clock to see how quickly all of the children can find and put on their shoes.

Music

Boys and Girls Come Out to Play. Here's a simple song about girls and boys, sung to the tune of "London Bridge is Falling Down." Invite children to make up additional verses.

Boys and girls come out to play,
out to play, out to play.
Boys and girls come out to play
so early in the morning.

Physical Development

Athletes. Invite the children to pretend to be athletes. Ask them what athletes or sports they know about and then encourage them to move their bodies as if they were playing that sport. Introduce sports that children may have missed or that they might not be familiar with.

Dance of the Dolls. Ask children to pretend that they are dolls and move their "doll bodies" to music. Play different types of music and encourage the children to move their bodies when the music is playing, and to stop moving when the music stops.

Boys and Girls March. Start this activity by walking around singing the following song as the children sit in a circle. At the end of the first verse, select a child to get up and join you. Insert the child's name and whatever play activity the child selects into the song. At the end of the song the child picks another child. Continue until the entire class is holding hands marching around the room.

(Teacher's name)
   went out to play
   (insert play activity).
I had such enormous fun,
   I called on a boy or girl
   to come.
Hey, (name of child
   picked)!
(Child's name) went out to play (activity child selects)
S/he had such enormous fun, S/he called on another girl or boy to
   come.
Hey, (name of child picked)!

Boys and Girls Together. Pair a boy with a girl. Play a variety of games that require cooperation. Possible games are a three-legged walk and a gunny sack run, or have the children walk with a ball between their foreheads, then move the ball from their foreheads down to their knees without using their hands.

Girls and Boys Stop and Go. Choose one child to be the caller. The rest of the children stand in a line. The caller turns her back to the others. When she says "girls," the girls can move forward. When she says "boys," the boys can move forward. When she says "Freeze!" and turns around, all of the children must stop. If the caller catches a child moving after she has said "freeze," the child has to go back to the starting line. The first child to reach the caller and tap her on the shoulder gets to take her place in the next round of the game.

Red Rover. Here's a cooperative twist on a traditional children's game. Ask children to form two lines that are facing one another, and at least 10 to 15 feet apart. The children in one line select a child in the line across from them to come and join them by saying, "Red Rover, Red Rover let (*child's name*) come over." In this version, change the word *come* to a movement, like jump, run, hop, crawl, dance, gallop, or crab walk, so the emphasis is on how the child gets from one side to the other. When the child reaches the other side, the children in that line clap and welcome the newcomer. Repeat the activity with the other line calling a child over. Continue until all of the children have had a turn.

Touching Game. Play a group game about finding and touching body parts. Invite the children to stand up. First ask them to find and touch different body parts on their own body. Then ask children to use their hands to touch various body parts (such as a foot, ear, and elbow) on a girl, then on a boy.

Science

Baby Bodies. Ask parents of children in the class or other familiar adults who have babies to bring them to class so that the children can observe babies being fed, bathed, and diapered. Be sure to have both mothers and fathers bring their babies in so that children can observe both genders providing loving, competent care. Encourage children to ask questions about what they see. Have both boy and girl babies so that you can talk about the similarities and differences of their bodies and the similarities in their wants, needs, and care.

Girl and Boy Bodies. Display a chart of a boy's body and a girl's body. If you don't have a commercially prepared chart, make one by tracing the outline of a boy's body and a girl's body. Present the body charts at large group time. Ask the children to name the parts on the bodies and write the name of the body part on the chart as the children identify them. Once the children have named the body parts, ask them if there are any parts that they forgot. Introduce private or sexual body parts. Ask the children if they know where the nipples, belly button or navel, vagina, and penis are located. This activity will help children recognize that boys' and girls' bodies are very similar, with one important difference: Boys have a penis and girls have a vagina.

Our Private Parts. Follow up the previous activity by posting two charts or flannel board figures of a boy's body and a girl's body. Make bathing suits to cover the private parts of each body. Ask the children to name the body parts they see. Then ask the children to name the body parts that are covered up by the bathing suit. Talk about how we cover up our private parts with clothes, and we don't show our private parts in public. Encourage children to draw a picture of their bodies with their private parts and then draw a bathing suit over the private parts.

Kite Flying. Bring a kite to school. Ask the children to help you put the kite together, following the directions on the package. Take the kite outside on a windy day. Ask the children how they could make the kite fly. Encourage the boys and girls to work together to fly the kite. Set out a science reference book that addresses the scientific properties of air and wind so children can learn about what makes the kite fly.

Windup Toys. Introduce children to the concepts of momentum and the force of air by helping them make a simple toy. Help each child make a wind hummer. Cut out a disk from a plastic container lid. Punch two holes near the center, about an inch apart. Cut a 16-inch length of string. Thread the string through the holes and tie the ends in a knot. Tell the child to hold the string in both hands and "wind up" the hummer by making the hummer go around and around until the string is twisted up tight. Then they can pull their hands apart to make the string unwind and the wind hummer hum like the wind.

Social Development

Boy and Girl Paper Dolls. Help children develop social skills with boys and girls. Take a full length picture of each child. Enlarge it on a color photocopier so that it is 10 inches high. Glue the photo to cardboard and cut it out. Make a stand for the doll and set them out in the block area to foster dramatic play.

Braiding. Make a braiding board by attaching three equal lengths of heavy yarn or narrow strips of cloths to one end of a rectangular piece of heavy cardboard or wood. Introduce children to braiding as a form of hair care. Braiding takes dexterity and fine-motor control. Show children how to braid and invite them to practice braiding.

 Everybody Can Play. Sometimes groups of children get into patterns of excluding others from their play. Hold circle time in the block area and set out tubs of blocks. Tell the children that there is enough for everyone—boys *and* girls. Give each child a pile of blocks, and invite the children to build something. As children are using the blocks, talk about how all of them are playing together in the same area.

 Our Wish for All Boys and Girls. Ask children if they know what *wish* means. Ask the children to name their wishes. Then ask the children what they wish for boys and what they wish for girls. Invite the children to make a poster or mural of all their wishes for boys and girls. Here is a poem that children can recite as they make wishes:

BIG AS LIFE

If my mind was a wishing well,
I'd find a wish that I could tell—
A thought from me to you,
A wish for smiles and fun—
Something you can do
To warm you like the sun.

(*The Peaceful Classroom*, Charles Smith. Beltsville, MD: Gryphon House, 1993; p. 163.
Used with permission.)

Partners. Introduce children to the term *partners* ("When two people work together, we call them partners"). Set out a heavy object that cannot be lifted by a child alone. Ask the children to see if they can lift and carry the object by themselves. Tell them that they could probably lift it and carry it away if they had a partner to work with. Ask children to find a partner. Give each of the pairs an opportunity to work together to lift and carry the block. Encourage the children to think of other things that they could do if they had a partner.

Photo Masks. Use a color photocopier to enlarge close-up photographs of a variety of boys and girls. Glue the photocopies of the faces to poster board. Punch eyeholes and holes near the edges to attach a string and make a mask. Encourage children to try on masks that represent both genders, look at themselves in the mirror, and engage in dramatic play.

Playground Problem Solving. Show the children a picture of a swing and ask them what would happen if everyone went out to the playground and there was only one swing. Discuss the children's answers and talk about how it would be a problem to have only one swing for a lot of children. Tell the children that they would need to decide what to do. Invite the children to do some problem solving. First, describe the problem ("We only have one swing and lots of kids want a turn"). Second, figure out what kind of solutions are available ("What could we do?"). Writing a list of all the possible solutions is often helpful. Third, vote on the possible solutions by giving a thumbs up (good choices) or thumbs down (poor choices). Use the vote to choose two or three of the best solutions.

Take Turns. Young children often have difficulty taking turns. Sometimes boys and girls fight with one another about who goes first and who gets a turn. Ask children if they know what taking turns means. Tell them, "Taking turns means first one person goes and then another, and we don't stop until everyone has had a turn." Girls and boys who are good at taking turns have patience and self-control. Ask children, "When do we need to take turns?" Invite the children to play a game that involves taking turns. It could be a board game, or taking turns could be practiced at the computer, or knocking over bowling pins with a ball. With younger children, you could play a simple ball-rolling game. Sit on the floor with two or three children and roll a ball back and forth. When you roll the ball to a child, say, "My turn." When they roll it to you or to each other, say, "Your turn," or use their names, for example, "Betsy's turn. Now it's Jamal's turn."

Who Is Missing? Help children recall members of a group. Set out an entire set of multicultural boy and girl dolls. Ask the children to hide their eyes while you take one away and rearrange the dolls. Ask children to look at the dolls and guess which one is missing. The child who guesses correctly can rearrange the dolls, take one away, and lay them out again.

We Are Growing Up Equal. Introduce children to the concept of equality. Talk about how boys and girls can do the same things in the classroom, in the community, and at work.

You Can Say No! Help children recognize that they can say no to others. Also help them realize that when they hear the word *no,* it means stop and they need to accept this. Bring a toy for each child to circle time. Ask the children, "When do you say no? What do you do when someone says no to you?" Tell the children that when someone says no they need to listen. *No* is like a stop sign telling us to stop. Invite children to practice saying no and putting their hand up like a police officer. To further illustrate this concept, give each child a toy and encourage the children to practice saying no. One by one, ask each child, "Can I have that?" If the child answers no, say "Okay." If the child answers yes. Take the toy and say, "Thank you." Ask the children, "What did I say and what did I do when you said no to me in that game? I stopped and I said, 'Okay.'" Play the game again, only this time invite each child to ask you for a toy. Invite the children to respond to being told no by answering "Okay." Teaching children the American Sign Language words for *no* and *stop* may give children who communicate best physically another option for successful communication in conflicts.

ACTIVITIES: AFFIRMING OURSELVES AND ONE ANOTHER

Human Rights

Everyone has the right to decide for themselves what they like to do, what they're good at, and who they want to play with.

BARRIER: Sometimes people think that whether you're a boy or a girl should make a difference in what you like to do, what you're good at, how you behave, or who you play with.

All children have the right to play.

BARRIER: Some children live in places where it's not safe to play or they have to work.

DISCUSSION QUESTIONS: Help children think about what girls and boys need to live and be healthy. Ask them, "What things do girls (or boys) need to live and be healthy? Why do you think girls (or boys) don't get what they need? What choices could people make to help girls (or boys) live and be healthy? How could we help girls (or boys) be healthy and happy?" Help them notice any basic inequities in the classroom—for example, if girls dominate the dramatic play area or boys dominate the block area. Ask them, "Do you think boys need to learn to take care of babies? Do you think girls need to learn about building? What could we do to make sure boys and girls get to use all the areas in the classroom?"

Cultural Identity

Children's Chants. Introduce children to traditional children's chants and rhymes from the cultures represented in your classroom.

Toys and Games. Introduce children to traditional children's games and toys from the cultures represented in your classroom. Ask the children, "Which toys and games are for both girls and boys? Which toys and games are traditionally played by girls? Which toys and games are traditionally played by boys?"

Traditional Dance and Dance Outfits. In many cultures there is a tradition of gender specific dance and dance attire. For example, at a powwow some dances are performed by Native American men, some dances are performed by Native American women, and other dances are performed by both men and women. In some tribes only men are drummers and in other tribes women drum. With the assistance of parents, explore the cultural traditions of dance. Which dances are for girls and women? Which dances are for boys and men? Which dances are for both men and women?

Diversity

Clothes. Explore all of the different ways that boys dress and girls dress. Ask the children to look at the clothes they are wearing. Chart the number of boys and girls wearing pants, short- or long-sleeved shirts, dresses, shoes or sandals, and other articles of clothing. Set out a flannel board, figures of boys and girls made from felt, and a variety of clothes for these figures. Invite the children to take turns dressing the boy or girl figures. Set out magazines and encourage the children to cut out pictures of men and women to make collages. Be sure that the magazines you supply are culturally diverse and show girls and women wearing pants and getting dirty, perhaps wearing clothes appropriate to tradeswomen (jeans, tool belts, hard hats, and so on); and show men wearing robes and other flowing clothing. When the collages are complete, ask the children to identify the different types of clothes boys and men wear and the different types of clothes girls and women wear.

Hair. Help children notice that hair can be a distinguishing physical characteristic. Show children pictures of a variety of adults and children with different hairstyles. Be sure to include pictures of women with very short hair and men with long hair. Pass around a hand mirror so that the children can take turns looking at and touching their own hair. Ask each child to describe her own hair.

Inside and Outside Play. Invite children to work together to make a mural or collage depicting all the different types of inside play that they enjoy. As a group, talk about all the different kinds of play the children enjoy when they are inside. On the next day, invite children to work together to make a mural or collage that shows all the different types of outside play that they enjoy. As a group, talk about all of the different kinds of outdoor play that they enjoy. Compare the two murals and ask the children, "How are inside play and outside play alike? How are they different?"

Models and Fashion Dolls. Very few people actually have bodies like models and fashion dolls—the average female model weighs 22 percent less than the average woman. Use this series of activities to help children understand how fashion models and fashion dolls are not realistic. Set out fashion magazines and news magazines or a photojournal. Show children photographs of women engaged in regular activities

and photographs of fashion models. Ask the children to find and cut out more pictures like these from the magazines.

Make a comparative poster with the photographs. Divide a sheet of poster board into two columns and put the fashion models in one and the women who are not models in the other. Talk with the children about the photographs, and help them notice similarities and differences. Take note of the models' skin colors and hairstyles. Notice that the models are probably thinner, situated in a variety of unnatural poses, and wearing makeup, clothes, and jewelry that are different from what most women wear. Tell the children that body fat is a normal and natural part of everyone's body; it provides us with energy and helps to keep us warm. Being too thin is not healthy.

Bring out a fashion doll. Compare the doll's body to the photographs of models and the photographs of women engaged in regular activities. Ask the children if they know anyone who has a body like the fashion doll. Talk about how the doll's body is out of proportion (long legs, small waist, large chest, big eyes, small nose). Repeat the activity with photographs of male fashion models and a male doll.

Pay attention to any stereotypes about body size that emerge from the children. You may hear that fat people eat too much, that it's not healthy to be fat, that fat people aren't active, that it's healthy to be thin. Give the kids correct information—that people's bodies are naturally different sizes, some people are fat and some are thin; that it's healthy to be the natural size of your body; that everyone needs to eat good food when they're hungry and exercise their bodies to stay healthy; that there are health benefits and drawbacks to being either fat or thin. You may want to read them *Belinda's Bouquet,* by Leslea Newman, which addresses these issues.

Toys. Encourage children to recognize all the different types of toys that boys and girls enjoy. Invite children to identify different categories of toys. They might identify toys by gender, age, inside and outside, school and home, type of play (dolls, balls, cars). Accept the categories that the children come up with. You could add a few of your ideas to expand their thinking, such as baby toys, toys from other cultures, old toys, toys for children with disabilities. Invite the children to find examples of the toys in each of the categories. They could trace the outlines of a real toy, draw a picture of it, or find and cut out a picture of a toy from a catalog, newspaper advertisement, or magazine. These images could be used to make a mural or collage, or mounted as part of a "Toys We Enjoy" display.

We Can Do Many Things. Explore all the different things that boys do and all of the different things that girls do. Divide the class by gender into two small groups.
Give the boys a large piece of butcher paper and markers and ask them to make a poster of all the things that boys do. Give the girls a large piece of butcher paper and markers and ask them to make a poster of all the things that girls do. Bring the groups together to look at and describe the two posters. Ask the children to compare all of the things that boys can do and all of the things that girls can do. Point out any limited or stereotypic thinking on the part of the children about what boys and girls can do. Be prepared to use this information to develop your curriculum further. For example, if you notice that children don't think of carpentry as something that girls can do, you may want to have a tradeswoman visit the class, or alternate boys' and girls' turns at the workbench.

We're All Human. Help children explore ways that boys are similar to and different from one another and the ways that girls are similar to and different from one another. Display pictures of boys and girls from many different cultures doing a variety of things. Show children the pictures and discuss them. Ask the children, "How are the boys and girls similar?" "How are you like the boys and girls in the pictures?"

Bias and Stereotypes

Bias in Children's Toys. Set out catalogues and toy wish books from local retailers. Ask children to find dolls, puppets, figures of people, and puzzles that represent different skin colors and cultures. Then ask them to find dolls, puppets, people figures, and puzzles that show children with disabilities. Ask the children, "What did you learn by looking through these catalogs?" "How would you feel if you couldn't find a doll or toy that looks like you?" Talk with the children about how toys that look like them help them to feel beautiful, proud, and special. Toys that represent lots of different types of people help children learn to play with all kinds of people and remember that there are all kinds of people in our world.

Can a Boy Play with Dolls? Read the book *William's Doll,* by Charlotte Zolotow. Set out a doll, a car, a ball, and crayons and paper. Show children each object and ask if a boy can play with them and why. Ask children why some people don't want boys to play with dolls. Ask them what William should do—should he play with dolls or not play with dolls?

Changing the Lead. Read a familiar children's story that has a male character and retell or act out the story with a girl in the lead role. Do the same with a familiar story that has a female as the lead character and retell or act out the story with a boy as the lead.

Gender Activity Hunt. Children may have very limiting views about what activities girls and boys can be involved in, or what toys they can play with. Take a walk through the center or school building and interview people that you come across. Ask them questions about the activities that they enjoy and record their answers. When you get back to the classroom, list all the things that the boys and men like to do, and list all of the things that the girls and women like to do. Ask the girls if there are things on the boys' list that they would like to add to their list, and ask the boys if there are things on the girls' list that they would like to add to their list. Talk about how stereotypes are limiting. If we believe stereotypes, we think that girls can only do certain things and boys can only do certain things.

Gender Stereotypes. As a class, go through the books in the book area and count how many have a main character that is a girl and how many have a main character that is a boy. Make a list of the things that the main characters do. Help the children decide if the activities are limited or stereotypic.

Is It a Boy or a Girl? Make up a variety of descriptions of children that challenge gender stereotypes. Describe a child by focusing on such things as likes, dislikes, favorite toys, favorite television shows, favorite people, and fears. Let children guess if the child is a boy or a girl. Talk with the children about why they think the child you described is a boy or a girl.

No Name-Calling. Introduce the concept that it is not acceptable to call people names or exclude someone because they are a boy or a girl. Use puppets or dolls to demonstrate a situation of name-calling and exclusion. Have one puppet say to the other puppet, "Hey, that looks like fun. Can I play?" The other puppet responds, "Get away. You're a girl, and girls can't play!" Ask the children, "What did the puppet just say? Is that okay? What could the puppet do instead?"

Gender Equality. Talk about how boys and girls are equal in your classroom. Ask children what they think boys' and girls' rights should be. You might want to introduce your ideas, such as boys and girls get to think for themselves, boys and girls in our class should get along with each other, boys and girls in our classroom have the right to be safe, it's not fair to call people names because they are a boy or a girl, it's not fair to say, "You can't play" because someone is a boy or a girl.

Community Service

Come Along. Invite a group of boys and girls from a homeless or battered women's shelter to go on a field trip with your class.

Toy Give Away. Ask children to bring in unwanted toys or toys that they have outgrown and donate them to children in a homeless shelter or shelter for battered women and children.

You're Invited. Make an invitation and distribute it around the neighborhood inviting all the boys and girls to a story time, video, or sing-a-long.

Social Action Suggestions

Playground Request. As a group, write a letter to local officials requesting that they turn a vacant lot into a playground.

School-Age Program. Identify the types of children's recreational programs and clubs in your neighborhood or community. Which ones are for boys and which ones are for girls? Which ones are for both boys and girls? If your program doesn't have a school-age child care program, children may want to petition the administration to add school-age care or write their local government to request that the city or public schools start a school-age child care program so that they will have a safe place to go before and after school. You might write a letter to the city requesting that an abandoned house be used to create an after-school recreational program for school-age children.

Young Children Are Important. Attend and participate in the local "Week of the Young Child" rally or some other community event that draws attention to the need for high-quality, accessible, and affordable early childhood programs.

ACTIVITIES: OPENING THE DOOR

Classroom Visitors

Ask local high school, amateur, and professional athletes to come and share their talents with the children. Make sure that you include both male and female athletes.

Invite women and men in nontraditional careers to talk about their jobs, how they chose their careers, what they do, the tools and equipment they use, and what they need to know to do their job.

Field Trips

Take a trip to a local YWCA or YMCA, Boys and Girl's Club, or health club.

Parent Involvement

Ask parents and grandparents to visit the classroom and share their ideas about what girls need to grow into womanhood, what boys need to grow into manhood, and what it means to be a woman or a man today.

Ask parents to come and show children how they care for and style their children's hair. Ask parents to talk about the names for the different styles of braiding and decorations that they use.

Encourage and support parents to work with the local crime prevention division of the police department to have their residences designated as McGruff Houses—safe places on the block for girls and boys to go in an emergency.

Parent Education

Invite an educator or psychologist to talk with parents about raising children free of gender bias, or invite a family life educator or sexuality educator to talk with parents about sexual development and learning in young children.

CLASSROOM RESOURCES

Children's Books

All The Colors Of The Earth, Sheila Hamanaka (New York: Morrow, 1994).

Allie's Basketball Dream, Barbara E. Barber (New York: Lee, 1996).

Amanda's Perfect Hair, Linda Milstein (New York: Tambourine, 1993).

Amazing Grace, Mary Hoffman (London: Magi, 1995).

The Bare Naked Book, Kathy Stinson (Toronto: Annick, 1986).

Baseball Ballerina, Kathryn Cristaldi (New York: Random, 1992).

Baseball Saved Us, Ken Muchizuki (New York: Lee, 1994).

Bet You Can't, Penny Dale (New York: Lippencott, 1987).

The Biggest Boy, Kevin Henkes (New York: Scholastic, 1995).

Bloomers! Rhoda Blumberg (New York: Atheneum, 1993).

Can't Sit Still, Karen Lotz (New York: Dutton, 1993).

A Carp For Kimiko, Virginia Kroll (Watertown, MA: Charlesbridge, 1993).

The Catspring Somersault Flying One-Handed Flip-Flop, SuAnn Kiser (New York: Orchard, 1993).

Children Do, Grownups Don't, Norma Simon (Morton Grove, IL: Whitman, 1987).

Con Mi Hermano/With My Brother, Eileen Roe (New York: Scholastic, 1991).

Cowboy Dreams, Dayal Kaur (New York: Potter, 1990).

Daniel's Dog, Jo Ellen Bogart (New York: Scholastic, 1990).

Diego Wants To Be, Doris Rodriguez (Fort Atkinson, WI: Highsmith, 1994).

Do Like Kyla, Angela Johnson (New York: Orchard, 1990).

Father Gander Nursery Rhymes, D. W. Larche (Santa Barbara: Advocacy, 1985).

Friends In The Park, Rochelle Bunnett (New York: Checkerboard, 1992).

Gina, Bernard Waber (Boston: Houghton, 1995).

The Girl Who Wore Snakes, Angela Johnson (New York: Orchard, 1993).

Harry's House, Angela Shelf Medearis.

Hello Amigos, Tricia Brown (New York: Holt, 1992).

I Am Not A Crybaby, Norma Simon (Morton Grove, IL: Whitman, 1989).

I Have A Sister, My Sister Is Deaf, Jeanne Peterson (New York: Harper, 1977).

I Want To Learn To Fly! Judy Barron (New York: Scholastic, 1995).

It's My Body: A Book To Teach Young Children How To Resist Uncomfortable Touch, Lory Freeman (Seattle: Parenting, 1983).

It's Raining Laughter, Nikki Grimes (New York: Viking, 1997).

Just Us Women, Jeannette Caines (New York: Harper, 1982).

Keepers, Jeri Hanel Watts (New York: Lee, 1997).

Lee Ann: The Story Of A Vietnamese-American Girl, Tricia Brown (New York: Putnam, 1991).

The Lesson, Pat Cummings.

Let The Celebrations Begin! Margaret Wild and Julie Vivas (New York: Orchard, 1991).

Let's Find Out About Bubbles, May Ebeltoft Reid.

Loving Touches, Lory Freeman (Seattle: Parenting, 1986).

Margaret And Margarita/Margarita y Margaret, Lynn Reiser (New York: Greenwillow, 1993).

Mirette On The Highwire, Emily Arnold McCully (New York: Scholastic, 1992).

Messy Bessey, Patricia McKissack and Frederick McKissack (Danbury, CT: Children's Press, 1997).

Messy Bessey's Closet, Patricia McKissack and Frederick McKissack (Chicago: Children's Press, 1989).

Messy Mark, Sharon Peters (Mahwah, NJ: Troll, 1980).

Mimi's Tutu, Tynia Thomassie (New York: Scholastic, 1996).

My Navajo Sister, Eleanor Schick (New York: Simon, 1996).

My Steps, Sally Derby (New York: Lee, 1996).

The Paper Bag Princess, Robert Munsch (Toronto: Annick, 1988).

Pueblo Boy: Growing Up In Two Worlds, Marcia Keegan (New York: Cobblehill, 1991).

A Rumbly Tumbly Gittery Gritty Place, Mary Lyn Ray (New York: Harcourt, 1993).

Sari Games, Naina Gandhi (London: André Deutsch, 1990).

Someone Like You, Dawn Kline (North Billerica, MA: Curriculum Associates, 1989).

The Streets Are Free, Kurusa (Toronto: Annick, 1995).

Through Our Eyes: Poems And Pictures About Growing Up, Lee Bennett Hopkins (Boston: Little Brown, 1992).

Together, George Ella Lyon (New York: Orchard, 1989).

When Frank Was Four, Alison Lester (Boston: Houghton, 1994).

Where's Chimpy? Berniece Rabe (Morton Grove, IL: Whitman, 1988).

Who Is Who? Patricia McKissack and Frederick McKissack (Danbury, CT: Children's Press, 1993).

Why Am I Different? Norma Simon (Morton Grove, IL: Whitman, 1987).

Wild Wild Sunflower Child Anna, Nancy White Carlstrom (New York: Macmillan, 1987).

William's Doll, Charlotte Zolotow (New York: Harper, 1972).

Music

Fink, Cathy, and Marcy Marxer. *Nobody Else Like Me* (A&M, 1994).

"Everything Possible"

"Hello, Hello, Hello"

Grammer, Red. *Hello World!* (Smilin' Atcha, 1995).

"Hello World"

"On The Day You Were Born"

———. *Teaching Peace* (Smilin' Atcha, 1986).

"With Two Wings"

Hartmann, Jack. *Let's Read Together* (Educational Activities, 1990).

"I Like"

———. *Make A Friend, Be A Friend* (Educational Activities, 1990).

"My Name Is Daniel"

———. *One Voice For Children* (Educational Activities, 1993).

"Positive Power"

Music For Little People. *Fiesta Musical,* with Emilio Delgado (Music for Little People, 1994).

"Una Melodia"

Shih, Patricia. *Big Ideas!* (Glass, 1990).

"Why Not?"

Thomas, Marlo, and Friends. *Free To Be… A Family* (A&M, 1988).

"Another Cinderella"

"Boy Meets Girl…Again"

Tune Into Kids. *Color The World* (Endeavor, 1992).

"Come On Over To My House"

Vitamin L. *Walk A Mile* (Lovable Creature, 1989).

"Family Feeling"

Visual Displays

Constructive Playthings
Friends Together Posters

Lakeshore
Children of the U.S. Poster Pack

National Black Child Development Institute
African American Sons Poster Series
Horizons Poster

Northern Sun Merchandising
Girlfriends Poster
Listen to Girls Poster

Syracuse Cultural Workers
Dancers Posters

Additional Resources

National Women's History Project
7738 Bell Road
Windsor, CA 95492-8518
(707) 838-6000
Fax: (707) 838-0478
Offers a catalog of books, posters, videos, and
classroom materials that celebrate women's
history.

COMMUNICATION

Infants can understand many more words than they can speak. Their use of language drastically increases during the second and third years of life. Along with learning how to speak, young children become interested in all forms of communication. At six in the morning, they're up pleading, "'Toons, Mom. 'Toons!" The conversation at the snack table centers around the latest children's video ("Did you see that movie? Do you have that tape at your house?"). Children also discover the world of books ("Will you read me this? Read it again!"). By age five they are learning to dial their best friend's phone number or calling grandma on the phone. Many children today also use computers to communicate.

A unit on communication celebrates all the ways that young children express themselves. It can be a way to recognize all the different languages and ways to communicate. A unit on communication can also help children begin to sort through difficult concepts, like real and pretend and fair and unfair, that are often presented in the media.

Unit 3:

COMMUNICATION

 Look for this symbol to find activities you can use for circle time.

WEB

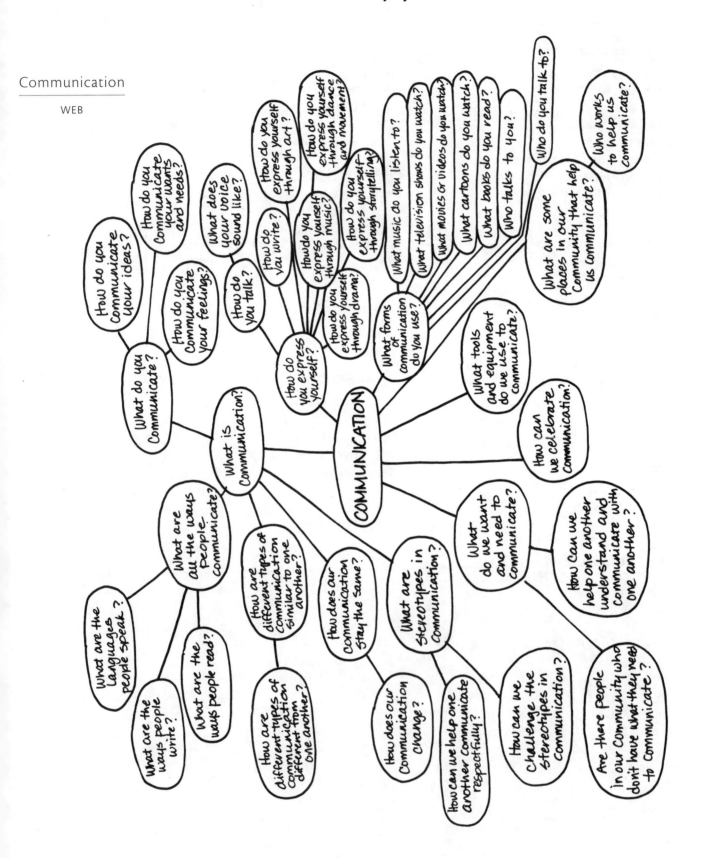

OUTLINE

I. How do you express yourself?
   A. How do you talk?
   B. What does your voice sound like?
   C. How do you write?
   D. How do you express yourself through art?
   E. How do you express yourself through music?
   F. How do you express yourself through dance and movement?
   G. How do you express yourself through drama?
   H. How do you express yourself through storytelling?

II. What forms of communication do you use?
   A. What music do you listen to?
   B. What television shows do you watch?
   C. What movies or videos do you watch?
   D. What cartoons do you watch?
   E. What books do you read?
   F. Who do you talk to?
   G. Who talks to you?

III. What are some places in our community that help us communicate?

IV. Who works to help us communicate?

V. What tools and equipment do we use to communicate?

VI. What is communication?
   A. What do you communicate?
      1. How do you communicate your ideas?
      2. How do you communicate your wants and needs?
      3. How do you communicate your feelings?
   B. What are all the ways people communicate?
      1. What are the languages people speak?
      2. What are the ways people write?
      3. What are the ways people read?
   C. How are different types of communication similar to one another?
   D. How are different types of communication different from one another?
   E. How does our communication stay the same?
   F. How does our communication change?

VII. What are stereotypes in communication?
   A. How can we challenge the stereotypes in communication?
   B. How can we help one another communicate respectfully?

VIII. What do we want and need to communicate?
   A. Are there people in our community who don't have what they need to communicate?
   B. How can we help one another communicate with and understand one another?

IX. How can we celebrate communication?

Materials List

ART

skin-colored paints, crayons, markers, felt, and craft paper

butcher paper roll

alphabet stencils and templates (for example, Alphabet Templates, *Lakeshore*)

alphabet stamps

alphabet cookie cutters

alphabet paint sponges

BLOCKS

a variety of multicultural people figures, including figures of people with disabilities

scissors, paper, tape and markers for making signs

traffic signs for block vehicles (for example, Mini Traffic Signs, *Edvantage*)

DRAMATIC PLAY

multiethnic baby dolls

multiethnic preschooler dolls (for example, Friends Dolls, Children with Hearing, Motor, and Visual Impairments Dolls, *People of Every Stripe*; Multi-Ethnic School Dolls, *Lakeshore*; Multi-Ethnic Dolls, *Constructive Playthings*)

adaptive equipment for dolls with disabilities (available from *Lakeshore*)

old phones or play phones (for example, Desk Phone, Talk 'n Listen Phone, Touch Tinkle Phone, *Beckley-Cardy*; Maple Cellular Phone, Touch Phone, *Constructive Playthings*; Push Button Phone, *ABC School Supply*)

pretend phone booth (for example, Telephone Booth, *Nasco* and *Constructive Playthings*; Double Sided Phone Booth, *Constructive Playthings*)

an old television set or pretend TV (for example, Count by Colors Musical TV, *Beckley-Cardy*; Television Set, *Sandy and Son*)

pretend video cameras, camcorders, record players, etc. (for example, Music Box Record Player, Video Camera, Camcorder, *Constructive Playthings*)

library: library sign, international library logo sign, librarian name tags, story time flyers, table, chairs, index cards for pretend library cards, card file box, stamp pads, date stamp, pencils, books, magazines, newspapers

television station: pretend microphones, pretend video cameras, head sets, career clothes, poster board and markers for making signs and headlines, maps, news magazines and newspapers that children can cut up for making headlines and visuals

post office: mailbox, mail carrier hats, mail sacks, name tags, post office signs, hours of operation sign, letters, bills, greeting cards, envelopes, padded mailing envelopes, boxes, craft paper, masking tape, self-stick mailing labels, stamps, pens and pencils, desk, service bell, cash register, scale, receipts, pretend money, rubber stamps and stamp pads (see also Fisher Price Post Office, *Beckley-Cardy*; Mail Carrier Costume and Mailbox, *Edvantage*)

home living: old or pretend television set, telephone, computer keyboard, transistor radios with headphones, newspapers, magazines, books, phone book, wall calendar, message board

LARGE MOTOR

materials that explore letters and language (for example, Alphabet Set Beanbags, *Constructive Playthings*; Alphabet Twist, Alphabet Carpet Squares, *Lakeshore*; Multi-Lingual Balls, *ABC School Supply*)

materials that support the mail theme (for example, Mailbox, *Beckley-Cardy*; U.S. Mail Delivery Trike, *ABC School Supply*)

LITERACY

children's books: fiction, nonfiction, and bilingual books about communication (see resource list at the end of the unit)

cassette player and theme-related storybook cassettes

blank cassettes

flannel board sets of communication workers

magnetic alphabet sets (for example, Magnetic Alphabet Boards and Letter Sets, *Lakeshore*; Magnetic Hebrew Letters, *Constructive Playthings*)

alphabet books in several languages, including American Sign Language

Braille alphabet book

alphabet and American Sign Language stamps and stamp pads

note cards, greeting cards, paper, envelopes, pencils

puppets (for example, Alphabet Finger Puppets, *Constructive Playthings*; Alphabet Puppets, *Lakeshore*)

MANIPULATIVES

alphabet sorting and matching games (for example, Alphabet and Number Stringing Beads, Alphabet Sorting Kit, *Lakeshore*; Finger Alphabet Cards, Finger Alphabet Lotto, *Sandy and Son*; Twisted Tales Games, Kids On Stage Game, *Childswork/Childsplay*)

pretend typewriter, microphone (for example, Radio with Microphone, My First Typewriter, Petite 800 Typewriter, *Beckley-Cardy*)

communications and alphabet puzzles (for example, "I Love You" Signing Puzzle, *Environments*; TV Reporter Puzzle, Learning the Alphabet Puzzle Set, Mail Carrier Puzzle, *Lakeshore*; Lineperson Puzzle, Mail Carrier Puzzle, Safety Signs Knob Inlay Puzzle, *Constructive Playthings*; Welcome Floor Puzzle, *Sandy and Son*)

SCIENCE

conch shell

a variety of tubes

megaphone

microphone

stethoscope

walkie-talkies

baby monitor

screwdrivers

old communication equipment like a radio, television, cassette player, or telephone

SENSORY

alphabet sand molds or cookie cutters (for example, Sand Mold Letters, available from *Constructive Playthings*)

Teaching Through the Interest Areas

Art

Set out alphabet stencils and templates, alphabet stamps, alphabet cookie cutters and playdough, and alphabet paint sponges.

Blocks

Encourage the children to make a television station or library with the unit blocks and people figures.

Set out a container with construction paper, markers, scissors, and masking tape to encourage children to make signs for the buildings they construct with the unit blocks.

Dramatic Play

Set up the dramatic play area as a library. Add a library sign, the international library logo, librarian name tags, story time flyers, table, chairs, index cards for pretend library cards, a card file box, stamp pads, a date stamp, pencils, books, magazines, and newspapers.

Set up the dramatic play area as a television station. Decorate a large appliance box as a television and encourage children to pretend they are television reporters. Add a stage, table, chairs, pretend microphones, pretend video cameras, head sets, career clothes, poster board and markers for making signs and headlines, maps, news magazines, and newspapers that children can cut up for making headlines and visuals. If you have the equipment, set up a video camera so that children can videotape and see themselves on television.

Set up a post office. Include the following: a mailbox, mail carrier hats, mail sacks, name tags, post office signs, hours of operation sign, letters, bills, greeting cards, envelopes, padded mailing envelopes, boxes, craft paper, masking tape, self-stick mailing labels, stamps, pens and pencils, a desk, service bell, cash register, scale, receipts, pretend money, rubber stamps, and stamp pads.

Add the following to the home living center: an old or pretend television set, telephone, computer keyboard, transistor radios with headphones, newspapers, magazines, books, phone book, wall calendar, and message board. Or make a simple cardboard television set for the home living area by cutting a screen-shaped hole in a piece of poster board. Draw buttons or knobs below the screen.

Literacy

Set out a collection of alphabet books in various languages. Include books in Braille and American Sign Language, bilingual books, a cassette player, storybooks and cassettes, cassette tapes of stories told in different languages, blank cassette tapes for the children to record their own stories, puppets of people, flannel board sets of communication workers, alphabet and American Sign Language stamps and stamp pads, a classroom post office box, note cards, greeting cards, paper, envelopes, and pencils, and materials for making books.

Manipulatives

Set out puzzles of communication workers and listening lotto games.

Music

Set out cassettes with songs in other languages and songs about using words.

Set out American Sign Language song charts.

Science

Set out a variety of materials used to listen to sounds. Include a conch shell, a variety of tubes, a megaphone, microphone, stethoscope, baby monitor, and walkie-talkies.

Sensory

Add water to the sand and use your fingers to write letters and numbers in it, or add alphabet sand molds or cookie cutters to make letters in the sensory table.

Activities: Investigating the Theme

Creative Development

Communicate. Ask children, "What are you thinking about today? How are you feeling today? What do you want and need?" Encourage children to express their thoughts, feelings, and wants and needs through art. Perhaps they could paint or draw a picture in response to these questions.

Greeting Cards and Envelopes. Set out paper, marking pens, crayons, collage materials, tape, and staplers. Invite children to make greeting cards and envelopes for family and friends.

Mail Bag. Set out brown paper sacks, construction paper, markers, glue, and scissors. Invite children to make a mail bag like the mail carrier uses to deliver the mail.

My Name. Cut out the letters of each child's name. Give each child the letters to his name. Set out a variety of art materials, and invite children to paint, color, or make a collage on each letter. When they are dry, help each child arrange the letters of his name on a large piece of paper and glue the letters in the correct sequence to spell it.

Megaphone. Invite children to experiment with construction paper to see if they can figure out how to make a megaphone. Set out a variety of paints and a stapler. Children can decorate their pieces of construction paper. When they dry, encourage children to roll the paper into a cone and help them staple it in place.

Newspaper Mosaic. Set out dark-colored construction paper, newspaper, scissors, and glue. Invite children to tear or cut the newspaper into small pieces and glue them onto the construction paper, leaving a small space between the pieces so that the dark construction paper shows through and provides a high contrast.

Secret Messages. Invite children to draw a picture or write a message to someone else in the class using a white or yellow crayon on a white piece of paper. The drawing or message will be almost invisible. When they are done, ask the children to give their messages to the recipient, who can expose the message by taking the paper to the art table and painting over the message with either black watercolors or a diluted wash of black tempera paint.

Secret Messages, Take Two. Use cooking oil to paint a picture or message on pieces of butcher paper. Hold the pictures up to the window. The light will shine through and illuminate the picture. Invite the children to take their pictures back to the art table and decorate them with watercolor paints.

Critical Thinking

Understanding Each Other. Take out play figures of children. Hold up two of the figures and explain that these two children speak different languages and they want to be friends with each other. Use examples of two languages currently spoken in your classroom. Ask the children, "What can these two children who speak different languages do together? How can they talk to each other? How does each know what the other one wants?" Repeat the discussion with a different situation. Present a friendship between a child who hears and a child who is Deaf.

What Is the Right Name? Use two dolls or puppets to introduce this discussion. Act out the following situation with the dolls or puppets. "Mary and Rosa are looking for something to write on. Mary is looking for a 'table' and Rosa for a 'mesa.' They see the table and they both say, 'That's what we need!' Rosa says, 'mesa,' and Mary says, 'table.' Then they start to argue about what it is really called. Who is right, Mary or Rosa? What is the real name of that object?" Children who are ready to do some switching of roles can consider what *mesa* means to Mary and what *table* means to Rosa.

Emotional Development

Body Talk. Encourage children to practice using their bodies to communicate their emotions. Ask children, "How do you communicate your wants and needs?" Invite children to take turns acting out what they want or need. The rest of the children can try to guess what the child is trying to communicate through pantomime.

Feeling Drum. Encourage children to express different emotions through music. Pass around a drum, and have children beat the drum in a happy, sad, afraid, or mad way.

I Can Communicate. Foster children's self-esteem and confidence in their verbal skills. At circle time, invite the children to show the class how well they can communicate. Some children may want to sing a song, tell a story, say something in another language, or recite a finger play, poem, or riddle.

Tattle Tale. Use a persona doll or puppets to tell the story of a child who constantly tattles on other children. He thinks it's his job to make sure all of the children play his way. Nobody can get too silly or have too much fun, because if they do, the child will tell on them. He runs to the teacher and whines,

"Teacher, teacher! They aren't playing the game right." Because this child tattles, the other children don't want to play with him. Stop the story and ask the children the following questions:

> How does this child feel?
>
> How do the other children feel?
>
> Why do you think he tattles?
>
> What can he do instead?

Conclude the activity by asking the children whether tattling gets the child in the story what he wants.

Health, Safety, and Nutrition

 Who Are You Going to Call? Help children recognize who they should call in emergency situations. Ask the children, "Who would you call if there is a fire? Who would you call if you hear gunfire? Who would you call if someone is sick or hurt?" Most communities have 911 service. Teach the children to dial 911. In many rural communities you still need to tell the 911 operator your location. Teach children to state the situation, state the location, and stay on the telephone. For example, "I can't wake up my mom. I live at 222 Maple Street in Springfield." Older children could be taught to tell the operator their names and ages as well. Remind children that calling 911 is not a game. They should only call 911 if there is a real emergency.

Language Development

> **Home Language.** *Learn and compare the American Sign Language finger spelling alphabet with the alphabets of the languages of the children in your class. Some languages, like Chinese and Japanese, don't have alphabets but instead have characters. Each character represents a whole word or idea. You may want to bring in a book or newspaper in one of these languages to allow children to examine the characters. Some languages are not traditionally written down at all (this is true of some Native American languages).*
>
> *Listen to and learn folk songs in the home languages of the children in the classroom.*

Class Communication. Make a classroom book that illustrates all the ways that children communicate. Include topics such as communicating through art, music, movement and dance, drama, puppets, and pretending, storytelling, and writing.

Communication Picture Cards. Glue magazine pictures of people communicating or working in communications-related jobs onto construction paper, or use a commercial set of teaching pictures. Hold up one picture at a time and ask open-ended questions:

Who can tell me about this picture?

What do you see?

What is this person doing?

What do you think this person is trying to say?

How is this person like you?

How is this person different from you?

What else can you tell me about this picture?

Communication Stories. Sit down with a small group of children and some pictures of people communicating in a variety of ways. Be sure to include pictures of people with disabilities, people using American Sign Language, and other people communicating nonverbally. Ask the children what they see in the pictures. Encourage the children to make up stories about the communication in the picture. If possible, write down the children's stories.

Individual Silly Putty. Make a visual recipe chart for the following recipe so that each child can make their own batch of silly putty. Use simple line drawings to illustrate each step. Arrange the drawings from top to bottom and left to right to foster prereading skills, and write the words next to the pictures to help children associate print with actions. Put 1 tablespoon liquid starch and 2 tablespoons white glue into a cup. Let it set five minutes. Add 2 drops of food coloring. Stir with a spoon. Mix it well so that all of the starch is absorbed. Store overnight in a jar or plastic egg. Use the silly putty to make prints from the newspapers and comics.

Lots of Literature. At group time, introduce children to a different form of literature each day. Include poetry, wordless books, fables, folktales, rhymes, fiction, and nonfiction. Set out samples of each type of literature. You might want to use small circle stickers to color code the books by type.

Mailboxes. Make simple mailboxes for each child. They could be paper pockets, decorated shoe boxes, or file folders. Write each child's name and address on the mailboxes and set them up in the language or writing area. Talk with the children about the role of mail carriers in delivering the mail each day. Encourage children to write one another letters and send one another mail.

Playdough Letters. Set out playdough, rolling pins, and plastic letter cookie cutters. Use a dark color of playdough, like black or brown, so that the playdough letters will stand out on a light-colored table and stand apart from bright-colored cookie cutters. Encourage children to spell out their names and words that they know, or are interested in.

Sing It! Here is a song and a finger play on the topic of communication which can be used at circle time and throughout the day.

CALL A FRIEND

Tune: *Row, Row, Row Your Boat*

Call, call, call a friend.
Friend, I'm calling you.
Hi, hello, how are you?
Very good, thank you!

(*Creative Resources for the Early Childhood Classroom*, second edition, Judy Herr and
Libby Yvonne. Albany, NY: Delmar Publishers, 1995; p. 147. Used with permission.)

MY HANDS

My hands can talk
In a special way.
These are some things
They help me to say:
"Hello" *(wave)*
"Come Here" *(beckon toward self)*
"It's A-OK" *(form circle with thumb and pointer)*
"Now Stop" *(hand out, palm forward)*
"Look" *(hands shading eyes)*
"Listen" *(cup hand behind ear)*
"It's far, far away" *(point out into the distance)*
And "Glad to meet you, how are you today?" *(shake neighbor's hand)*

(*Creative Resources for the Early Childhood Classroom*, second edition, Judy Herr and
Libby Yvonne. Albany, NY: Delmar Publishers, 1995; p. 148. Used with permission.)

Sound Choice. Make a cassette tape of people speaking in different languages and
accents. Include the languages represented in your program or community. Play the
tape and see if children can guess who it is or what language the person is speaking.

Story Writing. Have children take turns dictating stories to adults. Older children
will enjoy writing their own stories. At circle time the children can act out their
stories while they are read aloud.

Tag Team Stories. Start a story with a simple sentence—for example, you could say,
"I know a baby who is just learning to talk." Ask the child sitting next to you to add to
the story. Then go around the circle letting each child add a word or thought. You
might want to tape the story or ask another adult in the room to take dictation.

Television Shows. Make a television out of a
cardboard box. Cut out a screen-shaped hole
on one side. Add some dials or buttons to the
front. Cut out two holes large enough to insert
cardboard tubes or wooden dowels in the top
of the box, near the two front corners. Invite
children to draw a television show in scenes
on a long piece of butcher paper cut to the
width of the box TV. Start with the first scene
of the left-hand side of the butcher paper and
move across the paper to the right as the story

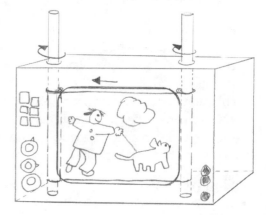

unfolds. When it's finished, tape the left and right edges of the story paper to cardboard tubes or wooden dowels. Roll the story paper up around the right-hand tube or dowel (the one with the end of the story), and insert the story roll into the box television from the inside so that the beginning of the story shows through the screen hole. Turn the dowels to wind the paper from the right-hand dowel onto the left-hand one, and tell the story from beginning to end.

We're on the Air. Tape record children's pretend telephone conversations. Also set out the tape recorder when you are having discussions with children. Label the cassette tapes of the children's discussion (for example, "Our Families," "Our Communities," "Our Workers," "Our Bodies, "Our Foods").

What Does the Camera Say?

Provide the children with disposable cameras, a Polaroid camera, or a video camera. Show the children how the camera works. Encourage them to select and take pictures of things that are important to them. You might want to look at books by noted photographers such as Tana Hoban and Anne Geddes. Make a book of the children's photographs.

Math

Cards and Envelopes. Make a simple matching game by setting out different sized greeting cards and corresponding envelopes. Ask children to try to match each greeting card with the envelope that fits.

Communication in Our Lives. Talk with the children about communication in their lives. Tell the children they are going to find out about one another. Ask questions such as

> How many languages do we speak?
>
> What is your favorite book?
>
> What is your favorite television show?
>
> What is your favorite song?

Ask the children what else they want to know about one another. Graph the answers.

Communication Match. Make four or more sets of communication matching cards. Find duplicate photos in magazines, or use a color photocopier to duplicate photographs of people singing, talking on the phone, using a typewriter, using a computer, reading a book, writing, listening with headphones, using sign language, and talking to one another. Place the cards in a basket and encourage the children to find the matching sets.

Communication Sort. Collect a variety of pictures of people communicating or pictures of communication-related objects. Make sure that the set reflects racial and cultural diversity and includes people with disabilities. Write the name of each object or communication act on the back of each card. Place the pictures in a basket, and set it out along with a sorting tray. Invite children to classify the pictures any way they like.

Computers 101. Introduce children to computers, if you have one in your classroom or school, or take them to the local library. Teach them about the parts of the computer, such as the screen, keyboard, CPU (central processing unit), disk drive, mouse, mouse pad, and disks. Show children how to turn the computer on and off. Introduce them to the icons on the screen. It's important for children to recognize the icon that tells the user to wait. Children who are not familiar with computers may press keys in rapid succession without waiting for the computer to respond. As a result, the computer will freeze up. Teach children how to take turns with the computer. Children also need to learn how to insert disks, use the keyboard, and click, double click, and drag the mouse.

Crayon Count. Set out a bowl of crayons, pencils, or other communication-related tools. Set out cards that have numerals on them and the corresponding number of dots. Invite children to count the crayons using the number cards.

Number Walk. With the children, take a walk around the classroom, building, and neighborhood and look for numbers. Make a list of all the places you find numbers.

Phone Numbers. Talk with the children about how many people have telephones in their homes and one way of communicating with others is to talk on the telephone. Show children how to pick up the receiver, dial the number, and call someone. With the children's help, make a classroom telephone book. Cut out the shape of a telephone from construction paper, and glue onto a 9-by-12-inch piece of construction paper for the cover. Write each child's name and telephone number on a separate sheet of paper, and staple the book together. Set out the book and two telephones and encourage the children to practice dialing their own and their friends' telephone numbers.

Read It. Ask the children, "How many books can you read in five days?" Make a chart to record how many books children read in a week. Place the chart in the book area. Give the children a sticker for each book they look at on their own during free-choice time. At the end of the week, count the stickers.

Music

A Song of My Own. Set out a variety of instruments and encourage children to create their own songs.

BIG AS LIFE

Communication Songs. Here are three songs about communication to teach to children at circle time and sing throughout the day:

MAIL A LETTER

Tune: *Frére Jacques*
by Pennie Smith and Donna Karnes

Mail a letter, mail a letter
To a friend, to a friend.
Going to the mailbox, going to the mailbox
around the bend, around the bend.
Get a letter, get a letter
From a friend, from a friend.
Look inside your mailbox, look inside your mailbox.
What did they send? What did they send?
Is it a letter? Is it a letter?
Addressed to you, addressed to you?
Do you know who sent it? Do you know who sent it?
Do you have a clue? Do you have a clue?
(Name) sent a letter, *(Name)* sent a letter
Just for me, just for me.
I will write a letter, I will write a letter
Wait and see, wait and see.

(*The Giant Encyclopedia of Circle Time and Group Activities for Children 3 to 6*, Kathy Charner, editor. Beltsville, MD: Gryphon House, 1996; p. 311. Used with permission.)

A GOOD DAY

Tune: *Auld Lang Syne*

This day is full of joy for me
I'll choose for love and peace
I'll bring good cheer to everyone
And let my worries cease.
I'll think good thoughts and speak good words
Of truth that sets us free
It's joy for me to be my best
Each day in harmony.

(*The Joyful Child: A Sourcebook of Activities and Ideas for Releasing Children's Natural Joy*, Peggy Jenkins. Tucson, AZ: Harbinger House, 1989; p. 98. Used with permission.)

COMMUNICATION

Tune: *You Are My Sunshine*

Communication gets information
Across to people both far and near.
May be a letter, a TV program, or a radio that you hear.
Communication is conversation
Between two people or maybe more,
By telephone or a walkie-talkie, or a neighbor standing at your door.
Communication can cross the nation

Or cross the ocean by satellite.
The world seems smaller, news travels quicker
than we ever dreamed it might.

(*Sing and Learn*, Carolyn Meyer and Kel Pickens. Carthage, IL: Good Apple, 1989; p. 46.
Used with permission.)

Physical Development

A Tisket, A Tasket. Invite children to form a circle and sit down on the floor. Choose one child to be "it." Give the child a small basket with an envelope in it and tell the child to skip around the outside of the circle while the children sing, "A tisket, a tasket a green and yellow basket. I wrote a letter to my mom and on the way I dropped it, I dropped it, I dropped it." At some point the child gently drops the basket behind a child sitting in the circle and begins running around the outside of the circle. The other child immediately gets up and chases the first child, trying to tag him. If the child who is "it" reaches the open space in the circle before being tagged, the other child becomes "it."

Alphabet Mix-Up. Make a set of alphabet cards. You will need one card for each child in the group, and two to four duplicates of each letter you include. (It's not necessary to use all the letters in the alphabet.) Ask the children to sit in a circle, and give each child a card. When you call out a letter, all the children who have that card jump up and exchange places. To make the game more complex, the teacher can take a seat after calling the first letter, which leaves one of the children without a place to sit. That child becomes the next caller.

Body Words. Challenge the children with the following situation. Ask them how they would say the following without using their voices: "I'm hot," "Please be quiet," "I'm hungry," "I have to go to the bathroom," "I want my mom," "I don't know," "Do you want to play with me?" and "Stop it!" Encourage the children to use their hands, bodies, and faces to communicate their thoughts, wants, and needs.

Breathing Exercise. This exercise helps children learn to project their voices. Invite everyone to stand in a circle and ask the children to put their hands on their abdomens and take a deep breath. Do they feel their diaphragms expand? Ask the children to exhale and feel their diaphragms contract. Let the children practice breathing in and out, feeling their diaphragms expand and contract. Then ask everyone to inhale and count to ten aloud, breathing out from their diaphragms. Next ask them to inhale and say, "Ha, ha, ha," from their diaphragms. End by going around the circle and asking each child to say, "My name is (*child's name*)," speaking clearly and strongly from his diaphragm.

Move to the News. Give each child a sheet of newspaper. Lead the children through creative movement. Begin by using the newspaper to define each child's space. Can they sit on it? Can they walk on it? Can they jump on it? Hop on it? Walk around it without touching it? Can they jump over it? Can they get under it? Can they pick it up and move it through the air? Can they crumple it into a ball and throw it into the basket?

People Communications Machine. Ask the children to figure out how they could make their bodies work together to form a typewriter, a telephone, a computer, a camera, or maybe a video game.

Sand Writing. Cover the bottom of a plastic cafeteria tray or a jelly roll pan with black construction paper. Pour a thin layer of clean beach sand or cornmeal over the construction paper. Invite the children to write letters and words in the tray. The dark construction paper shows through and provides a high contrast, making it easier for children to see the letters and words they write with their fingers. Gently lift and shake the tray from side to side to erase the writing and start all over again.

Sandpaper Letters. Use stencils to make a set of sandpaper letters and numbers. Glue the letters and numbers to poster board cards. Invite children to trace the letters and numbers with their fingers. Can they cover their eyes and identify the letter with their fingers? Set out newsprint and crayons. Show children how to place the sandpaper alphabet and number cards under the newsprint and rub the crayon back and forth to make rubbings.

Story Dancers. Introduce children to cultural dances that tell stories, perhaps by watching a video of dancers from one of the cultures represented in the classroom, or by having dancers from one of those cultures visit the class. Help the children understand that it may be disrespectful to perform dances from a culture of which you are not a member, but they can still use dance and movement to tell a story. Invite children to pick a familiar story or make up a new one and tell it through dance and movement.

Science

Name Reflections. Make a name card for each child by writing their names backward. Give the children their cards and ask them if they know what it is or what it says. You could ask them, "Did I write the letters correctly? Are the letters on your cards backward? How could we read the signs?" Invite children to hold their name cards up to a mirror and see what happens.

Paper Making. It is very easy to make recycled paper. Tear newspaper into small pieces and place them in a bowl. Pour 2 cups warm water over the paper. Beat the paper so that it turns to pulp. Add 2 teaspoons liquid starch. Use a hand beater or a blender to mix it thoroughly. Place a fine meshed screen on the rim of a jelly roll pan. Or, if you have an old window screen, set it up on blocks an inch above the pan, so that the liquid can drain through. Pour the paper pulp onto the screen in an even rectangular layer. Let it drain for a few minutes. Put the pulp-covered screen in between sections of newspaper and roll it with a rolling pin to squeeze out and soak up excess liquid. Remove the newspaper, peel the pulp off the screen, and lay it on dry newspaper to dry overnight. Children can experiment with texture and color by adding scraps of thread, yarn, or very small pieces of fabric to the pulp mixture.

Reflection Pictures. Give children an opportunity to experiment with mirrors and reflections. On each of a series of file cards, draw a half of a symmetrical shape (circle, heart, square, rectangle, etc.). You can also use the letters *H, A, T, X, U, V, W, M, I, O,* and *B* (divide the letters vertically and draw only half of each letter on the cards). Set out the cards and rectangular hand mirrors. Show children how to hold a mirror upright and at a right angle to the cards to make the pictures appear whole.

Super Sound Conductors. Set out a variety of tubes such as paper towel tubes, toilet paper tubes, wrapping paper tubes, vacuum cleaner hose, PVC pipe, plastic surgical tubing, piece of garden hose, and a cardboard cone or megaphone. Invite the children to talk and listen to each other through the tubes. Ask the children if they think the pipes will all work the same way. Which one works the best? Which one works the least? What do they think makes the difference?

Telephones. Cut a small hole in the bottom of each of two plastic drinking cups, and insert the ends of a length of plastic tubing into each hole. (Make the holes a little smaller than the tubing so that it will fit snugly.) Invite one child to talk into one cup while a second puts the other cup to his ear and listens. Talk with the children about how the sound of their voices travels. To extend this activity, have the children attempt to communicate with each other from various parts of the classroom. Try having one child stand outside the classroom and one child inside, or one child up in the loft and another child down on the floor, or one child in the block area and another in the dramatic play area.

Tubular Sounds. Get a mailing tube or some other piece of heavy cardboard tubing. Make sure that the diameter of the tube is large enough so that a plastic drinking cup can fit into the end of the tube, but not so big that it falls through. Ideally you want the lip of the cup to rest against the end of the tube. Poke a hole in the bottom of each cup, and push a 6-inch-long spring through one, leaving two coils on the inside. Push the cup into the end of the tube, with the spring hanging inside the tube. Pull the spring through the inside of the tube and push the loose end through the bottom of the second cup. Cover the ends of the spring with hot glue from a glue gun. This prevents them from falling out. Cover the ends of the tube with duct tape and decorate with contact paper. Shake the tube up and down to make sounds. Shake it really fast to make an interesting vibrating sound.

Social Development

Community Communicators. Introduce children to places and people in the community that help people communicate. Children could learn about the phone company, the library, the post office, the newspaper, the television station, the radio station, and the theater.

Hand Talk. Ask children to imagine how they might communicate if they couldn't hear or use their voices. Have they ever had a really bad cold and "lost" their voice? How did they let their parents know what they needed? If they don't come up with it, introduce them to the idea of talking with their hands, faces, and bodies. To extend this activity, tell the children that you will wear earplugs and not use your voice for the rest of the morning (or for half an hour), and that you will use your face, hands, and body to communicate with them. Explore with them the idea that you will not be able to hear them. How will they let you know what they need? At the end of the time, talk with them about the experience. What things were easy to communicate? What things were hard? Point out to them that Deaf people communicate easily with each other when they use ASL, and that hearing people communicate easily with each other using English, but both hearing and Deaf people have difficulty using the other's language. Sometimes special people called interpreters, who know both English and ASL, come to help hearing people and Deaf people talk to each other. You might have an interpreter come to visit the classroom and talk about her job.

Communication

SOCIAL
DEVELOPMENT

Hand Words. Learn simple sign language that you can demonstrate and teach to the children in your class. Introduce the children to the term *Deaf*. Talk about how some children and adults can't hear. You might need to help them understand what that means—that they can't hear the TV, or people talking, or music. Tell children that many Deaf people learn how to talk with their hands, using a language called American Sign Language (ASL). ASL is a different language from English, just like French or Spanish. Sign some simple words and ask children if they know what you are saying. Teach the children some simple and complex signs.

Deaf people also watch television with closed captioning, which displays the words that people are saying on the screen. Rent a children's video that has closed captioning from a video store and watch part of it with the sound turned off. How much of what's going on can the children catch? Deaf people use a teletypewriter (TTY) to talk on the phone. Bring a TTY into the classroom and demonstrate how Deaf people use the phone by typing. You might find an old TTY that can be left in the dramatic play area for children to experiment with.

I Heard You. Help children begin to learn that listening means hearing and understanding what others say to us. At circle time, ask the children to say something to the child on their right. They could say their favorite toy, their favorite book, or their favorite song. One child tells the other, "My favorite toy is… " The child who is listening responds, "I heard you say that your favorite toy is… "

My Voice. Tape the children's voices one at a time. With a small group of children, play the tape and see if they can guess whose voice they hear on the cassette tape. Ask them how they know who it is.

Talk on the Telephone. Introduce children to talking on the telephone. Bring a telephone to circle time. Ask the children if anyone knows how to use a telephone. Ask the children to demonstrate how to answer the telephone if it rings. Give each child a chance to practice picking up the receiver, holding it to his ear, and saying hello in a strong, clear voice. Then ask the children if they know how to call someone on the telephone. Demonstrate picking up the receiver, dialing the number, and speaking into the receiver. Give each child a chance to practice placing a telephone call. Set out telephones in the dramatic play area and encourage children to practice using the telephone.

Communication

SOCIAL
DEVELOPMENT

Talking Stick. Help children listen to one another and learn to speak one at a time. Introduce children to a talking stick or talking drum during group discussions. The child who is talking holds the stick or drum, and when finished, passes the stick to the next person who wants to speak. If no one wants to speak, the child can lay the stick down on the floor in the middle of the circle. The stick is a good visual reminder of who is speaking and who needs to be listening.

ACTIVITIES: AFFIRMING OURSELVES AND ONE ANOTHER

Human Rights

Each person has the right to speak, read, and write in his or her own language or the language of his or her family.

BARRIER: Many people only speak one language, so it's hard for people to talk to one another. Some people think that everyone should only speak English.

Everyone has the right to get public information in the language that they can best understand and to take part in public meetings. (This includes material being available on tape or in Braille for people who are visually impaired or blind and ASL interpretation for people who are Deaf.)

BARRIER: Some people think that everyone should speak only English. It's hard to find interpreters who can translate from one language to another.

DISCUSSION QUESTIONS: Help children think about what people need to be able to communicate. Ask them, "What things do people need to communicate with others? What is public information? Why is it important for people to be able to get public information the way they understand it best? What are public meetings? Why is it important for everyone to have access to public discussion? What happens when only some people have access to public discussion? What do people need to have access to public information and discussion? Why do you think some people don't get what they need? What choices can people make to help other people communicate with and understand one another? What can we do to make sure everyone has equal communications access? How can we communicate well with people who communicate differently from us?"

Cultural Identity

Folktales. Introduce children to folktales by explaining that folktales are very old stories. Folktales help us learn about how our relatives and ancestors lived a long time ago. Every culture has its own folktales. Read a selection of folktales from the cultures represented in your class. Talk about how the folktales are similar to and different from one another. Get out a globe or world map and help children find the countries where the folktales came from.

Many Languages. Explore the languages represented in your classroom, community, or region. You may want to read a story to the children in another language or use a storybook on cassette.

Music of My Culture. Introduce children to music as a form of communication. Choose a variety of songs from each child's home culture that tell a story or a message. Introduce children to songs from their home cultures.

 Rhythm Band. Introduce children to simple instruments from the cultures represented in your classroom. Ask an adult from the culture who plays that instrument to come in and demonstrate it for the children. Play folk music from the cultures and play the instruments along to the music.

Diversity

 Baby Talk. Explore how babies communicate and how our style of communication changes as we grow. Watch video tapes of babies and toddlers. Ask the children to look for ways that babies communicate without talking. Ask the children, "How do babies communicate like us? How do babies communicate in ways that are different from us?"

How Many Different Ways? Set out a variety of art materials, including string, glitter, craft dough, sandpaper, dried beans, rice, alphabet stencils, paint, markers, and crayons. Invite the children to make a set of alphabet letters by making each letter a different way.

Lots of Different Alphabets. Make an alphabet chart for different languages. Show the charts to the children. Tell them these are alphabet charts from different languages. Ask the children, "Does anyone recognize the alphabets?" Label each one for the children ("This is the Russian alphabet," "This is Hebrew," "This is Arabic"). Tell the children that not every language has an alphabet. Chinese and Japanese are examples of languages that have characters instead. Each character stands for a whole word or idea. Some languages are not written down at all. American Sign Language is an example of this kind of language, as are some (but not all) Native American languages. You may want to get a Chinese or Japanese newspaper or book and show the characters to the children or show them a video of a familiar story told in American Sign Language (available from Gallaudet University Bookstore).

ABCDEFG

АБВГДЕЖ

אבגדהוז

Lots of Ways to Communicate. Help children explore different ways of communicating and different styles of communication. Pick one concept or idea of interest to the children. It might be pets, babies, water, or the latest movie. Once you and the children have picked a topic, explore all the ways to communicate their interest in that topic. For example, they could talk about it, read about it, write about it, draw or paint a picture about it, act it out, sing a song about it, or watch a movie about it. Gather materials so that children have many choices to pick from, and invite them to pick one way to communicate their interest in the topic.

What Language Is That? Explore how languages are similar to and different from one another. Make a cassette tape of adults and children speaking different languages. If you don't know many people who speak a different language, contact a community English as a Second Language program. Play the tape and ask the children if they know what language the people are speaking. Can they tell when the language changes? Can they recognize when someone is speaking English? How do they know when someone is speaking a different language? What are some of the different languages spoken in the community? To extend this activity, explore how people's voices are similar to and different from one another, and how people can change their voices and talk in different ways.

Bias and Stereotypes

Don't Tease Me. Sometimes children are afraid of people whose communication pattern is different from their own. They may avoid or make fun of people who speak another language, with an accent, or with a speech impediment. Use a persona doll or puppet to introduce the concept of accents, different languages, and speech impairments and how it feels to be teased as a result. Help children find positive and respectful ways of interacting with people whose communication pattern is different from their own.

It's Just a Commercial. Watch some commercials that target children as consumers. Point out the things that are real and the things that are pretend in the commercial.

What's It Like? Invite children to put a piece of dental cotton or a large marshmallow in their mouths and try to talk. (You may want to model this first, and let the children experiment with trying to understand you.) Pair the children up and let them try to have a conversation, taking turns at being the one with the dental cotton in their mouths. Or hand the child a telephone and ask him to talk to his parent on the phone. Ask the children the following questions:

What was easy to communicate?

What was hard?

What did you do to try to make it easier?

What could the listener do to make it easier?

What was hard about listening?

They may say that it was easier if the other person was patient and took the time to listen, or that they had to find other ways to say difficult words. Listeners may say that they were frustrated, or that they wanted to laugh.

The subject of ridicule may come up, or you may want to bring it up. You might say, "Sometimes when we feel uncomfortable or embarrassed or we don't know how to handle a situation, it makes us want to laugh at a person who's having a hard time or make fun of them." Help the children explore alternative ways of behaving when they feel embarrassed or don't know what to do. Reinforce the idea that children with disabilities, speech delays, or speech impairments want to communicate, but have to do it more slowly or in different ways. Ask the children, "How can you make friends with someone who has a hard time talking?"

Who's Missing from the Magazines? Set out a variety of popular magazines. Ask the children to find pictures of different types of people. Paste the pictures to a chart. Include a column for men and a column for women who are European American, African American, Latino or Latina, Asian American, and Native American. Once the children have gone through all of the magazines and pasted their pictures to the chart, take a red felt tip marker and ask children to find all of the pictures of people with disabilities on the chart. Draw a circle around each picture of a person with a disability. Ask the children to look at the chart and count how many pictures there are for each group. Ask them the following questions:

Who are there the most pictures of?

Who doesn't have very many pictures?

Who has no pictures?

Why aren't there equal amounts of pictures?

How do you think the people with the most pictures feel?

How do you think the people with few or no pictures feel?

Tell the children that when people are missing from books, magazines, television shows, and movies, we can forget that they are an important part of our community. When we don't see people who look like us in books, magazines, television shows, and movies, we can feel left out and like we don't belong. Everybody belongs, and all types of people live in our community.

Where Are the Girls? Female characters are often missing from popular children's television shows and children's books. Watch some children's shows or set out some children's books and ask the children to look for girl characters and boy characters. Compare the number of girls to boys, the importance of the girl characters compared to the boy characters, and the roles that the girl characters play compared to the roles that the boy characters play.

You Don't Look Like an Indian! Young children often expect people who are Native American to look like the "Indians" that they see on television or in movies. Help children recognize the difference. Videotape segments of stereotypic portrayals of Native Americans on television and some accurate ones. Public television is a good source of accurate and contemporary programming about Native Americans. If this is too difficult, collect photographs from magazines that portray Native Americans in stereotypic ways. Entertainment guides and marketing materials that accompany popular children's cartoons can be good sources of these. Cut out photographs from magazines and newspapers that portray contemporary Native Americans in accurate ways. Show the photographs to the children and ask them to describe the pictures. How are they similar? How are they different? Talk about how the pictures of "Indians" with very red skin, feathers, teepees, bows and arrows, tomahawks, arms folded across their chests, and speaking in grunts are stereotypes. They are untrue pictures that make fun of Indians, and they confuse us. When we believe the stereotypes, it's hard for us to tell what is real and not real.

Community Service

Book Drive. Collect and donate books to your local library. Sponsor a book sale to raise money for local literacy programs.

Children's Video. Make a video for your local public television or community access station.

Social Action Suggestions

Access to Information. Appropriate communication systems and materials are very important for some people with disabilities or people whose home language is not English. Lack of appropriate translation methods or bilingual materials means people are at a disadvantage because they don't have access to information. As a group, advocate for bilingual, Braille, or taped materials for children and families in your program, school, or community, or for TTYs (teletypewriters) so Deaf people can access services by phone.

ACTIVITIES: OPENING THE DOOR

Classroom Visitors

Ask a person who uses sign language, or reads Braille, or uses other assistive communications equipment to share their experiences and skills with the children.

Field Trips

Take a trip to the local library, radio station, television station, or children's bookstore.

Parent Involvement

Ask parents to come into the classroom and read or tell favorite stories from their childhood. Or ask parents who are bilingual to share their home language with the children.

Parent Education

Invite a reading specialist or primary teacher to talk about helping children learn to read and write. Invite a children's librarian or children's bookseller to talk about choosing good books for children. Invite a bilingual educator to talk about the importance of maintaining home languages while learning English. Bring in an early childhood specialist or education coordinator from your local public television station to talk about the impact of violence and stereotypes in the media on children's development and how to use television as a learning tool. Have an early childhood educator talk about computers and young children and how to select developmentally appropriate software.

CLASSROOM RESOURCES

Children's Books

A To Zen: A Book Of Japanese Culture, Ruth Wells (New York: Simon, 1992).

Aaron And Gayla's Alphabet, Eloise Greenfield (New York: Writers and Readers, 1994).

ABCs The American Indian Way, Richard Red Hawk (New Castle: Sierra, 1988).

The Alaskan ABC Book, Charlene Kreeger (Homer, AK: Paw IV, 1993).

Alef-Bet: A Hebrew Alphabet Book, Michelle Edwards (New York: Morrow, 1992).

Albertina, Anda Arriba, Nancy Tabor (Watertown, MA: Charlesbridge, 1995).

The Alphabet Part, Cecilia Avalos.

Antler, Bear, Canoe, Betsy Bowen (Boston: Little Brown, 1991).

Arroz Con Leche, Lulu Delacre (New York: Scholastic, 1992).

At The Beach, Huy Voun Lee (New York: Holt, 1994).

Aunt Chip And The Great Triple Creek Dam Affair, Patricia Polacco (New York: Philomel, 1996).

A Bedtime Story, Mem Fox (Greenvale, NY: Mondo, 1996).

The Calypso Alphabet, John Agard (Littleton, MA: Sundance, 1996).

Chatterbox Jamie, Nancy Evans Cooney (New York: Putnam, 1993).

Cherry And Cherry Pits, Vera B. Williams (New York: Mulberry, 1986).

Communication, Aliki (New York: Greenwillow, 1993).

The Day Of Ahmed's Secret, Florence Perry Heide (New York: Lee, 1993).

The First Song Ever Sung, Laura Krauss Melmed (New York: Lothrop, 1993).

From Acorn To Zoo, Satoski Kitamura (New York: Farrar, 1992).

The Furry News: How To Make A Newspaper, Loreen Leedy (New York: Scholastic, 1990).

Grandmother's Alphabet, Eve Shaw (Duluth, MN: Pfeifer-Hamilton, 1996).

Grandmother's Nursery Rhymes, Nelly Palacio Jaramillo (New York: Holt, 1996).

The Handmade Alphabet, Laura Rankin (New York: Dial, 1991).

Handsigns: A Sign Language Alphabet, Kathleen Fain (New York: Scholastic, 1993).

Hello! Good-Bye! Aliki (New York: Greenwillow, 1996).

Hi! Ann Herbert Scott (New York: Philomel, 1994).

I Hate English! Ellen Levine (New York: Scholastic, 1995).

I Read Signs, Tana Hoban (New York: Morrow, 1983).

I Speak English For My Mom, Muriel Stanek (Morton Grove, IL: Whitman, 1989).

In The Snow, Huy Voun Lee (New York: Holt, 1995).

Incredible Ned, Bill Maynard (New York: Putnam, 1997).

It Begins With 'A,' Stephanie Calmenson (New York: Hyperion, 1993).

Jambo Means Hello, Muriel Feelings (New York: Dial, 1992).

K Is For Kiss Goodnight: A Bedtime Alphabet, Jill Sardegna (New York: Doubleday, 1996).

Keepers, Jeri Hanel Watts (New York: Lee, 1997).

Let's Go, Vamos: A Book In Two Languages, Rebecca Emberley (Boston: Little Brown, 1993).

Long Silk Strand, Laura Williams (Honesdale, PA: Boyds Mills, 1995).

Margaret And Margarita/Margarita y Margaret, Lynn Reiser (New York: Greenwillow, 1993).

Miz Berlin Walks, Jane Yolen (New York: Philomel, 1997).

Mouse TV, Matt Wovak (New York: Scholastic, 1994).

My Day, Mi Día: A Book In Two Languages, Rebecca Emberley (Boston: Little Brown, 1993).

Navajo ABC: A Dine Alphabet Book, Luci Tapahonso and Eleanor Schick (New York: Simon, 1995).

The Old Man And His Door, Gary Soto (New York: Putnam, 1996).

The Old, Old Man And The Very Little Boy, Kristine L. Franklin (New York: Atheneum, 1992).

Osa's Pride, Ann Grifalconi (Boston: Little Brown, 1996).

Pablo's World, Juan Farias.

The Palace Of The Stars, Patricia Lakin (New York: Tambourine, 1993).

The Path Of The Quiet Elk: A Native American Alphabet Book, Virginia A. Stroud (New York: Dial, 1996).

Recess Mess, Grace Maccarone (New York: Scholastic, 1996).

Richard Wright And The Library Card, William Miller (New York: Lee, 1997).

Say Hola To Spanish, Otra Vez (Again!), Susan Middleton Elya (New York: Lee, 1997).

Say It, Sign It, Elaine Epstein.

Secrets, Ellen Senisi (New York: Dutton, 1995).

Sesame Street Sign Language ABC, Linda Bove (New York: Random, 1990).

A Show Of Hands: Say It With Sign Language, Mary B. Sullivan (New York: Harper, 1992).

Sign Language Fun, Children's Television Workshop (New York: Random, 1980).

Signs For Me: Basic Vocabulary For Children, Parents And Teachers, Ben Bahan and Joe Dannis (San Diego: DawnSign, 1990).

Simple Signs, Cindy Wheeler (New York: Viking, 1995).

The Storyteller, Joan Weisman (New York: Rizzoli, 1993).

Talk To Me, Sue Brearly (London: A & C Black, 1996).

Tell Me A Story Mama, Angela Johnson (New York: Orchard, 1989).

Telling Isn't Tattling, Katherine Hammerseng (Seattle: Parenting, 1996).

Together We Are Together, The Children of St. Brigid's Head Start School (New York: Scholastic, 1992).

The Trouble With Secrets, Karen Johnson (Seattle: Parenting, 1986).

Turtle Island ABCs: A Gathering Of Native American Symbols (New York: Harper, 1994).

The Wednesday Surprise, Eve Bunting (New York: Clarion, 1989).

What's Your Name: From Ariel To Zoe, Eve Sanders and Marilyn Sanders (New York: Holiday, 1995).

Music

Fink, Cathy, and Marcy Marxer. *Nobody Else Like Me* (A&M, 1994).

"Hello, Hello, Hello"

"Kye Kye Kule"

"May There Always Be Sunshine"

Hartmann, Jack. *Let's Read Together And Other Songs For Sharing And Caring* (Educational Activities, 1990).

"Communication Connection"

"Going To The Library"

"Let's Read Together"

Grammer, Red. *Hello World!* (Smilin' Atcha, 1995).

"I Want You To Listen"

———. *Teaching Peace* (Smilin' Atcha, 1986).

"I Think You're Wonderful"

"Rapp Song"

"Say Hi!"

"Use A Word"

Hinojosa, Tish. *Cada Niño/Every Child* (Rounder, 1996).

"Escala Musical/Music Scales"

Hunter, Tom. *Bits And Pieces* (Song Growing, 1990).

"Lots Of Little Squiggles"

———. *Connections* (Song Growing, 1994).

"I Am One Voice"

"Weaving"

Rogers, Sally. *Peace By Peace* (Western, 1988).

"I've Got A Song"

Shih, Patricia. *Big Ideas!* (Glass, 1990).

"Speak Another Language"

Sweet Honey In The Rock. *I Got Shoes* (Music for Little People, 1994).

"African Numbers"

Vitamin L, *Walk A Mile* (Lovable Creature, 1989).

"That's The Truth"

Visual Displays

ABC School Supply
Spanish/English Alphabet Wall Cards

Educational Equity Concepts
Mainstreaming for Equity Posters

Knowledge Unlimited
The Arabic Alphabet

Cultural Kaleidoscope Poster: An American Alphabet

Organization for Equal Education of the Sexes
Linda Bove Poster

Sandy and Son
Alphabet Poster

Videos

A Kid's Guide to the Library (Kimbo Educational, 1989).

Sign Me A Story, by Linda Bove (Educational Record Center, 1987).

Sign Songs, by Kevin Lonquist (Educational Record Center, 1994).

Sing 'n Sign For Fun, by Gaia Tossing (Educational Record Center, 1996).

Computer Software

All-In-One Language Fun, by Syracuse Language Lab, Educational Record Center

Amazing Words and Pictures, by Dorling Kindersley, Educational Record Center

Kid Keys, Beckley-Cardy

Spanish/Español, by Twin Sisters Productions, Educational Record Center

The Magic Letter Factory CD-ROM, Constructive Playthings

Teaching Kits

Graeme, Jocelyn, and Ruth Fahlman. *Hand In Hand: Multicultural Experiences For Young Children* (Reading, MA: Addison-Wesley, 1990).

Sound Hearing Cassette Tape and Book, Sandy and Son

The 911 Project, Beckley-Cardy

Additional Resources

Gallaudet University Bookstore
800 Florida Avenue NE
Washington, DC 20002
(202) 651-5505
Gallaudet University is the only Deaf university in the United States. Its bookstore carries not only a selection of standard ASL texts and dictionaries, but also a wide variety of children's books with sign components, videos of children's stories and fairy stories told in ASL, videos of ASL literature, books about the Deaf liberation struggle, and the life stories of Deaf people. They have a catalog.

FAMILIES

A four-year-old girl dictated the following story to me, sharing her perceptions of her current family life and her dream of a new way for her family to be together: "My mommy spanks me. My daddy spanks me. My big brother yells at me. My baby sister breaks my toys. My mommy doesn't spank me. My daddy doesn't spank me. My brother doesn't yell at me anymore. My baby sister doesn't break my toys. The sun is out and we are a happy family."

Each child is born into a family. It's through our families that we learn how to be in relationships with others and first come to know ourselves. For young children, family is what they know of love and belonging.

Families take many forms. A unit on families strengthens children's connections to their home cultures and examines diversity. Every classroom represents diversity of family life. Often, however, units on family are very superficial. Here is a chance to explore more deeply what family means to children.

UNIT 4:

BIG AS LIFE

FAMILIES

Look for this symbol
to find activities you
can use for circle time.

WEB

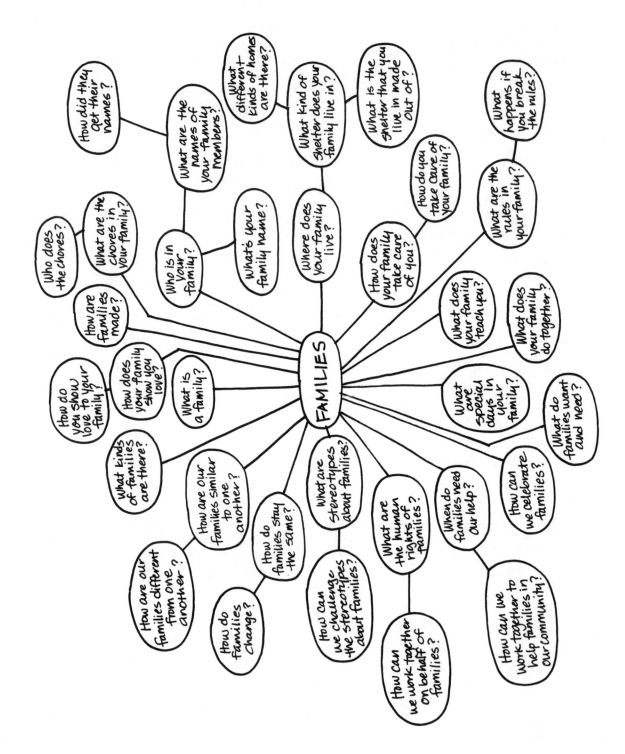

BIG AS LIFE

Outline

I. Who is in your family?
   A. What's your family's name?
   B. What are the names of your family members?
   C. How did they get their names?
II. Where does your family live?
   A. What kind of shelter does your family live in?
   B. What's the shelter that your family lives in made out of?
   C. What different kinds of homes are there?
III. How does your family take care of you?
   A. How do you take care of your family?
   B. What are the chores in your family?
   C. Who does chores?
   D. What are the rules in your family?
   E. What happens if you break the rules?
   F. What does your family teach you?
   G. How does your family show you love?
   H. How do you show love to your family?
IV. What does your family do together?
V. What are special days in your family?
VI. What is a family?
   A. What kinds of families are there?
   B. How are families made?
   C. How are families similar to one another?
   D. How are families different from one another?
   E. How do families stay the same?
   F. How do families change?
VII. What are stereotypes about families?
VIII. How can we challenge stereotypes about families?
IX. What do families want and need?
   A. When do families need our help?
   B. How can we work together to help families in our community?
X. What are the human rights of families?
XI. How can we work together on behalf of families?
XII. How can we celebrate families?

MATERIALS LIST

ART

skin-colored paints, crayons, markers, felt, and craft paper

butcher paper roll

baby care, family, and parenting magazines

people-shaped sponges for painting (for example, Home and Family Sponges, *Environments*)

BLOCKS

a variety of multicultural people figures, including figures of people with disabilities

a variety of domestic animal figures (for example, Classic Farm Animal Collection, *Lakeshore*)

small transportation vehicles

notepads

felt tip pens

two dollhouses

shoe boxes or pieces of cardboard

Lincoln Logs

pieces of canvas

string

masking tape

DRAMATIC PLAY

multiethnic baby dolls

multiethnic preschooler dolls (for example, Friends Dolls or Children with Hearing, Motor, and Visual Impairments Dolls, *People of Every Stripe*; Multi-Ethnic School Dolls, *Lakeshore*; Multi-Ethnic Dolls, *Constructive Playthings*)

adaptive equipment for dolls with disabilities (available from *Lakeshore*)

home living: cooking utensils, food sets, women and men's clothing, cookbooks, recipe cards, shopping lists, newspapers, magazines, books, telephone, phone books, coupons, and pretend money (see also Living Room Set, *Constructive Playthings* and *Nasco*)

baby care: baby dolls, baby blankets, baby bathtubs, washcloths, towels, crib, rocking chair, baby bottles, strollers, baby carriers, empty baby product containers, baby board books

LITERACY

children's books: fiction, nonfiction, and bilingual books about families (see resource list at the end of the unit)

cassette player and theme-related storybook cassettes

blank cassettes

flannel board sets of multicultural families (for example, Multicultural Flannel Board Concept Kits, *Constructive Playthings* and *Lakeshore*; Family Clings, *Sandy and Son*)

multicultural family puppets (for example, Family Puppets, available from *Constructive Playthings*, *Edvantage*, *Lakeshore*, and *Sandy and Son*)

writing, letter-writing, bookmaking, and journalling materials

MANIPULATIVES

multicultural and inclusive family puzzles (for example, Everyday Life Puzzles, Family Puzzles, *Constructive Playthings*; Houses Puzzle, *Animal Town*; Layered House Puzzle, *Environments*; Family Outing Puzzles, Wedding Puzzles, *Sandy and Son*)

household lotto games

SCIENCE

picture cards of animal families

SENSORY

cornmeal to fill sensory table

a variety of multicultural people figures, including figures of people with disabilities

Teaching Through the Interest Areas

Art

Set out baby care, parenting, and family magazines and skin-colored art materials.

Blocks

Add doll furniture, multicultural and inclusive people figures, small transportation vehicles, notepads, and felt tip pens to the block area to encourage family-related play.

Add two dollhouses to the block area so that children can role-play going to their relatives' homes.

Add shoe boxes or pieces of cardboard (for flooring) so that children can build apartment buildings.

Add Lincoln Logs, cardboard boxes, canvas, string, and masking tape to encourage house building.

Dramatic Play

Expand the dramatic play area to include a living, sleeping, and cooking area, adding props that reflect the home life of the children in your classroom. Include cooking utensils, food sets, women and men's clothing, cookbooks, recipe cards, shopping lists, newspapers, magazines, books, a telephone and phone books, coupons, and pretend money.

Set up two house areas side by side in the classroom so that children with extended, blended, or foster families can play going back and forth between their homes.

To encourage play around the theme of caring for babies, add props like baby dolls, baby blankets, baby bathtubs, washcloths, towels, crib, rocking chair, baby bottles, strollers, baby carriers, empty baby product containers, and baby board books.

Literacy

Set out a collection of fiction, nonfiction, and bilingual books on families. Include a tape player and family-related storybook cassettes in different languages, multicultural family puppets, flannel board sets of multicultural families, writing and letter-writing materials, and materials for keeping family journals and making books.

Manipulatives

Set out multicultural and inclusive family puzzles and household lotto games.

Music

Set out cassettes with family-related themes and songs.

Science

Set out picture cards of animal families.

Sensory

Add people figures to the sensory table filled with sand or cornmeal for family-related play.

Add cooking utensils to the sensory table.

ACTIVITIES: INVESTIGATING THE THEME

Creative Development

Build a House. Collect a variety of boxes, making sure you have more than enough for each child to have one. Set out the boxes, construction paper, tissue paper, glue, crayons, markers, and scissors. Encourage children to use the materials to make a house, trailer, duplex, or apartment building where a family might live.

Clean-Up Painting. Set out objects commonly used to clean homes. You might include a feather duster, sponge, rag, rubber gloves, and a spray bottle. Set out tempera paint in pie tins or other shallow containers. Invite children to experiment with using the household cleaning objects for painting.

Family Collage. Invite children to make collages representing their families. Encourage children to find and cut out magazine pictures to represent their family members and glue them onto construction paper.

Family Portraits. Encourage children to draw or paint a picture of their families. Encourage children to look at photographs of their families or think about all the people in their families before they begin.

Grandparents Collage. Set out a large piece of butcher paper and magazines. Invite the children to find and cut out pictures of grandparents to glue onto a collage. Invite children to finish the sentence, "A grandparent is… " and write their answers on the collage.

House Collage. Draw a picture or floor plan of a house on a large sheet of butcher paper. Include a kitchen, living room, bathroom, bedrooms. If you want, you could add an attic, basement, garage, or laundry room. Set out newspaper advertisements and catalogs from department stores, furniture stores, and discount stores. Invite children to cut out pictures of things they might find in a home and glue them in the room where they think they belong.

We Welcome All Families. Invite the children to make a mural to celebrate and welcome all kinds of families. Remind children of all the different types of families. There are adoptive, foster, single-parent, two-parent, blended, interracial, gay or lesbian, extended, and communal families. Some families may fall into several categories. Set out magazines and newspapers that you know have pictures of families. Invite the children to cut out and glue pictures of families, or draw pictures of families, on a large sheet of butcher paper. Write "Welcome All Families" across the top of the mural. Display it outside the classroom or just inside the door.

Where I Live. Set out easel paper and paints. Invite children to paint pictures of the buildings where they live.

Critical Thinking

Find a Way. Facilitate a discussion on communication in families with a member who is Deaf. Challenge children to take another perspective by asking questions like, "If you couldn't hear, how would your family tell you it is time for dinner? How would they tell you it's time to get ready for bed? How would they tell you that they love you?"

Family Discussions. Following are three possible topics of discussion for small groups or circle times on the subject of family, with suggested scenarios and questions. These discussions help children think about the complicated web of relationships involved in being a family and hear from each other how families are different from and similar to each other.

Be aware that this kind of discussion may raise issues for children, parents, or teachers about what are appropriate ways of showing affection and enforcing rules in families. Children may name ways their families show affection or provide discipline that are unfamiliar or uncomfortable for you. Parents and teachers may have different beliefs about how children should be disciplined or affection expressed in families. In addition, our culture and class backgrounds influence what we think is okay in these areas. It's also possible that this kind of frank discussion in a nonjudgmental atmosphere will make it safe enough for children to disclose physical or sexual abuse. Be prepared for a variety of responses from children. Follow up as appropriate by asking further open-ended questions (for example, "How do you feel when your mom tells you that you can't watch television?"), reflecting children's feelings back to them (for example, "It sounds like that makes you mad."), and providing them with opportunities to represent their experiences and feelings through art, story-writing, and dramatic play. If you have reason to believe that a child is being physically or sexually abused, you will also need to follow your state's guidelines for reporting the abuse to the appropriate agency.

Love and Affection. Bring a set of family figures to a discussion. Show the children the grandparent figure and ask them, "Who is this in your family? How does your grandmother show that she loves you? How does your grandfather show that he loves you?" Continue with each of the family figures.

Rules and Discipline. Ask the children, "What are the rules at your house? Why do families have rules? How do the rules help you?" Show them the family figures. Hold up the grandmother figure and ask, "What does your grandmother do if you break the rules?" Continue through various family members.

How Do You Show Love? Ask the children such questions as, "How do you use your words to show your family that you love them? How do use your body to show your family that you love them? What things can you do to show your family that you love them?" After the group discussion, children might identify something they would like to make or do for their families to show them love.

What Is a Family? Lead a discussion on the topic of family. Ask questions like, "What is a family? What makes a family? Who is in your family? How does your family work together?"

Who Would You Ask? Family members represent a variety of ages. Help children explore their ideas about age-related behavior by presenting a variety of situations and asking them who they would go to in each. For example:

You run, fall, and scrape your knee. Who in your family could help you put a bandage on the cut? Why would they be a good person to ask?

You get a new toy and don't know how to make it work. Who could show you how it works? Why do you think they would be able to help you?

You want to play with someone. Who in your family could play with you? You are hungry and need someone to help you get a snack. Who would you ask? Why?

Emotional Development

Brothers and Sisters. Young children may experience feelings of jealousy in their relationships with brothers and sisters. Ask the children such questions as

> How many of you have a brother or sister?
>
> How do you feel about your brother or sister?
>
> When do you feel love for your brother or sister?
>
> When do you feel mad at or jealous of your brother or sister?

Set out "preschool" dolls or puppets. Role-play common situations of sibling rivalry—taking toys, breaking toys, fighting over a seat at the table, who sits in the front seat of the car, or which television station to watch. Invite the children to think of positive ways to work out problems with their brothers and sisters.

Fears in the Night. Young children are often scared by the household sounds they hear in the night. Make a cassette tape of sounds children might hear from their beds. You could include creaking floors or roof, doors opening and closing, the toilet flushing, the telephone ringing, the television or radio, people fighting, dogs barking, cats meowing, the wind blowing, thunder, sirens, airplanes flying overhead, or gunfire. Ask the children what kinds of things scare them when they are in their beds at night. Play the cassette and see if the children can identify the sounds on the tape. Emphasize that some of the sounds are scary because we don't know what is making the sound, and once we learn what that sound is, we aren't afraid anymore because we know it won't hurt us. Some sounds, like gunfire, are scary because they are dangerous. Cover a table with a sheet and unroll sleeping bags on the floor under the table to re-create a dark bedroom. Play the cassette tape and invite the children to pretend they are going to sleep and hear the scary sounds. One child could pretend to be the parent who comforts the scared children.

I Want You All to Myself. Sometimes children feel jealous of their brothers and sisters because they want their moms or dads to give them all of their attention. Ask the children, "Do you know what feeling jealous is? It's when you feel hurt and mad and disappointed because someone else is getting all of the attention. Sometimes children feel jealous when there is a new baby at their house. They feel mad, hurt, and left out because their mom is spending lots of time with the new baby. They feel ignored, like nobody is paying any attention to them. When do you feel jealous? What are some things that we can do when we feel jealous?"

I'm a Member of a Family. Foster children's self-esteem and confidence in their participation in their families. At circle time, ask each child to tell the class a way in which she is a helpful member of her family.

Love, Love, Love. Ask the children, "What is love? Who do you love? What are ways that we can show our family members that we love them?" Invite children to dictate a story about love or paint a picture of love in their family.

Puppet Play. Set out puppets of family members and encourage children to act out how their families make them feel. Give children some situations to get them started:

> How do you feel when it's time to go to bed and your mom gives you a bath, reads you a story, and tucks you into bed?

> How do you feel when your sister takes your toys?

> How do you feel when your mom or dad takes you to the park to play?

> How do you feel when you are at the store with your mom and she says you can't buy a treat?

Show How It Feels. Invite the children to take turns showing how they would feel in a variety of situations. Suggest a number of situations, such as the following:

> Show us how you would feel if you got a new puppy.

> Show us how you would feel if your puppy ate your shoe.

> Show us how you would feel if your mom had a new baby.

> Show us how you would feel if your big brother shared a piece of cake with you.

> Show us how you would feel if your sister took you to the park to play.

> Show us how you would feel if your dad lost his job.

> Show us how you would feel if your mom said, "No television because you didn't listen to me."

Why's That Baby Crying? Make a cassette recording of a baby crying. Play the tape, and ask the children if they have ever heard a baby crying. Why do they think the baby is crying? What might the baby want? How might the baby be feeling? What could they do to help care for the baby?

Health, Safety, and Nutrition

Poisons at Home. Ask children if they know what a poison is. Tell them that a poison is something that can make us sick if we taste it or eat it or sometimes if we touch it. Ask children if they know any poisons. Help children identify common household poisons. Collect samples or pictures of common household poisons like cleaners, medicines, mothballs, plants, fertilizer, pesticide, or soap. Show the samples to the children, one at a time, and see if the children can identify them. See if they can identify where these items might be found in a home. Talk to the children about the importance of storing these poisons out of the reach of children, storing them in a locked cupboard, and keeping them out of their mouths. Contact your local poison control center for educational resources.

Language Development

> **Home Language.** *Learn the words for family members (*mom, dad, brother, sister, grandmother, grandfather, aunt, uncle*) in American Sign Language and the home languages of the children in your classroom.*

All Our Families. Make a classroom book with a page or two on each child's family. Encourage children to write stories about their families. Ask them to think about who is in their family, what they like about their family, how their family cares for them, teaches them, and loves them. Include a photograph or the child's drawing of his or her family.

Family Picture Cards. Use a commercial set of family pictures or make your own set by cutting out large magazine pictures of all types of families and gluing them onto construction paper. Hold up one picture at a time and ask open-ended questions:

> Who can tell me about this picture?
>
> What do you see?
>
> What kind of family is it?
>
> What are the family members doing?
>
> How do you think they are feeling?
>
> How is this family like your family?
>
> How is this family different from your family?

Family Picture Stories. Sit down with a small group of children and some family pictures. Show the children one picture at a time. Ask the children what they see in the pictures. Encourage the children to make up stories about the families in the pictures. If possible, write down the children's stories.

Family Poems. Here are five poems about family life. Introduce them at circle time. Ask the children to help you create motions for the first two.

I LOVE MY FAMILY

Some families are large
Some families are small
But I love my family
Best of all.

(source unknown)

GRANDMAS

Some grandmas live near
Some grandmas live far
But grandmas love you
Wherever they are.

Grandpas, aunts, and uncles, too
Always want to know about you
These are special people for you and me
For they are part of our family.

(Busy Fingers Growing Minds: Finger Plays, Verses and Activities for Whole Language Learning, Rhoda Redleaf. St. Paul: Redleaf Press, 1993; p. 144. Used with permission.)*

Families

LANGUAGE
DEVELOPMENT

BROTHERS AND SISTERS

Brothers and sisters are lots of fun
They play with you and chase and run *(run in place)*
But sometimes they tease and call you names
And won't let you play some of their games *(shake finger)*
But most of the time it's nice to be
With brothers and sisters in a family *(make hugging gestures)*

(Busy Fingers Growing Minds: Finger Plays, Verses and Activities for Whole Language Learning, Rhoda Redleaf. St. Paul: Redleaf Press, 1993; p. 145. Used with permission.)*

A GOOD HOUSE

This is the roof of the house so good *(make roof with hands)*
These are the walls that are made of wood *(hands straight, palms parallel)*
These are the windows that let in the light *(thumbs and forefingers form window)*
This is the door that shuts so tight *(hands straight side by side)*
This is the chimney so straight and tall *(arms up straight)*
Oh! What a good house for one and all *(arms at angle for roof)*

(Finger Frolics, Liz Cromwell and Dixie Hibner. Livonia, MI: Partner Press, 1976; p. 10. Used with permission.)*

KITTEN IS HIDING

A kitten is hiding under a chair, *(hide one thumb in other hand)*
I looked and looked for her everywhere. *(peer about with hand on forehead)*
Under the table and under the bed, *(pretend to look)*
I looked in the corner and then I said,
"Come, Kitty, come, Kitty, I have milk for you." *(cup hands to make dish and extend)*
Kitty came running and calling, "Mew, mew." *(run finger up arm)*

(Creative Resources for the Early Childhood Classroom, second edition, Judy Herr and Libby Yvonne. Albany, NY: Delmar Publishers, 1995; p. 104. Used with permission.)*

Last Names. Help the children begin to recognize their families' last names. Make flash cards with each child's last name on it and see if the children can guess whose is whose.

What's My Address? Help children learn to recognize and eventually recall their street addresses. At circle time, tell the children, "Our houses are on streets that have a name, and our houses have a number. The house number and name of the street is called our address. We can learn our street address." Print each child's address on an envelope. Show an envelope to the group. Read the address and see if the children can guess whose address it is. Give clues about the child's identity, if necessary. When the children correctly identify the child, give the child the envelope to hold.

Math

Family Chart. Explain to children that they are going to make a chart of all their families. Make a chart with a column for each child and write each child's name across the top. Work individually with children to chart their families. Chart the number of moms, dads, siblings, grandparents, aunts, uncles, cousins, or friends that live in the child's home, using a different colored sticker or marker for each category of family member. For example, you might use a red circle for each mom, a green circle for each aunt, uncle, cousin, or friend, and so forth. When complete, help the children count the number of family members and discuss the similarities and differences of the families in your class.

Family Match. Make four or more sets of family matching cards. Find duplicate photos of families in magazines, or use a color photocopier to make duplicates. You could take family teaching pictures and use a color photocopier to reduce the pictures to a size suitable for games. Make sure that your collection of pictures represents cultural diversity and many different family forms. Place the cards in a basket and encourage the children to find the matching sets.

Family Member Count. Set out multicultural family figures and felt, wooden, or plastic numerals. Assist children in counting out the family figures and matching the correct number of family figures to the corresponding numeral. You could also play a counting game by placing the numerals in a left column and lines of family figures in the right column. Children can find the correct match and lay a piece of yarn from the numeral to the family figures.

Family Outlines. Trace around a set of family figures on oaktag or poster board. Be sure to use a diverse set of figures that includes people of color and people with disabilities, as well as a variety of adults and children. If you trace the figures in family groupings (more than one figure on the same card), be sure to do several groupings and reflect diverse family structures, including families with single parents of both genders, extended families, and families with two mommies or two daddies. Set out the outlines of the family members and the figures. Invite the children to match each family figure to the corresponding outline.

Family Sort. Collect a variety of pictures of family members. Place the pictures in a basket. Make sure that the set reflects racial and cultural diversity and includes people with disabilities. Set out the basket along with a sorting tray. Invite children to classify the family member pictures any way they like. You could also do this activity with a large collection of wooden or plastic block play family members.

Family Tree. Display children's family photos on a bulletin board. With the children, count the number of people in each child's family. Make a chart showing how many people are in each family. Ask the children, "Who has the most people in their family? Who has the fewest people in their family? What are all the names we use to describe family members?" Talk about how there are many different ways of being a family.

Household Match. Make four or more sets of household matching cards. Find duplicate photographs in magazines or department store catalogs, or use a color photocopier to make duplicates. Include appliances and items found in the kitchen, bathroom, bedroom, and family room. Place the cards in a basket and encourage the children to find the matching sets.

Shape Houses. Set out glue, construction paper, and a variety of geometric shapes cut out of construction paper. Invite children to make a building where families might live by gluing the shapes to the construction paper.

Music

Music from Home. Invite children to bring in samples of music that they listen to in their family.

Songs about Families. Here are some songs about families and pets you can sing with the children.

PEOPLE AT MY HOUSE
Lyrics adapted by Paul Fralick

Who are the people at my house,
at my house, at my house?
Who are the people at my house,
The people that I see each day?
(*Child's name*) is a person at my house,
At my house, at my house,
(*Child's name*) is a person at my house,
A person that I see each day.

(*Make It Multicultural—Musical Activities for Early Childhood Education*, Paul Fralick. Hamilton, Ontario, Canada: Mohawk College, 1989; p. 49. Used with permission.)

SIX LITTLE PETS
Tune: *Six Little Ducks*

Six little gerbils I once knew, fat ones, skinny ones, fair ones too.
But the one little gerbil was so much fun.
He would play until the day was done.
Six little dogs that I once knew, fat ones, skinny ones, fair ones too.
But the one little dog with the brown curly fur,
he led the others with a grr, grr, grr.

Six little fish that I once knew, fat ones, skinny ones, fair ones too.
But the one little fish who was the leader of the crowd,
he led the others around and around.
Six little birds that I once knew, fat ones, skinny ones, fair ones too.
But the one little bird with the pretty little beak,
he led the others with a tweet, tweet, tweet.
Six little cats that I once knew, fat ones, skinny ones, fair ones too.
But the one little cat who was as fluffy as a ball,
he was the prettiest one of all.

(*Creative Resources for the Early Childhood Classroom*, second edition, Judy Herr and Libby Yvonne. Albany, NY: Delmar Publishers, 1995; p. 433. Used with permission.)

FAMILY HELPER

Tune: *Here We Are Together*

It's fun to be a helper, a helper, a helper.
It's fun to be a helper, just any time.
Oh, I can set the table, the table, the table.
Oh, I can set the table at dinnertime.
Oh, I can dry the dishes, the dishes, the dishes.
Oh, I can dry the dishes, and make them shine.

(*Creative Resources for the Early Childhood Classroom*, second edition, Judy Herr and Libby Yvonne. Albany, NY: Delmar Publishers, 1995; p. 235. Used with permission.)

Physical Development

Blanket Play. Many young children have favorite blankets. Set out some blankets or invite the children to get out their naptime blankets. Invite the children to show one another something they can do with their blankets. Ask the children to roll up in their blankets and see if they can roll across the floor. Invite them to find a friend and see if they can work together to bounce and rock a teddy bear on one of their blankets.

Bouncing on the Bed. Set out the trampoline. Invite the children to pretend the trampoline is a bed and role-play jumping on the bed.

Creative Movement. Invite children to act out family situations. They can pretend they are a parent putting their children to bed at night, eating a meal with their families, or going somewhere with their families.

Mother May I? Mark off a start and finish line. Select one child to be the "mother" and ask her to stand on the finish line. The rest of the children stand along the start line. Each child takes a turn asking "mother" if she can move forward. The child has to include in the question the number of steps and the way they want to move. For example, "Mother may I take four baby steps?" "Mother may I take two hops?" The "mother" answers either, "Yes, you may," or "No, you may not." If a child tries to move forward without asking, she has to go back to the starting line. The first child to reach the finish line gets to be the next mother.

Rock-a-Bye Baby. Place a parachute on the ground and have the children sit in a circle around it. Choose one child to lie on top of the parachute. Sing a lullaby from the child's home culture. As you sing, have the children slowly lift the parachute off the ground and gently rock the child as you sing.

Simon Says. Play a different version of this traditional game. Use the format to invite children to role-play being a family member. For example, "Simon says, be your little sister. Simon says, be your mom. Simon says, be your grandmother. Simon says, be your big brother."

This Is the Way... Teach children the traditional nursery song "This Is the Way We..." to the tune of "Here We Go 'Round the Mulberry Bush." Insert family-oriented verses—for example, "This is the way we wash our clothes (go to bed, catch the bus, clean the house, watch TV, take our baths)." Invite children to make up their own verses of things they do each day at home and act out the motions as they sing the song.

Science

Hatch Baby Chicks. Purchase or borrow an incubator and buy some fertilized eggs. When you buy the fertilized eggs, you'll need to ask the date of conception so that you can chart their development. Eggs hatch twenty-one days after conception. You may need to turn the eggs one or two times a day. Once hatched, place the chicks in a large cardboard box with a 60-watt light bulb to keep them warm. They will need water daily and feed which can be purchased from a farm supply store or large pet store. Find a farm for the chicks' new home. Take a field trip to deliver the chicks to their new family.

Snails. Snails are mollusks that carry their houses around with them. Invite the children to help you gather three or four snails in damp shady areas where plants grow. Add them to your terrarium, though they might eat up your plants. Or put them in an old aquarium or other large glass container. Feed them leafy vegetables like lettuce, spinach, and celery tops. Invite the children to feed the snails daily and remove dried out leaves. Take the snails out and place them on a piece of black construction paper and watch them move across the paper, leaving a snail trail of mucous secretion on the paper. Release the snails when you are finished observing them.

The Truth About Cats. Many families have a cat for a family pet. Invite a parent, staff person, or friend to bring their cat to school. Make sure the cat is used to being around people and doesn't mind being petted. Children could also take a trip to a pet store to observe a cat. Talk about what the cat eats and drinks, the sounds it makes, how it moves its body and tail, how it cleans itself, what it likes and doesn't like, toys it likes to play with. Use a stamp pad to make a footprint of the cat's paws. Children may want to touch the cat's fur, whiskers, and tongue.

The Truth About Dogs. Many families have a dog for a pet. Ask a parent, staff person, or friend to bring their pet dog to school to visit. A local nursing home might be able to put you in touch with someone whose dog is registered as a therapeutic dog. This way you'll be sure that the dog is calm and will enjoy being petted. Invite children to pet the dog. Some children will be afraid, others will assume that the dog is mean and out to get them. Encourage children to feel the dog's nose and talk about how dogs have a well-developed sense of smell. Use a stamp pad to make a footprint of the dog's paws so that you can compare them to those of the cat. Watch the dog's ears and how they move when it hears a sound. Observe the different noises the dog makes. Ask the owner what sounds the dog makes when it's hungry, hurt, excited, or mad. Also encourage children to observe the dog's tail.

Social Development

Babies! Invite a parent and baby to visit your class. Ask the parent to introduce the baby to the children. Ask the parents such questions as

> What's its name?
>
> How old is it?
>
> Is it a boy or a girl?
>
> What does it like to do?
>
> What sounds does it make?
>
> What does it eat?

Ask the parent to show children all the things in the baby's diaper bag. If possible, invite the children to touch the baby, one at a time, or hold the baby on their laps while they are sitting down. Ask children how mothers and fathers care for babies. Ask them what they would do with a baby if they were its older brother or sister.

Family Rules. Discuss rules and why we have rules in families. As a group, brainstorm a list of family rules. Then discuss what happens if you break the rules. Introduce the concept of consequences.

Felt Families. Gather felt squares in a variety of skin colors. Ask the children to pick out the colors that are like the skin colors of their family members. Give them gingerbread cookie cutters in different sizes and markers to trace them on the felt. Help them cut out a felt person to represent each member of their families. You might want to give them fabric paint to paint faces on the felt families and write their names on the back. Set out the felt families with a flannel board for dramatic play.

Growing Up in Families. Invite children to work together to make a time line collage of how we grow up in families. Set out a large sheet of butcher paper. Invite children to cut out pictures of infants, toddlers, young children, school-age children, teenagers, adults, and elderly people. Help the children sequence the pictures along the chart from young to old.

I Can't See You. Ask children if they know anyone who is blind, and if they know what blind means. Ask, "What do you think your mom or dad might need to do differently around the house if they couldn't see? How do you think they would shop at the grocery store? How do you think they might cook?" Tell the children that there are descriptive videos that blind people use to "watch" movies, so they know what is happening on-screen. Descriptive videos can be rented at Blockbuster Video stores—you may want to bring one in and have the children close their eyes and listen to the video. Read a book about a family with a member who is blind. Show children a blindfold and tell them you are going to wear

the blindfold for part of the morning (like during circle time and free-play time). Put the blindfold on. Remind the children that you cannot see them, but that you can hear them, feel them, and smell them. Coach them in adjusting their interactions with you. After an hour or so, take off the blindfold. As a group discuss what each of you learned from the experience. You may want to give the children the opportunity to wear the blindfold too. Ask them, "How do you think we could mark our room so you could find it by yourself if you were blind? How do you think you could do a puzzle if you couldn't see?"

 Our Wish for Our Families. Ask children if they know what a wish is. Ask each child what their wish is. Then ask the children what their wish is for their family members. Invite the children to make a poster or mural of all their wishes for their families. Here is a poem that children can recite as they make wishes:

> If my mind was a wishing well,
> I'd find a wish that I could tell—
> A thought from me to you,
> A wish for smiles and fun—
> Something you can do
> To warm you like the sun.

> (*The Peaceful Classroom*, Charles Smith. Beltsville, MD: Gryphon House, 1993; p. 163.
> Used with permission.)

We Help Our Families. Explore all the chores or jobs in a family. Discuss cooking, cleaning, shopping, yard work, and repairing things. Talk about how children can begin to help out with family chores. Have each child identify one to three chores that she could do around the house to help her parents.

ACTIVITIES: AFFIRMING OURSELVES AND ONE ANOTHER

Human Rights

Every person has the right to decide who they want to love and who they want to make a family with.

BARRIER: Some people think only certain kinds of families are okay. It's very hard to find books and pictures about some kinds of families, and some kinds of families face discrimination. This means that because of who is in their family, they might be called names, made fun of, or have difficulty getting the things all families need: safe homes and neighborhoods, health care, good food.

Families need places to live, food to eat, and support to be healthy.

BARRIER: Some families don't have what they need, because it isn't available or is too expensive, or because they face discrimination because of their family.

DISCUSSION QUESTIONS: Help children think about what families need to live and be healthy. Ask them, "Why do you think families don't have what they need? What choices could people make to help families be strong and healthy? How could we help families be strong and healthy?"

Cultural Identity

Family Days. Ask families to share family photos. Invite parents and grandparents to share special days in their families with the class.

Family Ways. Invite parents and family members to share cultural objects from their homes that they use on a regular basis and that might not be familiar to all of the children.

Family Photos. Collect photos of the children and photos of their parents. Play a guessing game using the photos of the parents. Hold them up one at a time and see if the children can guess whose parent it is. Put each photo in a small resealable bag and make a matching game. See if the children can match the picture of the child with the picture of the parent.

Family Roots. Invite children to explore where their grandparents came from. Send a note home asking parents where their parents were born and lived as children. Set out a globe or a map and ask the children if they know where their grandparents came from. Tell them that you found out by asking their parents and you can look on the map to see where they came from. Together with the children look on the map or globe and find where the grandparents were born. You may want to display a world map and mark where the children's grandparents were born or make a chart to hang on the wall.

Diversity

All Kinds of Families. Explore different kinds of families. At circle time, read a book about different types of families. Consider *Your Family, My Family*; *Families: A Celebration of Diversity, Commitment, and Love*; or *Families* (see the resource list at the end of this unit). Afterward, ask the children to describe the different kinds of families presented in the book. Set out a tub of people figures. Encourage the children to arrange the figures into family structures that match those presented in the book. Label the different types of families—adoptive, foster, single-parent, two-parent, blended, interracial, gay or lesbian, extended, and communal. End the activity by teaching children this rhyme:

> Different families, different day,
> Different people and different ways.
> When we live and grow together,
> Everything's a whole lot better.

> (*One World, Many Children: A Multicultural Program for Early Childhood Education,* Turney, Monica. Miami, FL: Santillana/Smithsonian, 1994; p. 21. Used with permission.)

Families Change. Explore ways that families stay the same and change. Ask children if they know what change means. Tell them that changes are like differences; when something changes, it's not the same anymore. Children change when they grow taller and bigger. They outgrow their clothes and their shoes. The seasons and the weather change. One day it is sunny and warm outside, and then the weather changes, and it is cold and rainy. Ask the children, "Was there a time in your family when things were different than they are now? What are some changes in your family?" Children may have experience with changes like moving, a new baby, divorce, marriage, adoption, getting a pet, a parent going to work or losing a job, other family members moving

into their homes, or the death of a family member. Help children recognize that all families change. You might want to ask children which changes feel good and make them happy and which changes feel bad and make them sad or mad. Also help children recognize that many things about families stay the same, especially the love that family members feel for one another.

Homes. Help children understand that families live in different kinds of dwellings. Gather pictures of different types of homes: houses, apartment buildings, high-rises, houseboats, huts, trailers, tents, cabins, cottages. Show the children the pictures of different types of homes in which families live. Ask the children to talk about what kinds of homes their families live in. Display the pictures in the block area and encourage the children to build different types of homes during free-choice time.

Interracial Families. Set out a variety of multiethnic people figures, all mixed up. Tell children that families can be interracial. Families can have members with different skin colors and different cultural backgrounds. Invite children to pick out two or more figures to create an interracial family.

The Colors We Are. Set out skin-colored paints at the easels. Encourage children to paint using all the colors of their family members' skin.

We're All Human. Help children explore ways that families are similar to and different from one another. Display pictures of families from many different cultures and with many different structures. Show children the pictures and discuss them. Ask children, "How are the people in these families similar to one another? How are the families in these pictures similar to your family? How are the families in these pictures different from your family?"

Bias and Stereotypes

Daddies Care for Babies. Children may have the gender stereotype that boys and men don't hold babies and don't care for babies; and therefore boys don't play with dolls. Invite children to bring in photographs of their dads or another male member of their family holding them and caring for them when they were babies. You may also want to add photographs cut out of magazines to the collection.

Rewrite the Books. Look through children's books about families with the children. See if you can find things that aren't true for your families or families you know. Invite children to rewrite the stories so that they reflect the children's reality of family life.

You Can't Have Two Mommies! Some children live with parents who are gay or lesbian and have two mommies or two daddies at home. Others have friends or family members who are gay or lesbian. They may naturally want to play house with two mommies or two daddies. Children may also occasionally announce that they love and want to marry a same-sex friend, whether or not they are familiar with gay and lesbian people. Other classmates may attempt to deny or reject this reality with protests of, "You can't have two mommies" or "Boys don't marry boys." If this happens, intervene and assure the children that they can love whomever they want and there are many different kinds of families.

Community Service

Clothes Drive. Collect clothes and donate them to a local shelter.

Play Kits. Make play kits for families who are living in homeless shelters. Gather things that families could use to spend time together. You could include a deck of cards, coloring books and crayons, children's books, and games, and see if a local fast food restaurant would donate meal coupons.

Social Action Suggestions

Homeless Shelter. As a group, support a drive to get a homeless shelter for families in your community, or work to encourage your community to adopt family-friendly policies.

ACTIVITIES: OPENING THE DOOR

Classroom Visitors

Ask parents and family members to visit the classroom. Perhaps a parent could bring a baby and show how she cares for the baby. Another child's big brother, grandma, or great-grandma could come to class.

Field Trips

Charter a bus and take a tour of the community, stopping by each of the places the children in your class live. Bring along a camera and take a picture of each child's home.

Parent Involvement

Ask parents to share photographs of their families.

Ask parents from a variety of family situations to visit the classroom and share their experiences with the children in your class. Include the parents of adoptive or foster children, gay or lesbian parents, and single parents. Invite parents of families in which a person has a disability, and parents who live in extended, interracial, blended, and two-parent families.

Parent Education

Invite a parent educator or family therapist to talk about the traits of healthy families, disciplining young children, teaching children values, or building strong families.

CLASSROOM RESOURCES

Children's Books

Families

Abuela, Arthur Dorros (New York: Dutton, 1991).

Adoption Is For Always, Linda Walvoord Girard (Morton Grove, IL: Whitman, 1986).

All Kinds Of Families, Norma Simon (Morton Grove, IL: Whitman, 1987).

Allison, Allen Say (Boston: Houghton, 1997).

Always My Dad, Sharon Dennis Wyeth (New York: Knopf, 1995).

Anna In Charge, Yorkio Tsutsui (London: Viking Kesterel, 1988).

Asha's Mums, Rosamund Elwin and Michele Paulse (Toronto: Women's Press, 1990).

Asleep In A Heap, Elizabeth Winthrop (New York: Holiday, 1993).

At Daddy's On Saturdays, Linda Walvoord Girard (Morton Grove, IL: Whitman, 1987).

Aunt Flossie's Hats (And Crabcakes Later), Elizabeth Fitzgerald Howard (New York: Clarion, 1991).

Baby-O, Nancy White Carlstrom (Boston: Little Brown, 1992).

The Baby Sister, Tomie de Paola (New York: Putnam, 1996).

Beginnings: How Families Come To Be, Virginia Kroll (Morton Grove, IL: Whitman, 1994).

Being Adopted, Maxine Rosenberg (New York: Lee, 1984).

The Best Time Of Day, Valerie Flournoy (New York: Random, 1978).

Bigmama's, Donald Crews (New York: Greenwillow, 1991).

A Birthday Basket For Tia, Pat Mora (New York: Simon, 1992).

The Birthday Swap, Loretta Lopez (New York: Lee, 1997).

Black Is Brown Is Tan, Arnold Adoff (New York: Harper, 1973).

Born In The Gravy, Denys Cazet (New York: Orchard, 1993).

Boundless Grace, Mary Hoffman (New York: Dial, 1995).

Calling The Doves, Juan Felipe Herrera (San Francisco: Children's Book, 1995).

Celebrating Families, Rosmarie Hausherr (New York: Scholastic, 1977).

Clean Your Room, Harvey Moon, Pat Cummings (New York: Simon, 1991).

Con Mi Hermano/With My Brother, Eileen Roe (New York: Simon, 1991).

A Crack In The Wall, Mary Elizabeth Haggerty (New York: Lee, 1993).

Daddies, Adele Aron Greenspun (New York: Philomel, 1991).

Daddy And Me In The Morning, Patricia Lakin (Morton Grove, IL: Whitman, 1994).

Daddy Makes The Best Spaghetti, Anna Grossnickle Hines (Boston: Houghton, 1986).

Daddy's Roommate, Michael Willhoite (Boston: Alyson Wonderland, 1990).

Daddy's Wedding, Michael Willhoite (Boston: Alyson Wonderland, 1996).

Do Like Kyla, Angela Johnson (New York: Orchard, 1990).

Evan's Corner, Elizabeth Starr Hill (New York: Puffin, 1993).

Families, Meredith Tax (New York: Feminist Press, 1996).

Families: A Celebration Of Diversity, Commitment, And Love, Aylette Jenness (New York: Orchard, 1989).

Families Are Different, Nina Pellegrini (New York: Holiday, 1991).

Families: Poems Celebrating The African American Experience, Dorothy S. Strickland and Michael R. Strickland (Honesdale, PA: Boyds Mills, 1994).

Family Pictures/Cuadros De Familia, Carmen Lomas Garza (San Francisco: Children's Book, 1990).

Fathers, Mothers, Sisters, Brothers: A Collection Of Family Poems, Mary Ann Hoberman (New York: Scholastic, 1993).

Fly Away Home, Eve Bunting (New York: Clarion, 1991).

A Forever Family, Roslyn Banish (New York: Harper, 1992).

Free To Be…A Family, Christopher Cerf, ed. (New York: Bantam, 1987).

Good-Bye Daddy, Bridgette Weninger (New York: North South, 1995).

Gramma's Walk, Anna Grossnickle Hines (New York: Greenwillow, 1993).

Grandpa's Face, Eloise Greenfield (New York: Philomel, 1988).

Heather Has Two Mommies, Leslea Newman (Northampton, MA: In Other Words, 1989).

The House I Live In: At Home In America, Isadore Seltzer (New York: Macmillan, 1992).

A House Is A House For Me, Mary Ann Hoberman (New York: Scholastic, 1993).

How My Family Lives In America, Susan Kuklin (New York: Simon, 1992).

I Have A Sister, My Sister Is Deaf, Jeanne Peterson (New York: Harper, 1977).

I Love My Family, Wade Hudson (New York: Scholastic, 1995).

I Remember "121," Francine Haskins (San Francisco: Children's Book, 1991).

I Visit My Tutu And Grandma, N. Mower (Kailua, HI: Press Pacifica, 1984).

In My Family/En Mi Familia, Carmen Lomas Garza (San Francisco: Children's Book, 1996).

Jennifer Has Two Daddies, Priscilla Galloway (Toronto: Women's Press, 1985).

Jenny Lives With Eric And Martin, Suzzane Bosche (London: Gay Men's Press, 1981).

The Keeping Quilt, Patricia Polacco (New York: Simon, 1988).

Kenya's Family Reunion, Juwanda G. Ford (New York: Scholastic, 1996).

A Koala For Katie: An Adoption Story, Jonathon London (Morton Grove, IL: Whitman, 1993).

Lee Ann: The Story Of A Vietnamese-American Girl, Tricia Brown (New York: Putnam, 1991).

Living In Two Worlds, Maxine Rosenberg (New York: Lothrop, 1984).

Lots Of Moms, Shelly Rotner and Sheila Kelley (New York: Dial, 1996).

Mama, Do You Love Me? Barbara M. Joosse (San Francisco: Chronicle, 1991).

Mama Zooms, Jane Cowen-Fletcher (New York: Scholastic, 1992).

Mom And Dad Don't Live Together Anymore, Kathy Stinson (Toronto: Annick, 1984).

Mom And Me, John Kaplan (New York: Cartwheel, 1996).

Mommy And Me By Ourselves Again, Judith Vigna (Morton Grove, IL: Whitman, 1987).

My Dad Takes Care Of Me, Patricia Quinlan (Buffalo, NY: Firefly, 1987).

My Daddy And I, Eloise Greenfield (New York: Black Butterfly, 1991).

My Kokum Called Today, Iris Loewen (Winnipeg, Canada: Pemmican, 1993).

My Mother's House, My Father's House, C. B. Christiansen (New York: Puffin, 1990).

Mycca's Baby, Rinda Byers (New York: Orchard, 1990).

Never, No Matter What, Maryleah Otto (Toronto: Women's Press, 1988).

One Hundred Is A Family, Pam Mñoz Ryan (New York: Hyperion, 1994).

One Of Three, Angela Johnson (New York: Orchard, 1991).

Our Baby From China: An Adoption Story, Nancy D'Antonio (Morton Grove, IL: Whitman, 1997).

Our Brother Has Down's Syndrome, Shelley Cairo (Toronto: Annick, 1985).

Our Granny, Margaret Wild (New York: Ticknor, 1994).

Pablo's Tree, Pat Mora (New York: Simon, 1994).

The Patchwork Quilt, Valerie Flournoy (New York: Dial, 1985).

Priscilla Twice, Judith Casely (New York: Greenwillow, 1995).

The Quilt Story, Tony Johnston (New York: Putnam, 1995).

Sam Is My Half Brother, Lizi Boyd (New York: Viking, 1990).

Shoes From Grandpa, Mem Fox (New York: Orchard, 1990).

Sitti's Secrets, Naomi Shihab Nye (New York: Simon, 1994).

Special Parents, Special Children, Joanne Berstein and Bryna J. Berstein (Morton Grove, IL: Whitman, 1991).

Families
—
CHILDREN'S BOOKS

Sunday, Synthia Saint James (Morton Grove: Whitman, 1996).

Tar Beach, Faith Ringgold (New York: Crown, 1992).

Tell Me Again About The Night I Was Born, Jamie Lee Curtis (New York: Harper, 1996).

Things I Like About Grandma, Francine Haskins (San Francisco: Children's Book, 1992).

This Is My House, Arthur Dorros (New York: Scholastic, 1992).

Through My Window, Tony Bradman (Parsippany: Silver Burdett, 1986).

Tiger Flowers, Patricia Quinlan (New York: Dial, 1994).

Together We Are Together, The Children of St. Brigid's Head Start School (New York: Scholastic, 1992).

Too Many Tamales, Gary Soto (New York: Putnam, 1993).

Two Mrs. Gibsons, Toyomi Igus (San Francisco: Children's Book, 1996).

Veronica's First Year, Jean Sasso Rheingrover (Morton Grove, IL: Whitman, 1996).

Wait And See, Virginia Bradley (New York: Cobblehill, 1994).

We Are All Alike…We Are All Different, The Kindergartners at Cheltenham Elementary School (New York: Scholastic, 1991).

Welcoming Babies, Margy Burns Knight (Gardiner, ME: Tilbury, 1994).

When I Am Old With You, Angela Johnson (New York: Orchard, 1990).

When We Married Gary, Anna Grossnickle Hines (New York: Greenwillow, 1996).

Who's In A Family? Robert Skutch (Berkeley, CA: Tricycle, 1995).

Will There Be A Lap For Me? Dorothy Corey (Morton Grove, IL: Whitman, 1992).

William And The Good Old Days, Eloise Greenfield (New York: Harper, 1993).

Yonder, Tony Johnston (New York: Dial, 1988).

You Be Me And I'll Be Me, Pili Mandelbaum (Brooklyn, NY: Kane/Miller, 1990).

Your Family, My Family, Joan Drescher (New York: Walker, 1980).

Music

Fink, Cathy, and Marcy Marxer. *Nobody Else Like Me* (A&M, 1994).

"Everything Possible"

"May There Always Be Sunshine"

"Twins"

Hartmann, Jack. *Make A Friend, Be A Friend* (Educational Activities, 1990).

"It's Not Your Fault"

Hinojosa, Tish. *Cada Niño/Every Child* (Rounder, 1996).

"Siempre Abuelita/Always Grandma"

Music For Little People. *Peace Is The World Smiling* (Music for Little People, 1989).

"Make Peace"

Pirtle, Sarah. *Two Hands Hold The Earth* (Gentle Wind, 1984).

"May There Always Be Sunshine"

———. *Big Ideas!* (Glass, 1990).

"Daddy's Song"

"First, Middle, Last, Only"

Visual Displays

Lakeshore
Families Poster Pack

Nasco
The Family Album Cards

Syracuse Cultural Workers
Babies Poster

Feelings

"I hate you!" "You poopy face!" Young children have big feelings. Each child's family has different rules regarding the expression of feelings. Often these expectations of behavior are culturally based. A child's home culture influences the meaning, value, and expectations for expressing one's feelings.

Today children are coming into our classrooms emotionally charged. Many children are stressed, angry, depressed, or confused. A unit on feelings provides children with an opportunity to learn about feelings, clarify their confusion, and gain acceptance for and explore nonviolent ways of releasing their feelings.

UNIT 5:

Feelings

TABLE OF CONTENTS

FEELINGS

 Look for this symbol
to find activities you
can use for circle time.

Web

How can we tell what someone is feeling?

What are the consequences of our actions?

What are healthy ways of showing feelings?

How do your brothers and sisters show their feelings?

What makes you have strong feelings?

What are ways we act out our feelings?

What are hurtful ways of showing feelings?

How can we celebrate our feelings?

How do your parents show their feelings?

How do you show your feelings?

What are feelings?

How are you feeling?

What do people want and need?

How can we work together to help people in our community who are feeling sad, scared or lonely?

FEELINGS

What are our human rights?

How do people feel when they don't get what they want and need?

What are all the different kinds of feelings?

How are feelings similar to one another?

How do feelings stay the same?

What are stereotypes about feelings?

How can we respect one another's feelings?

How are feelings different from one another?

How do feelings change?

How can we challenge stereotypes about people with disabilities?

OUTLINE

   I. How are you feeling?
- A. How do you show your feelings?
- B. How do your parents show their feelings?
- C. How do your brothers and sisters show their feelings?
- D. How can we tell what someone is feeling?

  II. What makes you have strong feelings?
- A. What are ways we act out our feelings?
- B. What are the consequences of our actions?
- C. What are hurtful ways of showing feelings?
- D. What are healthy ways of showing our feelings?

 III. What are feelings?
- A. What are all the kinds of feelings?
- B. How are feelings similar to one another?
- C. How are feelings different from one another?
- D. How do feelings stay the same?
- E. How do feelings change?

 IV. What are stereotypes about feelings?

  V. How can we challenge the stereotypes about feelings?

 VI. What do people want and need?
- A. How do people feel when they don't get what they want and need?
- B. How can we work together to help people in our community who are feeling sad, scared, or lonely?

 VII. What are our human rights?

VIII. How can we respect one another's feelings?

 IX. How can we celebrate our feelings?

MATERIALS LIST

ART

skin-colored paints, crayons, markers, felt, and craft paper

butcher paper roll

magazines with pictures of people expressing feelings

chart of feelings

BLOCKS

a variety of multicultural people figures, including figures of people with disabilities

two dollhouses

DRAMATIC PLAY

multiethnic baby dolls

multiethnic preschooler dolls (for example, Friends Dolls or Children with Hearing, Motor, and Visual Impairments Dolls, *People of Every Stripe*; Multi-Ethnic School Dolls, *Lakeshore*; Multi-Ethnic Dolls, *Constructive Playthings*)

adaptive equipment for dolls with disabilities (available from *Lakeshore*)

bedroom and bedtime props, including bedtime storybooks

moving: suitcases, backpacks, boxes, change-of-address cards, maps, wagon, for rent, for sale, and sold signs

LARGE MOTOR

equipment that supports children's moving their bodies to show how they're feeling (for example, No-Fail Streamer Set, *Lakeshore*) or fosters helping, cooperation, and kindness (for example, Tandem Trike or Twosome Trike, *Constructive Playthings*)

LITERACY

children's books: fiction, nonfiction, and bilingual books about feelings (see resource list at the end of the unit)

cassette player and theme-related storybook cassettes

blank cassettes

hand puppets showing different feelings (for example, Feelings Hand Puppets, *Edvantage*)

feelings cut-outs (for example, Everybody's Beautiful Children's Feelings Cut-Outs, *ABC School Supply* and *Sandy and Son*)

MANIPULATIVES

puzzles having to do with feelings (for example, "I Love You" Signing Puzzle, *Environments*)

matching, lotto, and board games about feelings (for example, Feelings and Faces Games, *Lakeshore*; Guess How Much I Love You Game, *Constructive Playthings*; My Home and Places Board Game, *Animal Town*; Not So Scary Things Board Game, The Great Feelings Chase Game, The Nurturing Game, *Childswork/Childsplay*)

SCIENCE

books about weather
wave bottles
weather teaching pictures

SENSORY

bubble solution
bubble wands and pipes
cornstarch

Teaching Through the Interest Areas

Art

Set out magazines with pictures of people expressing various emotions and a chart of feelings with labels and faces that children can refer to.

Blocks

Set out two dollhouses so that children can play sleeping over at someone's house, visiting friends and families, going to a foster family, or going back and forth between mom's house and dad's house.

Dramatic Play

Set out props to encourage dramatic play that centers around common experiences that generate strong feelings in young children. For example, you could add bedroom and bedtime props, including bedtime storybooks, to foster play around going to bed and putting children to bed. Or add suitcases, backpacks, boxes, change-of-address cards, maps, a wagon to facilitate pretending to move, and for rent, for sale, and sold signs.

Literacy

Set out a collection of literacy materials that deal with feelings. Include fiction, nonfiction, and bilingual books, a tape player and storybook cassettes in different languages, hand puppets, flannel board sets, picture sets, and materials for making greeting cards and books.

Manipulatives

Set out materials on the subject of feelings: puzzles, matching games, lotto games, and board games.

Music

Add a variety of cassettes about self-esteem and feelings to the music area.

Set out different types of instrumental music that can influence our feelings.

Science

Set out weather teaching pictures, books on weather, and wave bottles.

Sensory

Add materials to the sensory table that might generate strong sensations or responses. Try bubbles and bubble wands, pipes, and bubble makers or cornstarch and water.

ACTIVITIES: INVESTIGATING THE THEME

Creative Development

Be a Clown. Talk about how sometimes people dress up as clowns in order to make people laugh and smile. Set out face paints and a mirror and encourage children to paint their faces to make themselves look like clowns.

Feelings Drawings. Each day, set out painting or drawing materials: drawing paper and crayons; easel paper and paints; or drawing paper and pastels. On one day, invite children to draw a happy picture. The next day, ask them to draw a sad picture. On the third day, ask children to draw a mad picture, and on the fourth day, ask children to draw a scared picture.

Feelings Puppets. Invite the children to make feelings puppets. Set out small paper bags, felt tip markers, glue, construction paper scraps, and yarn. When the children are done, invite them to give their puppets names and describe how they are feeling.

Happy and Sad. Set out paper plates, skin-colored crayons, and color crayons. Invite children to take two paper plates and draw a happy face on one plate and a sad face on the other. Staple the plates together so that the happy face is on one side and the sad face is on the other.

My Peaceful Place. Invite children to think of a place that makes them feel peaceful. Encourage children to draw and describe their peaceful place.

BIG AS LIFE

Paint a Feelings Rainbow. Remind children of how rainbows are bands or rows of colors. Invite them to paint a band of color to represent each of the following feelings: happy, sad, mad, tired, afraid, worried, excited.

Paint to the Music. Over a period of several days or weeks, play a variety of music while the children are at the easels. Each time ask the children to paint the way the music makes them feel. On one occasion you might want to play a march and another time a lullaby or dance music.

Critical Thinking

What Would You Do? Help children associate behavior with feelings. Ask the children the following questions:

> What are some things you would do if you were feeling happy?
>
> If you like someone, how would you show it?
>
> If you love someone, how would you show it?
>
> If you are afraid of someone or something, what would you do?
>
> If you are feeling sad, what might you do?

Emotional Development

Affirmation Jar. Find a large jar or box to hold simple affirmations. Once a week, at circle time, invite children to reach into the jar and pull out an affirmation. Read each child's affirmation out loud to them, and then ask them to say it out loud. Encourage the children to sit quietly for a moment to think about what the affirmation means. Here are some sample affirmations: I use my words, I am a good listener, I put my toys away, I am friendly, I am helpful, I am a winner, I am lovable, I am capable, I am patient, I am kind to others, I try hard, I do my best.

How Do You Show Your Feelings? Ask the children what they do and say when they are angry, sad, or happy. What do they do when they love somebody or when they feel proud? You might ask such questions as, "When you are angry, what do you do? What do you say? How do you think you look? Can you show us how you look?" Pass a mirror around the circle and invite children to look at themselves making "feelings faces."

How Does That Feel? Help children become aware of feelings associated with prejudice and increase their sensitivity to the feelings of others. Cut out an 8-inch circle out of oaktag and divide the circle into six sections. In each section draw a face that represents a different emotion. Make a spinner for the feelings circle. Present a variety of common classroom scenarios in which children ignore, tease, or reject one another. Pass the feelings circle around and ask children how they would feel in that situation. They can either tell you or use the spinner to point to the facial expression that matches how they would feel.

Hug Me. Ask children if anyone has ever given them a hug. When do people give them a hug? What does *hug* mean? How does getting a hug make them feel? Tell children they can use their arms and hands to give themselves a hug. Ask children to think of who they could hug. Remind them that they can always hug themselves. Teach them this poem:

> I can't hug a bug,
> I can't hug a rug,
> But I can always hug me.
> When I'm feeling glad,
> When I'm feeling sad,
> I can always, always hug me.

(*Everybody Has a Body*, Robert E. Rockwell, Robert A. Williams, and Elizabeth A. Sherwood. Beltsville, MD: Gryphon House, 1992; p. 57. Used with permission.)

I'm Mad! Help young children learn how to manage their anger without becoming aggressive or violent. Ask the children what makes them really mad. What's it like to feel mad? What do they want to do when they are mad? Tell the children that you have an idea of a way to deal with their angry feelings: (1) Stop what you are doing. (2) Take two deep breaths. (3) Count to three. (4) Say how you feel and what you need. (5) Listen to others. (6) Try to work it out.

Picture Yourself. Ask children if you can take their picture. Tell them you would like them to make "feelings faces." Take a picture of each child's happy face, mad face, sad face, and scared face. Write the name of the emotion on the back of each photograph. Children can compare their photographs, match photographs of similar feelings, and identify the feeling being expressed in each picture.

 Strong Voices. Help children learn to use their strong voices when they are mad or have an immediate need, or want to influence someone. Invite children to stand up and talk from their throats in their high, squeaky voices. Show them how to put their hands around their throats to feel the vibrations there. Talk about how this voice is hard to listen to and sounds whiny. Then invite the children to stand tall, put their shoulders back, and talk from their diaphragms in their strong voices. Show them how to put their hands on their chests to feel the vibrations.

 What a Wonderful Person You Are. Begin each morning's circle time by welcoming each child individually and identifying one positive physical trait, personality trait, or skill. For example, you might say, "Good morning, Mandell. I really like the way you tie your own shoes" or "Brianna, I really like those strong arms of yours."

What Are Feelings? Facilitate a series of discussions with children to introduce them to basic feelings. Begin with feeling happy. Ask children what being happy means. Ask them the following questions:

> What makes you happy?
>
> How do you act when you are happy?

How do you look when you are happy?

How can we show others that we are feeling happy?

What can we do when we are happy?

You might want to tape record the conversation so that children can listen to it again later. Repeat the discussion with other basic emotions, like sadness, anger, fear, surprise, frustration, relaxation, worry, silliness, patience, shyness, excitement, boredom, hope, hopelessness, shame, love, loneliness, embarrassment, and pride. More complex feelings include contentment, grief, disgust, hate, terror, intimidation, amazement, annoyance, peace, relief, confidence, and superiority.

What Feeling Is This? Children need to learn how to recognize basic emotions in others. Show children three different photographs of people expressing the same feeling. Ask children to look at the pictures and identify the feeling.

Health, Safety, and Nutrition

Relax. Teach children how to relax their bodies when they are feeling stressed. Invite children to find places on the floor where they can lie down and not touch anyone else. Dim the lights and play soft instrumental music. Ask the children to lie quietly and take big slow breaths. Have them tense different body parts for five seconds, and then relax them. For example, say, "Now I want you to tighten up your feet and toes. Make them just as tight as you can…that's right. Hold them tight just a little longer.…Now let them relax. Let them get soft and relaxed." Repeat this for a series of other body parts. Ask the children to tense and then relax their feet and toes, legs, bottom, back, shoulders, hands, arms, and faces. Then ask the children to lie quietly and breathe deeply.

Stress Release. Help children explore ways of dealing with stress or problems. Ask the children to think of all the things they can do when they are feeling frustrated or upset. The list might include taking a break, running, crying, taking a walk, and talking to someone. Introduce classroom materials that children can use to calm themselves. Set out the water table, freshly made playdough, woodworking materials and hammers, crayons and paper, and relaxing instrumental music. Invite the children to choose a calming activity.

Language Development

> **Home Language.** *Learn the words for feelings, like* happy, sad, mad, scared, *and* worried, *in American Sign Language and the home languages of the children in your class.*

Feelings and Actions. Play a guessing game. Describe a series of actions or behaviors that illustrate a feeling, then ask the children, "How am I feeling?" For example, you might use this situation to illustrate happiness: "I'm playing with my toys and I'm singing my favorite song and I'm moving my head from side to side as I sing and play." Here is a scenario to illustrate fear: "If I don't play with someone, if I don't want to sit next to them at the snack table, and if I don't ever talk to them, how might I be feeling?" Curiosity could be described by the following: "How am I feeling if I peek inside a package to see what's inside, or if I ask questions like, 'What's that?' and 'What are you doing?'"

Feelings Picture Cards. Use a commercial set of pictures showing feelings, or make your own by cutting out large pictures of people with different facial and bodily expressions from magazines and gluing them onto construction paper. Hold up one picture at a time and ask open-ended questions:

> Who can tell me about this picture?
>
> What do you see?
>
> What is this person doing?
>
> How do you think they are feeling?
>
> How do you know?
>
> When have you felt like the person in this picture?

Feelings Picture Stories. Sit down with a small group of children and some pictures of people expressing different emotions. Show the children one picture at a time. Ask the children what they see in the pictures. Encourage the children to make up stories about how the people in the pictures are feeling. If possible, write down the children's stories.

How Do You Feel About Color? Help children express the feelings they associate with different colors. Ask the children, "What do you think of when you see the color blue? How does blue make you feel?" Repeat the questions with many different colors. Invite the children to make a color book, with a page for each color.

 Use Your Words. Give children an opportunity to practice using words to say how they are feeling. Each morning at circle time or at the snack table, go around and ask each child to say how he is feeling. During the day you can take the pulse of the group and announce, "Feelings check!" Once again, quickly ask each child how he is feeling.

Math

Alike and Different Feelings Faces. Make game cards to help children find the feeling that doesn't belong. Cut 10- to 12-inch lengths of oaktag sentence strip. Draw a total of four faces on each strip. Make three of the "feelings faces" exactly alike and one different. For example, you could have three happy faces and one sad face. Vary the types of feelings and their arrangement on each strip. Set out the game strips and some poker chips or juice can lids for markers. Ask children to look at the faces and see if they can find the one that doesn't belong and put a marker on top of it.

Feelings Dominoes. Make a set of domino cards that show a variety of feelings. Draw two faces next to each other on blank index cards, with each face expressing a different feeling. Use skin-colored markers to make the "feelings faces" multicultural. Draw a line down the middle of each card to separate the two faces. Invite children to play dominoes. One child begins the game by placing a card faceup on the floor. The next child places a card next to it so that there are matching faces next to each other.

Feelings Match. Make four or more sets of feelings matching cards. Find duplicate photos in magazines, use a color photocopier to make duplicates of photos, or draw simple facial expressions that reflect different feelings. Make sure that your set of matching cards reflects cultural diversity and includes both boys and girls and children with glasses. Place the cards in a basket and encourage the children to find the matching sets.

Feelings Shapes. Set out a variety of geometric shapes cut from construction paper, and glue. Invite children to arrange and glue the shapes on construction paper to make a feeling face. Ask them, "How would you make a happy face, or a sad face, or a mad face?"

Feelings Sort. Collect a variety of pictures of people expressing different feelings. Make sure that the set reflects cultural diversity and includes people with disabilities. Write the name of the feeling on the back of each card. Place the pictures in a basket. Set out the basket along with a sorting tray. Invite children to classify the feeling pictures any way they like.

How Many? Ask children, "How many different feelings can you name?" and make a list of all of them. Go back through the list and count how many feelings they know. You might also want to write the numerals 1, 2, 3, etc., along the left side of the feelings list to help children match rote counting with numerals.

Music

Feelings Sound. Set out a variety of musical instruments. Invite children to make the sounds of different feelings with their instruments. Ask them if they can make happy sounds, sad sounds, angry sounds, joyful sounds, proud sounds, and fearful sounds.

Feelings Songs. Here are three simple songs about feelings to teach children at circle time and sing throughout the day.

I Am Happy

Tune: *Frére Jacques*

I am happy, I am happy
Yes, I am, Yes, I am
I am fun and cheerful
I am fun and cheerful
Joy, Joy, Joy
Joy, Joy, Joy

(Replace "happy" with other feelings, such as loving, peaceful, and grateful.)

(*The Joyful Child: A Sourcebook of Activities and Ideas For Releasing Children's Natural Joy*, Peggy Jenkins. Tucson, AZ: Harbinger House, 1989; p. 94. Used with permission.)

I Have Feelings

Tune: *Twinkle, Twinkle, Little Star*

I have feelings. You do, too.
Let's all sing about a few.
I am happy. *(smile)*
I am sad. *(frown)*
I get scared. *(wrap arms around self)*
I get mad. *(make a fist and shake it)*
I am proud of being me—*(hands on hips)*
that's a feeling too, you see.
I have feelings. You do, too.
We just sang about a few.

(*Creative Resources for the Early Childhood Classroom*, second edition, Judy Herr and Libby Yvonne. Albany, NY: Delmar Publishers, 1995; p. 255. Used with permission.)

If You're Happy and You Know It

If you're happy and you know it, clap your hands.
If you're happy and you know it, clap your hands.
If you're happy and you know it, then your face will surely show it.
If you're happy and you know it, clap your hands.

Additional verses (and add your own):
If you're angry and you know it, stop and breathe.
If you're angry and you know it, stop and breathe.
If you're angry and you know it, you don't really need to blow it.
If you're angry and you know it, stop and breathe.

If you're mad and you know it, stomp your feet…

If you're sad and you know it, say boo hoo…

(*Peacemaker's A, B, Cs for Young Children: A Guide for Teaching Conflict Resolution with a Peace Table*, Rebecca Ann Janke and Julie Penshorn Peterson. Marine-on-St. Croix, MN: Growing Communities for Peace, 1995; p. 44. Used with permission.)

Physical Development

Balloon Toss. Balloons are often associated with cheering people up, celebrations, and happy feelings. Give each child an inflated balloon. Encourage children to explore the color, weight, and shape of their balloons. Invite children to form a circle, toss their balloons in the air, and catch them. How many times can they toss their balloons without dropping them? You could also have the children play catch with each other, or pass the balloons to the left and right around the circle.

Class Clown. Have the children sit in a circle. Select one child to be the clown. The clown walks around the circle and stops in front of one child, who then must say, "I won't smile" three times. The clown must try to make the child laugh. The first person to laugh becomes the next clown.

Feelings Express. Invite the children to express various feelings through creative movement. Ask the children to move their bodies in ways that show they are happy, mad, scared, tired, excited, proud, thankful, patient, and feeling loved.

Guess That Feeling. Invite the children to take turns acting out feelings for the rest of the children to guess. You could use a set of feeling face cards and have the child draw a card and act out the feeling on the card for the other children to guess.

Science

Are You Wound Up? Sometimes children feel like they have a lot of energy inside that needs to come out. Objects store energy inside and the objects can release it. Put a block inside a plastic bag. Hold the top of the bag and twist the bottom where the block is many times. Let go and watch the bag spin around and around. Set out a variety of bags and objects. Invite the children to experiment with twisting and releasing the bags.

Blowing Bubbles. Blowing bubbles is fun and always makes people laugh and smile. Make bubble solution by mixing dish soap, water, and a few drops of glycerin (available at drug stores). Experiment with blowing bubbles with a variety of objects. Try wooden spools, paper tubes, straws, bubble wands, and plastic six-pack holders.

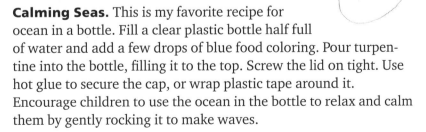

Calming Seas. This is my favorite recipe for ocean in a bottle. Fill a clear plastic bottle half full of water and add a few drops of blue food coloring. Pour turpentine into the bottle, filling it to the top. Screw the lid on tight. Use hot glue to secure the cap, or wrap plastic tape around it. Encourage children to use the ocean in the bottle to relax and calm them by gently rocking it to make waves.

Surprise! We can mix chemicals together and create a gas. A gas is invisible (air, for example). You can't see it. Ask the children, "What do you think will happen if I mix baking soda and vinegar? Are you feeling curious?" Pour ½ cup of baking soda into a plastic soda bottle. Add ½ cup vinegar and quickly insert a cork into the opening. The gas will pop the cork. Afterwards, ask the children if they were surprised by the experiment. Did they expect the gas to be so powerful that it could push the cork out?

Thunder and Lightning. Young children are often frightened by thunder and lightning. Help them develop an understanding of this natural phenomenon by exploring static electricity. Have them rub their feet on the carpet. Then explain that, "During a storm, strong winds make the water droplets in clouds rub against each other. This causes sparks of electricity, called lightning, that shoot out of the cloud. Lightning is very hot. It heats the air around it. As the hot air pushes out against the cooler air, it makes a loud noise called thunder."

Volcano. Sometimes when we are really mad, we feel like we want to explode. We might even feel like a volcano, which erupts when gases build up enough pressure inside to force the liquid out the top. Set a baking pan on a table. Place a pop bottle in the center of the pan. Mound damp soil around the bottle so that it is hidden and looks like a volcano. Pour 1 tablespoon baking soda into the bottle. Measure 1 cup vinegar and color it with red food coloring. Pour the vinegar into the bottle, and stand back. The mixture will create a red foam that will spray out the top of the volcano and run down the sides.

Social Development

Feelings in My Family. Ask the children how they know when their parents are happy with or mad at them. What do their parents do or say? Also ask the children what kinds of things make their parents happy or make them mad.

How Are You Feeling? Help children recognize how others might be feeling. Ask children to look at pictures of people expressing various emotions. See if the children can recognize the emotions. Ask them, "How is this person feeling? What do you see that makes you think that?"

How Would You Feel If...? Invite children to think of situations that foster strong feelings. Here are some examples:

How would you feel if your friend shared a cookie with you?

How would you feel if your friend took your toy?

How would you feel if your friend asked if he could sit by you?

How would you feel if your friend called you names?

How would you feel if your friend ran up to greet you when you first came to school and said, "I'm so glad to see you"?

How would you feel if your friend pushed you down?

How would you feel if your friend asked you to come to his house to play?

How would you feel if your friend said, "If you don't give me that toy, I'm not going to be your friend"?

Let's Lift Up Others. Help children learn to recognize when people are feeling sad, down, or depressed. Ask children what can they do when someone they know is feeling sad or down. What could they do to help someone who is depressed feel better? Invite children to role-play helping cheer up someone.

Photo Masks. Use a color photocopier to enlarge close-up photographs of people expressing a variety of feelings. Glue the photocopies of the faces to poster board. Punch eyeholes and holes near the edges to attach a string and make a mask. Encourage children to try on the different masks, look at themselves in the mirror, and engage in dramatic play.

Sharing. Bring a tub of toys to circle time. Pretend to play with the toys and tell the children, "These are my toys. I want them all to myself, and I'm not going to let anyone else have them." Stop playing and ask the children, "What am I doing? How am I feeling?" Then role-play a different scenario. Tell the children, "Let's suppose I was feeling differently and I said, 'Hey, look at this bucket of toys. Would you like to play with me? I've got plenty. There's enough for me and you. Would you like some?'" Give each child a toy. Ask the children, "What did I just do? How am I feeling now?" Talk about how you shared your toys, how you were feeling, and how sharing makes you feel.

ACTIVITIES: AFFIRMING OURSELVES AND ONE ANOTHER

Human Rights

People have a right to know what their feelings are, to be able to name them, and to have them respected by others. People have the right to express their feelings in the ways that are comfortable for them and come from their home culture.

BARRIER: Strong feelings are uncomfortable for some people. People from different cultures have different ways of expressing feelings, and people can misunderstand one another. Sometimes people are taught not to show their feelings.

People have a right to respect.

BARRIER: Sometimes we get frustrated and think that our way of expressing feelings is the only way or the best way. Sometimes we don't understand one another's ways of expressing feelings.

DISCUSSION QUESTIONS: Help children think about what people need to feel respected around their feelings. Ask them, "What makes you feel respected? How do you like to be treated when you're mad (or sad, or afraid, or happy)? What makes you feel disrespected? What don't you like people to say or do to you when you're mad (or sad, or afraid, or happy)? Why do you think people don't get what they need? What choices could people make to respect other people's ways of expressing their feelings? How can we respect others' feelings?"

Cultural Identity

Folk Music. Different types of music are often associated with different types of feelings. Introduce children to music from the cultures of the children in your class.

I've Got the Blues. Introduce children to blues and rap music, which originated in the African American culture. Invite children to write their own blues or rap. You may want to make a cassette recording of children performing their blues or rap.

Silly Songs and Silly Stories. Read folktales that are silly, or listen to silly folk songs from the cultures represented by the children in your class. Talk about how the stories and songs make them feel. Ask the children, "How do you feel when you laugh? How does a silly song or a silly story help us?"

Diversity

Attitudes Toward Diversity. Explore feelings children have about differences among people. Show children photographs of a variety of people. Include photographs of both genders, and of people of different ages, races, socioeconomic classes, and disabilities. For each picture, ask the child a series of questions:

Who is in the picture?

What can you tell me about the person in the picture?

How is that person like you?

How is that person different from you?

How does that person make you feel?

If the child has any misconceptions that are prejudicial, give the child simple accurate information.

Feeling Different. Introduce the children to the concept of feeling left out or excluded. Ask them, "Did you ever feel like you didn't belong or weren't wanted?" Sometimes other people leave us out because we are different from them. Ask the children, "Can any of you think of a reason why you might feel like you didn't fit in?" Maybe we wear different clothes, or our skin color is different from someone else's, or we talk or move differently from them. They might not know how to behave with us, or be afraid of differences, or feel embarrassed. Ask the children, "What could you do if someone else is treating you like you don't fit in? What could you say to them? Who could you get to help you?" Sometimes we exclude other people for the same reasons. Maybe they eat different foods, or celebrate different holidays, from us. Help children understand that difference enriches us all. Ask them, "What could you do if you were feeling uncomfortable with someone else's difference? How can we make sure there's room for everyone to belong? How can we help someone who feels left out?" Use a persona doll to help you tell a story about exclusion, or ask the children to help you make up a story.

New Things. Explore feelings children have about trying new things. Ask the children, "How would you feel if I told you we were going on a field trip to someplace that you have never been before? If we were going to get a new child in our classroom? If I put something in the sand and water table that you hadn't played with before? If we had a snack that we hadn't eaten before?" Plan a "Try New Things Day." Set out new toys to play with, new activities that you haven't done before, and a new snack the children haven't had before. Teach the children a new song, and read them a new book. At the end of the morning, talk with the children about how it felt to try new things.

Similar and Different. Help children recognize that people can have similar feelings and show them in different ways. Show the children pictures of people expressing a variety of emotions. Hold up each picture and ask the children how the person is feeling. Then invite them to make up a story about why the person in the picture is feeling that way. Then go around the group and ask the children what they would do if that had happened to them. Ask the children, "How are the ways we show our feelings similar to one another? How are they different from one another?"

Bias and Stereotypes

It's All Right to Cry. Tell the children that some people believe a stereotype that boys and men don't cry. Ask them, "Is that true? What boys do you know who cry or have cried? What men do you know who cry or have cried? It's okay for boys and men to cry." You might want to make a list or chart of all the men the children know who cry, and when they have cried.

True or False. Help children tell the difference between respectful and stereotypic (false) pictures of people. Show children accurate and stereotypic pictures of people one at a time. As you show them each picture ask, "What is this a picture of? Is this picture true or false?" After children answer, summarize why the picture is accurate or stereotypic.

 Unfair Behavior. Help children make the connection between stereotypes, feelings, and behaviors. Provide the children with several situations that involve stereotypic attitudes using dolls or puppets to role-play them. For example, one puppet has a disability and the other puppet thinks he's a baby and can't do anything. The able-bodied puppet doesn't like the puppet with the disability and feels superior to the other puppet. So he ignores the puppet with a disability and refuses to talk to him. Another situation might be a doll who is African American thinking that an Asian American child in her class looks and talks funny. The African American doll is afraid of the Asian American doll and avoids any contact with her. She doesn't talk to her and she's afraid to sit by her.

Community Service

 Cheer Up. Are there people in the community who are sad or lonely? What could you do to cheer them up? Cheer up the residents of a nursing home by bringing them artwork, singing songs, and doing finger plays for them.

Social Action Suggestions

 Don't Leave Me Out. Show children wall calendars of babies or children. See if any culture, race, gender, or disability is missing or underrepresented. Talk about what it feels like to be left out. As a group, write a letter to the company that manufactures the calendars and request that they make their calendars more inclusive.

BIG AS LIFE

ACTIVITIES: OPENING THE DOOR

Classroom Visitors

Ask a drummer or a musician to come to your classroom, play his instrument, and talk about how making music makes the children feel.

Field Trips

Attend a concert, play, or other cultural event in your community that everyone can enjoy.

Parent Involvement

Invite parents to share their hobbies, personal interests, or things they do for fun and relaxation.

Parent Education

Invite a child psychologist, psychotherapist, social worker, or parent educator to talk about helping children cope with stress, fostering emotional intelligence in children, or helping children deal with anger.

CLASSROOM RESOURCES

Children's Books

Feelings

CHILDREN'S BOOKS

Alexander And The Terrible, Horrible, No Good, Very Bad Day, Judith Viorst (New York: Atheneum, 1972).

All About You, Catherine Anholt and Laurence Anholt (New York: Viking, 1991).

Babushka's Doll, Patricia Polacco (New York: Simon, 1990).

The Bear Under The Stairs, Helen Cooper (New York: Dial, 1993).

The Bracelet, Yoshiko Uchida (New York: Philomel, 1993).

C Is For Curious: An ABC Of Feelings, Woodleigh Hubbard (San Francisco: Chronicle, 1990).

Cat's Got Your Tongue? Charles Shaefer (Milwaukee: Stevens, 1993).

The Chocolate-Covered-Cookie Tantrum, Deborah Blumenthal (New York: Clarion, 1996).

Daniel's Dog, Jo Ellen Bogart (New York: Scholastic, 1990).

Dark Day, Light Night, Jan Carr (New York: Hyperion, 1995).

Barney Is Best, Nancy White Carlstrom (New York: Harper, 1994).

Double Dip Feelings: Stories To Help Children Understand Emotions, Barbara Cain (New York: Magination, 1990).

Even If I Did Something Awful, Barbara Shook Hazen (New York: Atheneum, 1981).

Everett Anderson's Goodbye, Lucille Clifton (New York: Holt, 1993).

Everybody Has Feelings, Charles E. Avery (Seattle: Open Hand, 1992).

Everybody Needs A Rock, Byrd Baylor (New York: Atheneum, 1974).

Feelings, Aliki (New York: Greenwillow, 1984).

Feelings Inside You And Outloud Too, Barbara Kay Pollard (Millbrae, CA: Celestial Arts, 1975).

Go Away, Big Green Monster, Ed Emberly (Boston: Little Brown, 1992).

Grandfather's Lovesong, Reeve Lindbergh (New York: Viking, 1993).

Gustavo And The Fears, Ricardo Alcántara.

Honey I Love And Other Love Poems, Eloise Greenfield (New York: Harper, 1978).

How Would You Feel If Your Dad Was Gay? Ann Heron and Meredith Maran (Boston: Alyson Wonderland, 1991).

I Am Not A Crybaby, Norma Simon (Morton Grove, IL: Whitman, 1989).

I Like Me, Deborah Conner Coker (Racine, WI: Golden, 1995).

I Like Me! Nancy Carlson (New York: Viking, 1988).

I Was So Mad, Norma Simon (Morton Grove, IL: Whitman, 1974).

I Want To Be, Thylias Moss (New York: Dial, 1993).

I'm Frustrated, Elizabeth Crary (Seattle: Parenting, 1992).

I'm Mad, Elizabeth Crary (Seattle: Parenting, 1992).

I'm Proud, Elizabeth Crary (Seattle: Parenting, 1992).

Laney's Lost Momma, Diane Johnston Hamm (Morton Grove, IL: Whitman, 1991).

Less Than Half, More Than Whole, Kathleen Lacapa and Michael Lacapa (Flagstaff, AZ: Northland, 1994).

Linda Saves The Day, Lawrence Balter (New York: Barron's, 1989).

Loving, Ann Morris (New York: Lothrop, 1990).

Make Someone Smile, Judy Lalli (Minneapolis: Free Spirit, 1996).

Mama, Do You Love Me? Barbara M. Joosse (San Francisco: Chronicle, 1991).

Mommy And Me By Ourselves Again, Judith Vigna (Morton Grove, IL: Whitman, 1987).

My Many Colored Days, Dr. Seuss (New York: Knopf, 1996).

Not Yet, Yvette, Helen Ketterman (Morton Grove, IL: Whitman, 1992).

Now Everybody Really Hates Me, Jane Read Martin (New York: Harper, 1993).

The Palm Of My Heart, Davida Adedjouma, ed. (New York: Lee, 1996).

Pierre, Maurice Sendak (New York: Viking, 1984).

So Much, Trish Cooke (Cambridge, MA: Candlewick, 1984).

Sometimes I Feel Like A Mouse, Jeanne Modesitt (New York: Scholastic, 1992).

Sometimes I Like To Cry, Elizabeth Stanton and Harry Stanton (Morton Grove, IL: Whitman, 1978).

The Storm, Marc Harshman (New York: Cobblehill, 1995).

The Temper Tantrum Book, Edna Preston Mitchell (New York: Puffin, 1978).

Thunder Cake, Patricia Polacco (New York: Philomel, 1990).

Tucking Mommy In, Morag Loh (New York: Orchard, 1987).

The Underbed, Cathryn Clinton (Intercourse, PA: Good Books, 1990).

We Got My Brother At The Zoo, John Hassett and Ann Hassett (Boston: Houghton, 1993).

What Is A Feeling? David W. Krueger (Seattle: Parenting, 1993).

What Makes Me Happy? Catherine Anholt and Laurence Anholt (Cambridge, MA: Candlewick, 1995).

Whitle Home, Natalie Honeycutt (New York: Orchard, 1993).

Will There Be A Lap For Me? Dorothy Corey (Morton Grove, IL: Whitman, 1992).

Willie's Not The Hugging Kind, Joyce Durham Barrett (New York: Harper, 1989).

Music

Allen, Lillian. *Nothing But A Hero* (Redwood, 1991).
   "If You See The Truth"

Bonkrude, Sally. *Celebrating Differences With Sally B* (Musical Imaginings, 1992).
   "Share A Little Love"

The Children of Selma. *Who Will Speak For The Children* (Rounder, 1987).
   "I Just Want To Be Me"

Grammer, Red. *Hello World!* (Smilin' Atcha, 1995).
   "When I Get A Feeling"
———. *Teaching Peace* (Smilin' Atcha, 1986).
   "See Me Beautiful"

Hartmann, Jack. *Make A Friend, Be A Friend* (Educational Activities, 1990).
   "Its Not Your Fault"
   "Just Laugh"
   "Sunshine Sun On Me"
   "You've Got Personality"
———. *One Voice For Children* (Educational Activities, 1993).
   "Respect Yourself And Others Too"

Hinojosa, Tish. *Cada Niño/Every Child* (Rounder, 1996).
   "Simplemente Por Amor/Simply For Love"

Hunter, Tom. *Bits And Piece* (Song Growing, 1990).
   "Starlight, Starbright"
———. *Connections* (Song Growing, 1994).
   "Tears"

Lefranc, Barbara. *I Can Be Anything I Want To Be* (Doubar, 1990).
   "I Am Me"
   "The Angry Rap"

Murphy, Jane. *I Like Myself* (Kimbo Educational).
———. *Songs For You And Me* (Kimbo Educational).

Music For Little People. *Fiesta Musical,* with Emilio Delgado (Music for Little People, 1994).
   "Happy Bomba"
   "No Llora Más"
———. *Peace Is The World Smiling* (Music for Little People, 1989).
   "Find A Peaceful Thought"
   "Peace Is The World Smiling"

Rogers, Sally. *Peace By Peace* (Western, 1988).
   "I'm So Lucky To Be In This World"
———. *What Can One Little Person Do?* (Round River, 1992).
   "P Is For Peace"

Stitchie, Lt. *Positively Reggae* (Sony, 1994).
   "Be Humble"

Vicious, *Positively Reggae* (Sony, 1994).
  "Respect"
Vitamin L. *Walk A Mile* (Lovable Creature, 1989).
  "Joy, Joy, Joy"
  "The Bright Side"
  "Think For Yourself"

Visual Displays

Childswork/Childsplay
The Emotions Poster
Everyone Has Feelings Poster

Constructive Playthings
Moods and Emotions Picture Packets

Lakeshore
How Do You Feel Today Mirror Poster
Let's Talk About Feelings Photo Cards
Moods and Emotions Poster Pack

Videos

Mr. Rogers Music and Feelings (Kaplan).

Computer Software

Pajama Sam—Who's Afraid of the Dark? CD-ROM, Childswork/Childsplay

Teaching Kits

I Am Amazing, AGS
ABC Feelings Kit, ABC School Supply
My Friends

MY PEOPLE

"I'm LaTonya and I'm African American." This is how a friend's daughter introduced herself to others when she was three years old. Participation in an early childhood program may be a child of color's first experience with European American culture—and she may experience culture shock. Sometimes biracial children, and children who have been adopted into families from a culture other than their own, experience denial or confusion about their cultural identity. They may be told by their families that they belong to one culture or the other, or they may feel as though they are not fully at home in either. Often, European American children experience another form of denial and confusion. They might mistakenly think that European Americans don't have a culture and only people of color have a culture. Or they may have adopted the attitude that European American ways are normal and other cultural practices are weird.

Teachers often find that there are many languages and cultures represented in their classrooms. A unit on my people gives you the opportunity to bring all of the cultures to the table, and to get to know each child and family in a deeper, more meaningful way. It's also a way for each child to get to know herself as a cultural being, and to learn to appreciate the values and beliefs of her own and other cultures and the contributions that each culture makes to society. Finally, it's a chance to build children's capacity for cross-cultural relationships.

UNIT 6:

My People

 Look for this symbol to find activities you can use for circle time.

WEB

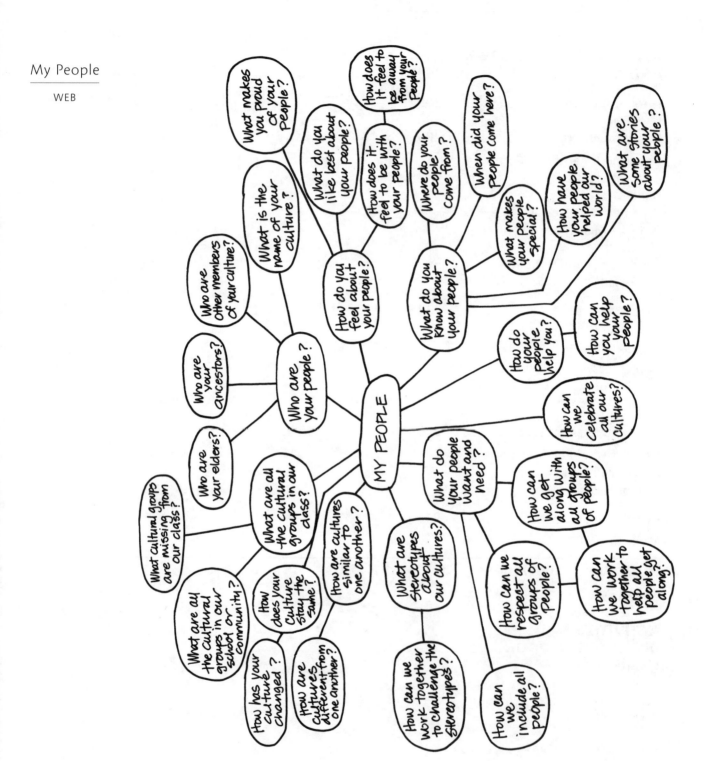

OUTLINE

I. Who are your people?
   A. Who are your elders?
   B. Who are your ancestors?
   C. Who are other members of your culture?
   D. What is the name of your culture?

II. How do you feel about your people?
   A. What makes you proud of your people?
   B. What do like best about your people?
   C. How does it feel to be with your people?
   D. How does it feel to be away from your people?

III. What do you know about your people?
   A. Where do your people come from?
   B. When did your people come here?
   C. What makes your people special?
   D. How have your people helped our world?
   E. What are some stories about your people?

IV. How do your people help you?

V. How can you help your people?

VI. What are all the cultural groups in our class?
   A. What are all the cultural groups in our school or community?
   B. What cultural groups are missing from our class?
   C. How are cultures similar to one another?
   D. How are cultures different from one another?
   E. How does your culture stay the same?
   F. How has your culture changed?
   G. What are stereotypes about our cultures?
   H. How can we work together to challenge the stereotypes?

VII. What do your people want and need?
   A. How can we show respect to all groups of people?
   B. How can we get along with all groups of people?
   C. How can we include all people?
   D. How can we work together to help all people get along?

VIII. How can we celebrate all our cultures?

MATERIALS LIST

ART

skin-colored paints, crayons, markers, felt, and craft paper

butcher paper roll

scraps of fabric from different cultures (for example, batik from Indonesia and Malaysia; gauze and madras from India; tie-dye from Africa; mud cloth and corte cloth from West Africa; jaspe cloth and kente cloth from Guatemala; see also Assorted Fabric Scraps, available from *Environments*)

ethnic magazines (for example, *Indian Artist, American Indian Art, Native Peoples, Colors, Latina, Moderna, Heart & Soul, American Legacy, Black Enterprise, Hispanic, Ebony, Essence, Asian Business*—see the "Classroom Resources" list at the end of the unit for addresses)

puppet-making materials

weaving boards and yarn

BLOCKS

a variety of multicultural people figures, including figures of people with disabilities

small transportation vehicles

notepads

felt tip pens

shoe boxes or cardboard boxes

pretend airplanes, trains, and buses

DRAMATIC PLAY

multicultural cooking sets

multicultural play food sets

multiethnic baby dolls

multiethnic preschooler dolls (for example, Friends Dolls, Children with Hearing, Motor, and Visual Impairments Dolls, *People of Every Stripe*; Multi-Ethnic School Dolls, *Lakeshore*; Multi-Ethnic Dolls, *Constructive Playthings*)

home living: cooking utensils, eating utensils, empty food containers, pretend food, cookbooks, baby dolls, fabric pieces, clothing, ethnic newspapers and magazines (see above for a list, but also look for local neighborhood papers that are specific to your community), other cultural items that would be found in children's homes

celebration: invitations, envelopes, pencils, paper decorations, crepe paper, gift bags, party hats, party favors, party plates and napkins

LITERACY

children's books: folktales, fiction, nonfiction, and bilingual books on culture (see resource list at the end of the unit)

cassette player and theme-related storybook cassettes in different languages

blank cassettes

a set of multiethnic pictures of people

multicultural puppets, including elder or grandparent puppets (for example, Children of America Doll Puppets, *Lakeshore*; Multi-Ethnic Family Puppets, *Constructive Playthings, Edvantage, Lakeshore, Sandy and Son*)

multicultural flannel board sets (for example, White Family, Black Family, Hispanic Family Flannel Board Concept Kits, *Lakeshore*)

materials to make journals and books

MANIPULATIVES

games from children's home cultures

people matching cards

multicultural puzzles (for example, Celebrations Puzzles, People of the World Puzzles, People Puzzles, Wedding Puzzles, *Sandy and Son*; Faces Puzzle, *Animal Town*; Kinara Puzzle, Multicultural Children Puzzle, *Constructive Playthings*)

SCIENCE

smelling jars

labeled herb plants

labeled raw fibers (wool, silk, and cotton)

reference books

SENSORY

a variety of multicultural people figures, including figures of people with disabilities

essential oils from the cultures represented in the classroom

Teaching Through the Interest Areas

Art

Set out ethnic fabric scraps (for example, scraps of kente cloth, mud cloth, batik, jaspe cloth, macana cloth, corte cloth, and tie-dye), ethnic magazines (for example, *Indian Artist, American Indian Art, Native Peoples, Colors, Latina, Moderna, Heart & Soul, American Legacy, Black Enterprise, Hispanic, Ebony, Essence, Asian Business;* see the resource section for addresses), skin-colored art materials, puppet-making materials, yarn, and a weaving board.

Blocks

Add people figures, small vehicles, boxes, paper, and felt tip pens to the block area so that children can create a neighborhood, extended family, or clan living situation with the blocks.

Set out people figures, airplanes, trains, buses, and cars for children to use with the unit blocks to encourage play around the theme of visiting our people.

Dramatic Play

Add party props to the dramatic play area to encourage children to pretend they are having a party or a celebration. Include invitations, envelops, pencils, paper decorations, crepe paper, gift bags, party hats, party favors, party plates and napkins.

Set up the home living area with cooking utensils, eating utensils, empty food containers, pretend food, cookbooks, baby dolls, fabric pieces, clothing, ethnic newspapers and magazines (see above for a list, but also look for local small neighborhood papers that are specific to your community), and other cultural items that would be found in children's homes.

Literacy

Set out a collection of folktales and fiction, nonfiction, and bilingual books on culture. Add a tape player and storybook cassettes in different languages, a set of multiethnic pictures of people, multicultural puppets, elder (grandparent) puppets, multicultural flannel board sets, and materials to make books and journals.

Manipulatives

Set out multicultural puzzles, board and card games from children's home cultures, and people matching cards.

Music

Set out rhythm instruments and cassettes with children's music and instrumental music from the cultures represented in your classroom.

Science

Fill jars with scents that are common to the cultures of the children in the classroom, and label them. Set out these smelling jars, a collection of labeled herb plants, a collection of raw fibers (for example, wool, silk, or cotton), and reference books.

Sensory

Add a variety of people figures to the sensory table.

Fill the sensory table with water and scent it with essential oils from the cultures represented in your classroom.

ACTIVITIES: INVESTIGATING THE THEME

Creative Development

Batik Printing. Cover the table with many layers of newspapers. Peel the paper off crayons, separate them by color, place them in a muffin tin, and melt on a warming tray. Set out old 100 percent cotton sheets or unbleached muslin. Paint the melted crayon heavily on the fabric so that it soaks through. Remove the excess wax after it dries.

Candlemaking. Collect half-pint milk cartons for each child in the classroom. To make a candle, open the top of the milk carton all the way to make a box. Tie a string to a craft stick and lay the stick across the top of the carton so that the string hangs down inside. This will be the candle wick. Melt old candles in a coffee can that is set inside a larger pan of water. When the wax is melted, pour it into the milk carton and let it harden. The next day, peel the milk carton away from the candle, and cut the string off the stick.

Carving. Explore carving as a form of folk art. Show children pictures of carvings from their cultures, and ask parents to share examples of carvings or statues. Set out sandstone, plastic knives, and toothpicks, and encourage the children to carve the stone.

Individual Weavings. Set out enough clean Styrofoam meat trays for each child. Make slits in the top and bottom edges 1 inch apart, directly across from one another.

String a strong thin yarn around the tray, using the slits to hold the string in place. Set out a variety of yarns, and invite children to weave the yarn in and out of the string.

Pottery. Encourage children to experience the sensation of working with natural clay. Cover a table with oilcloth or plastic, or set out plywood boards for children to work on. Show children several samples of pottery from other cultures. Parents may have examples to share with the class. Set out potter's clay, a small bowl of water, plastic knives, and toothpicks. Encourage the children to work with the clay. They can add water if the clay begins to dry out, wet their hands to smooth the clay, and make decorations in the clay with the knives and toothpicks.

Sock Puppets. Set out felt scraps, fabric trim, yarn, buttons, glue, and a variety of socks in different shades of brown. Encourage children to make a sock puppet that looks like someone from their culture.

Tie-Dye Cloth. Fold or twist fabric pieces, and secure with rubber bands. Dip the fabric into bowls of fabric dye. Cut off rubber bands, unfold the cloth, and hang it up to dry. After the children have had some practice with the process, try tie-dying a large piece of cloth for a classroom banner or a cotton T-shirt for each child.

Wall Hangings. Gather large pieces of scrap fabric or sheets. Cut them into large rectangles. Attach the fabric to a dowel, hanger, or large stick. Decorate the fabric with paint, fabric crayons, ribbons, and trim. You might want to make a wall hanging to honor and recognize each of the cultures present in your classroom.

Critical Thinking

Are We All the Same? Help children differentiate between an individual's behavior and an entire group's behavior. Ask the children, "What do some kids do that you don't like?" Their answers might include things like hit, take toys, call names. Use puppets or persona dolls to present scenarios for children to think about. For example, show the children a boy doll, and say, "This is Marcus. Marcus hit another child. Marcus is in kindergarten. What if I thought to myself, *Marcus hit somebody, so I think all kindergartners hit. I'm not going to play with any kindergartners.*" Ask the children, "What do you think of that? Is that true? Do all kindergartners hit? Be careful. Don't think that all people in a group are the same." Repeat the process with different scenarios. For example, "Here is Jenny. Jenny pushed three children out of the way because she wanted to be first in line. Jenny is European American. What if I thought to myself, *I'm not going to play with any European Americans because they all push and have to have their own way?*" A third example is Kenny. "Kenny uses bad words. He is Asian American and I decide that I don't want to play with any kids who are Asian American because I think all Asian Americans use bad words. Is that true?" Encourage children to think of their own examples.

You Belong. Ask the children if they have ever felt like they didn't belong. You might ask, "What made you feel left out, or like you didn't fit in?" Sometimes we feel like we don't belong when we are different in some way from other people around us—if we use a wheelchair and other kids in the class don't, or if we speak a language that our friends don't know, or if our skin color is different from the other kids in our school.

Ask, "What kinds of things might make us feel better? And remember that we are all different from one another and we all belong." Pose a problem to the children like this one: "Let's pretend a new child named Luz joined our class, and she's Latina and speaks Spanish. Do other kids in our class speak Spanish? How could we get to know Luz if we don't speak Spanish? What could we do to help her know that she's welcome here and she does belong?" You could repeat this process with other examples.

Emotional Development

Homesick. Help children recognize that being away from our people can make us feel sad, lonely, or depressed. Introduce children to the concept of moving away from our families and friends. Ask them if any of them has moved away from their families and friends. You might want to introduce children to the terms *immigrant* and *refugee*, especially if you have children or families for whom this is their experience. An immigrant is someone who moves from one country to another. It's their choice to move. Even though they want to move, they might feel scared in their new country, or sad because they miss their family, friends, and their old country. A refugee is someone who is forced to leave their country and move to a new one. They don't have a choice. They have to move because of things like war or not having enough food to eat. Often, they have to move quickly and leave all their things behind. Read *Angel Child, Dragon Child* or another story about a family who had to leave their homeland and move to a new country. Help the children identify with the feelings often associated with leaving our people behind. Ask, "How would you feel if you had to move away from your family and friends? How can we be friends to people who have just moved here?"

 I Have a Culture. Foster children's self-esteem and pride in their home culture. At circle time, ask the children to tell or show the class something about their home cultures. Send a note home or talk to parents ahead of time asking them to help their children pick out objects, stories, songs, or poems to share. You could take a picture of each child sharing her culture and display them on a bulletin board.

 I've Got Pride. Introduce the concept of feeling proud. Feeling proud is feeling good about yourself. Ask children what makes them feel proud of themselves. Talk about how we can be proud of our culture. Ask children, "How do you look when you feel proud?" Invite children to stand up and show everyone how they look when they are proud. Play the song "Walking Tall, Walking Proud," by Jack Hartmann, and invite children to move to the music.

Quality Cards. Ask the parents of the children in your class which personal qualities they would like to foster in their children (honor, pride, honesty, independence, responsibility). Write the name of each personal quality on an index card. Place the cards in a basket. Invite a child to pick one card at morning circle time. Read the quality out loud. Ask the children if they know what it means. Make the quality your group's thought for the day. Try to incorporate the quality into conversations, teachable moments, and activities.

Health, Safety, and Nutrition

Good Grooming. Introduce children to the habits of good grooming. Grooming is a way of showing pride in ourselves by taking care of our bodies. Teach children how to wash their hands and faces. Encourage children to wash their faces after messy meals or snacks. Talk about the importance of caring for their hair. Give the children combs to keep in their cubbies and comb their hair after nap. Invite children to look at their fingernails, and show them how to keep their nails clean and smooth using nail clippers and nail brushes.

Language Development

Home Language. *Learn the names of the cultures represented in your classroom. Learn the words for* people, culture, *and* country *in American Sign Language and the home languages spoken in your classroom.*

Cultural Diversity Picture Cards. Use a commercial set of multicultural pictures or make your own set by cutting out large magazine pictures of American people from many different cultures and gluing them onto construction paper. Hold up one picture at a time and ask the children open-ended questions:

> Who can tell me about this picture?
>
> What do you see?
>
> What is this person doing?
>
> Where does this person live?
>
> Who else does this person look like?
>
> How is this person like you?
>
> How is this person different from you?
>
> Notice and counter any stereotypes that emerge during the discussion.

Folktales. Introduce children to folktales by explaining that folktales are very old stories. Folktales help us learn about how our relatives and ancestors lived a long time ago. Every culture has its own folktales. Read a selection of folktales from the cultures represented in your class. Get out a globe or world map and help children find the countries where the folktales came from.

My People Picture Stories. Sit down with a small group of children and some pictures of people from a variety of cultures celebrating or at cultural events. Show the children one picture at a time. Ask the children what they see in the pictures. Encourage the children to make up stories about the people in the pictures. If possible, write down the children's stories.

Where Does My Family Come From? Help children understand that every family has a cultural heritage. Invite the children to make books about their families, ancestors, and ethnic groups. Each page could include their drawings and responses to the following questions:

> Who are your people?
>
> What's the name of your ethnic group?
>
> Which ancestors came to America?
>
> When did they come here?
>
> Where did they come from?
>
> What language do your people speak?
>
> What are your favorite ethnic foods?
>
> What are some ethnic customs practiced at home?
>
> Who are members of your ethnic group?
>
> How does it feel to be with your people?
>
> What do you like best about your people?
>
> What's special about your people?
>
> How can you show that you are proud of your people?

Math

Concentration. Use the pattern cards (see below) to play a memory game. Arrange the cards facedown in rows. Each player gets a chance to make a match by turning over two cards. If the cards match, the player continues playing. If the cards do not match, the player returns the cards to their facedown position and the next child makes a guess.

Culture Match. Use pictures of a variety of people to make eight or more sets of matching cards. Find duplicate photos in magazines, or use a color photocopier to make duplicates. Include pictures that represent the different cultures present in your classroom, community, or American society at large. Place the cards in a basket and encourage the children to find the matching sets.

Fabric Lengths. Cut strips of fabric from different cultures, each an inch longer than the previous. Set the strips out in a basket. Invite children to take the strips, lay them side by side on the floor, and then order them from shortest to longest.

Fabric Shapes. Purchase 2 to 3 yards each of several fabrics that are created in and used by different cultures. Your collection might include cotton gauze, tie-dye, batik, mud cloth, kente cloth, jaspe cloth, macana cloth, or corte cloth. Cut the fabric into different shapes: triangles, squares, rectangles, circles. Encourage the children to identify the shapes and think of different ways they can use the fabric to wrap themselves. Keep the fabric in the dramatic play area.

Multicultural Sort. Collect a variety of pictures of people representing the major cultural groups present in the United States. You might include pictures of European Americans, African Americans, Latinos, Asian Americans, Native Americans, and Arab Americans. Place the pictures in a basket. Set out the basket along with a sorting tray. Invite the children to classify the pictures any way they like.

Necklace Patterns. Make simple necklaces by stringing 10 to 20 beads on a piece of string. Punch two small holes in a piece of poster board, about half an inch from each edge, and drape the necklace across it. String each end of the necklace through the poster board. Tie each end in a knot on the back side of the poster board so the necklace is securely attached. Display these necklace patterns, and encourage children to make matching necklaces. Cut necklace lengths of yarn. Make a masking tape "needle" at one end of each piece of yarn and tie the other end in a knot. Set out a variety of beads and encourage children to string beads to match the pattern of one of the necklace templates.

Object Count. Collect an inexpensive object from each child's culture. Set out the collection of objects, paper, and pencils. Invite children to count the objects and write down the number on the paper.

Pattern Cards. Make matching cards by tracing or photocopying design patterns found on fabric, traditional dress, beadwork, tapestry, or pottery. Make two cards of each pattern. Write the name of the pattern and the culture that it comes from on the back of the cards. Place the cards in a basket and encourage the children to match the patterns and talk about the designs and the cultures they come from.

Who Is Missing? Collect pictures of people representing each of the cultural groups in your community. Try to have at least nine different pictures. Begin by setting out four of the pictures. Ask children to close their eyes. Take one picture away and mix up the remaining ones. Ask the children, "Who is missing?" Repeat the activity and increase the total number of pictures that are set out at a time until you can set out nine pictures (three rows of three) and the children are able to recognize who is missing.

Music

Folk Music. Ask parents to share examples of music from their home cultures. Listen to a variety of folk music. Learn a song from each of the cultures in your classroom. Invite children to talk about the similarities and differences in the music.

Joy, Joy, Joy. Here's a variation of a traditional song to celebrate and honor the role of culture in our lives.

> I've got the joy, joy, joy, joy down in my heart,
> down in my heart, down in my heart!
> I've got the joy, joy, joy, joy down in my heart,
> down in my heart, down in my heart to stay!
>
> Additional verses:
> I've got the knowledge of my people…
> I've got the pride of my people…
> I've got the strength of my people…
> I've got the love of my people…
> I've got the dreams of my people…

Paint to Music. Invite children to paint to the traditional music of the cultures represented in your classroom. Explore the similarities and differences of the paintings that result.

Physical Development

Creative Movement. Play selections of instrumental music from the cultures represented in your classroom. Invite children to listen to the music, think about how the music makes them feel, and move their bodies creatively to the music. You might want to repeat this activity many times, using selections of music from a different culture each time.

Games. Invite the children to share their favorite games from home or games that children play during cultural celebrations. With the help of the children's parents, introduce the children to a traditional children's game from the cultures represented in your classroom or community.

Multicultural Musical Chairs. Here's a new twist on an old game. The goal is to make sure everyone has a place to sit. Set a group of chairs in a circle or line. Start with one chair for every child. Play music from the children's home culture while the children walk around the chairs. When the music stops, everyone needs to find a seat. Remove a chair each time you start the music, making it more and more difficult for children to find a place to sit. By the end of the game, everyone should be piled on top of one another on the same chair.

Physical Fairy Tales. Read a fairy tale or folktale from children's home cultures that contain very large or very small characters, like giants or fairies. Guide the children through a movement activity where the children move like the characters in the folktale. For example, you might ask the children, "How might the giant walk? Can you walk like that giant? Can you make your body huge like a giant's?"

Science

Hair. Help children notice that hair can be a distinguishing physical characteristic. Sometimes hair style is a way of expressing our culture. Show children pictures of a variety of adults and children of both genders with different hairstyles. Be sure to include pictures of women with very short hair and men with long hair. Pass around a hand mirror so that the children can take turns looking at and touching their own hair. Ask each child to describe her own hair. Talk about how hair has texture and curl; how some people have fine hair and some people have coarse hair. Some people have straight hair and other people have curly hair. Talk about how people can have different color hair and different length hair.

Mud Houses. Here's a chance for children to learn about a very old building technique. Mix clay-based dirt with water in a tub so that it looks like pancake batter. Add handfuls of dried straw or grass clippings. Talk about how the grass will help hold the dirt and water together. Cut the tops off 1-pint milk cartons so they are about 1 inch high, spoon the mud mixture into them, and set the cartons in the sun to bake until they dry out. Build a simple house with the bricks using mud as mortar to hold the bricks together.

Smelling Jars. Introduce children to the smells of one another's cultures. Ask parents what spices they cook with and what oils or perfumes are common in their culture. Gather a number of small containers such as margarine tubs or film containers. Place one spice, incense, or essential oil in each container. Ask the children to close their eyes and smell the contents of each smelling jar. Encourage the children to guess the smell. Talk about how people from different cultures use different spices to cook with and have different smells in their homes.

Candles. Set out a variety of candles. Ask children if they know what they are and if they celebrate any special days when their families light candles. Introduce children to wax. Some wax comes from petroleum oil and some comes from bees. Set out a variety of wax products like Chapstick lip balm, crayons, paraffin, waxed paper, honey comb, and cheese covered with wax. Invite the children to feel the objects, and ask them the following questions:

> How are these alike?
>
> How are these different?
>
> Which of the wax objects are soft and which of the wax objects are hard?
>
> Can you think of anything else that has wax in it? (crayons)
>
> Can you think of a place in your body where there is wax? (ears)

Cotton, Wool, Silk, and Leather. Set out raw cotton, wool, and silk fibers, fabric and yarn made from them, and pieces of leather and suede. You may also want to include a sheepskin, cotton plant, and silkworms or pictures of the plants and animals that the fibers come from. Label the items and set out reference books. Invite children to examine the materials, and to match fabric and yarn to the raw materials used to make them.

Social Development

Baby Care. Explore how parents from the cultures represented in your classroom or community care for, carry, and play with their babies. Invite parents and extended family members to bring their babies to class to talk with the children about how they care for their babies. Talk with the children about what they can do to help care for babies.

Do My Part. Cut gingerbread people shapes out of skin-colored construction paper. Invite children to name at least one way they can make their people proud. Write the children's answers on the people shapes and display them on the walls around the room.

Fables and Morals. Collect a variety of children's fables representing the cultures present in your class. Introduce children to the fables and tell them that fables are stories that teach us how we are supposed to behave. Each fable has a lesson for us to learn good behavior. Make a list of the lessons your class learns by reading fables from different cultures.

Listen to Your Elders. Ask children if they know what *elder* means. Elders are adults, who have lived a long time and are wise because they have done many things in their lives. Elders deserve our respect. Ask the children if they know how to treat and talk to an elder. Invite the children to role-play greeting an elder. Invite elders in the children's families or from the community to visit your classroom. Give the elders a place of honor in the classroom. Children could draw pictures, write stories, and learn songs to present to the elders.

Our Wish for All Our Relations. Ask children if they know what a wish is. Ask the children what their wishes are. Then ask them what they wish for their families and all of their people. Invite the children to make a poster or mural of all their wishes for all of their relations. Here is a poem that children can recite as they make wishes:

> If my mind was a wishing well,
> I'd find a wish that I could tell—
> A thought from me to you,
> A wish for smiles and fun—
> Something you can do
> To warm you like the sun.

(*The Peaceful Classroom,* Charles Smith. Beltsville, MD: Gryphon House; p. 163, 1993. Used with permission.)

BIG AS LIFE

ACTIVITIES: AFFIRMING OURSELVES AND ONE ANOTHER

Human Rights

Everyone has the right to speak their own language, follow their cultural beliefs and practices, and feel good about their culture and background.

> **BARRIER:** It's easy to feel that our way of doing things is the only way or the best way. There are lots of messages in our society that tell us that one way is the best way or the right way and that disrespect other ways.

All people are equal and have equal rights.

> **BARRIER:** There is a history in our country of people not having equal rights or an equal say, and so we have to work to overcome these old ways of thinking and doing things.

DISCUSSION QUESTIONS: Help children think about what people need to be able to respect and get along with one another. Ask them, "What things do people need to respect one another? What things do people need to get along with one another? Why do you think some people don't respect or get along with others? What are some of the ways that people are treated unfairly in our society (or in our community)? What could we do to change these? What choices could people make to encourage respect? How could we help people respect one another? How could we help people get along with one another?" Make a group flyer or poster that could be distributed to all the families and displayed throughout the school.

Cultural Identity

Accomplishments and Contributions. Introduce the children to members of their home culture who have accomplished great things and made important contributions to American society. You might include famous scientists, inventors, educators, authors, artists, entertainers, sport legends, religious leaders, political and civic leaders, and activists. Be careful to avoid stereotypes; for example, in addition to choosing African Americans who are athletes or musicians, include those who have excelled in other fields.

Cultural Colors. Help children recognize common color combinations within their culture by including flags or artifacts from the cultures in the classroom and talking about the colors with the children. Reference books such as encyclopedias may explain the meaning of the colors, or you may be able to get this kind of information from adults who share a given culture. For example, part of my family is Dutch and I love the combination of blue and white. Blue and white is prominent in delft pottery and represents the land, sky, and sea of the Netherlands. The colors red, black, and green are associated with the continent of Africa. In this combination, red symbolizes the blood of African people, black stands for their faces, and green is for hope.

Dances. Help children recognize that many celebrations involve dancing, singing, and wearing special clothing. Invite parents and members of cultural communities to demonstrate traditional dances from their home cultures, describe the traditional dress they wear, and when and why they dance.

Dreams of My People. Help children identify their cultural identity. Set out cultural and travel magazines and invite the children to make collages of their culture's homeland. Ask the children to think about their ancestors, members of their families who lived long ago, and who used to live in their homelands. Ask children, "What do you think they dreamed of? What are your dreams for your people? What are your dreams for your family's homeland?"

Just Like Me/Just Like You. Help children explore the concept of alike and different. Display pictures of people that represent different cultures and abilities. Set out a mirror so that children can look at themselves. Ask the children to pick out all the pictures of people who look like them. If a child seems unsure about selecting a particular picture, encourage her to look in the mirror. Talk about the common features between the people in the pictures and the child. For example, "Your hair is curly like this girl's, but your skin is like that boy's." To extend this activity, ask the children to find a friend and pick out all of the pictures of people who look like their friend.

Match-Ups. Set out photographs of people and cultural objects. Encourage the children to match the photographs of people with the photographs of objects from the corresponding culture.

Special Days and Holidays. Introduce children to the concept of holidays. There are special days when we set aside our daily routine to celebrate, remember, or honor a special event or a special person. Some holidays are national holidays which the government chooses, like Labor Day, Memorial Day, and Martin Luther King Day. Each of us may also celebrate special days that are specific to our family's culture or religion. Invite parents to share their family's special days with the class. Here is a poem to teach children as they learn about the holidays they celebrate.

A Holiday Is a Special Day

A holiday is a special day
To celebrate with family
In your own special way;
Some families get together
While others go away.
Schools and stores and businesses say:
"Closed for the holiday."
Some holidays are times to play
While some may be a time to pray.
Some holidays are in honor of someone great,
Some are to remember a special date.
There may be parties or picnics or a parade
There may be special foods or decorations made
Some holidays have presents to share,
Or special cards to show you care.
All over the world people celebrate
But their holidays have a different name and date.
No matter how you spend the day
We hope you have a happy holiday.

(*Busy Fingers Growing Minds: Finger Plays, Verses and Activities for Whole Language Learning*, Rhoda Redleaf. St. Paul: Redleaf Press, 1993; p. 149. Used with permission.)

Diversity

Group Tree. Help children become aware of cultural groups and recognize that groups are made of individual people. Make a "tree" for each cultural group represented in your class, school, or community. Begin to fill each tree with photographs of children and staff in your class. Then invite the children to look in magazines for pictures of people or objects that represent each of the cultures, and add them to the trees.

Similar to Me. Tape a large piece of paper to the wall, and show children pictures of people representing a variety of cultures. Ask the children to see if they can name all of the ways people from different cultures are similar to one another. Write the children's answers on the paper.

Skin Color Match-Ups. Set out a collection of knee-high stockings in shades of tan, white, black, yellow, and red. Encourage children to put the stockings on their hands to find a color that matches their skin color. Explore lighter and darker shades. Talk about how we are all shades of brown and that nobody's skin color is really white, red, or yellow.

Two Cultures. Introduce children to the concept of being biracial or bicultural. Tell them that some families are made of people who come from more than one culture. You might want to show children pictures of and read stories about biracial/bicultural families, such as *Black is Brown is Tan.*

We're All Human. Help children explore ways that people are similar to and different from one another. Make a collage of pictures of people for each culture. Select pictures to represent the variety and diversity present within a cultural group. Show the pictures to the children and ask them the following questions:

How are the people in these pictures similar to one another?

How are they different from one another?

How are you like the people in these pictures?

How are you different from the people in these pictures?

Bias and Stereotypes

Daily Life and Celebrations. Sometimes young children think that people of different cultures wear traditional dress and celebrate all of the time. Make a file folder sorting game to help children differentiate everyday life shared by Americans of all cultures and the holidays, celebrations, and traditions specific to each culture. Label one side of the folder "Everyday Life" and the other side "Celebrations." Collect photographs of people of different cultures performing daily activities and celebrating special events. Make sorting cards by gluing the pictures onto index cards, and invite the children to use the file folder to sort the pictures.

Real and Pretend. Make a sorting game to help children begin to tell the difference between real images of people and pretend images that are unfair (stereotypic). Label one side of a manila file folder "Real" and the other side "Pretend." Gather a variety of images (photographs, drawings, and cartoons) of people from different cultures—some that are realistic and depict the way people actually live today, and some that are stereotypic, such as a drawing of a cartoon bear wearing an Indian headdress. Talk about how stereotypes make fun of peoples and hurt people's feelings. Invite the children to sort the pictures using the file folder.

True or False. Help children tell the difference between respectful and stereotypic (false) pictures of people. Show children accurate and stereotypic pictures of people one at a time. As you show them each picture ask, "What is this a picture of? Is this picture true or false?" After children answer, summarize why the picture is accurate or stereotypic.

BIG AS LIFE

Community Service

Multicultural Fair. Plan a cultural fair or multicultural celebration. You may want to celebrate a different culture represented in your school each year or you could celebrate and recognize many cultures at the same time.

Social Action Suggestions

Racism-Free School. Work together to rid your center or school of racism. Children could write a letter to the principal requesting a racial harassment policy similar to the school's sexual harassment policy.

ACTIVITIES: OPENING THE DOOR

Classroom Visitors

Invite representatives from the cultures represented in your classroom to share their heritage and talents with the children. You could invite a musician, dancer, artist, storyteller, community worker, or a museum curator.

Field Trips

Take a trip to visit a museum or an exhibit that highlights a culture in your community.

Parent Involvement

Invite grandparents and elders from the cultural communities in your area to visit the classroom and tell stories about their childhoods.

Invite parents, grandparents, and leaders from cultural groups in your area to visit the class and talk about how they and their culture are a part of the community.

Invite grandparents and elders to share toys from their childhood and cultures.

Invite parents to share their cultures with the children. They could visit the class, give presentations, and help make books about their cultures that could stay in the classroom. Ask them to share the names of their cultures, their home languages, special holidays and customs, and some forms of traditional dress. If possible, ask parents to bring examples of music, food, and games that are popular within their culture.

Invite parents and grandparents to share a proverb or words of wisdom that they remember their parents and grandparents saying to them. Make a book of the sayings and talk with the children about what they mean.

Parent Education

Invite a multicultural specialist from your local public school district to talk to parents about preserving and celebrating their culture with their children.

CLASSROOM RESOURCES

Children's Books

A To Zen: A Book Of Japanese Culture, Ruth Wells (New York: Simon, 1992).

ABCs The American Indian Way, Richard Red Hawk (Sacramento: Sierra, 1988).

Angel Child, Dragon Child, Michele Maria Surat (New York: Scholastic, 1983).

Africa Brothers And Sisters, Virginia Kroll (New York: Simon, 1993).

Africa Dream, Eloise Greenfield (New York: Day, 1977).

Arielle And The Hanukkah Surprise, Devra Speregan and Shirley Newberger (New York: Scholastic, 1992).

Aunt Flossie's Hats (And Crabcakes Later), Elizabeth Fitzgerald Howard (New York: Clarion, 1991).

Baseball Saved Us, Ken Mochizuki (New York: Lee, 1994).

Big Mama And Grandma Ghana, Angela Shelf Medearis.

Black Is Brown Is Tan, Arnold Adoff (New York: Harper, 1973).

Bigmama's, Donald Crews (New York: Greenwillow, 1991).

A Birthday Basket For Tia, Pat Mora (New York: Macmillan, 1992).

Caravan, Lawrence McKay Jr. (New York: Lee, 1995).

Caribbean Counting Book, Charles Faustin (Boston: Houghton, 1996).

Chave's Memories, Maria Isabel Delgado (Houston: Arte Publico, 1996).

Dancing With The Indians, Angela Shelf Medearis (New York: Holiday, 1991).

The Day Gogo Went To Vote, Elinor Batezat Sisulu (Boston: Little Brown, 1996).

Dia's Story Cloth: The Hmong People's Journey Of Freedom, Dia Cha (New York: Lee, 1996).

Doesn't Fall Off His Horse, Virginia Stroud (New York: Dial, 1994).

Down Buttermilk Lane, Barbara Mitchell (New York: Lothrop, 1993).

Dreamcatcher, Audrey Osofsky (New York: Orchard, 1992).

Dumpling Soup, Jama Kim Rattigan (Boston: Little Brown, 1993).

A First Clay Gathering, Nora Naranjo Morse (Cleveland: Modern Curriculum, 1994).

A First Passover, Leslie Swartz (Cleveland: Modern Curriculum, 1992).

From Far Way, Robert Munsch and Saoussan Askar (Toronto: Annick, 1995).

Giving Thanks: A Native American Good Morning Message, Chief Jake Swamp (New York: Lee, 1995).

Going Home, Eve Bunting (New York: Harper, 1996).

Grandfather Drum, Ferguson Plain (Winnipeg, Canada: Pemmican, 1994).

Grandfather's Journey, Allen Say (Boston: Houghton, 1993).

Grandmother's Nursery Rhymes, Nelly Palacio Jaramillo (New York: Holt, 1994).

Green Snake Ceremony, Sherrin Watkins (Tulsa: Council Oaks, 1995).

Gung Hay Fat Choy, June Behrens (Danbury, CT: Children's Press, 1982).

Halmoni And The Picnic, Sook Nyul Choi (Boston: Houghton, 1993).

Happy New Year, Beni, Jane Breskin Zalben (New York: Holt, 1993).

How Many Days To America? A Thanksgiving Story, Eve Bunting (New York: Clarion, 1988).

How My Family Lives In America, Susan Kuklin (New York: Macmillan, 1992).

I Am Native American, Ana Saage (New York: PowerKids, 1997).

Joshua's Masai Mask, Dakari Hru (New York: Lee, 1993).

The Journey, Sheila Hamanaka (New York: Orchard, 1990).

Juneteenth Jamboree, Carole Boston Weatherford (New York: Lee, 1995).

Just Plain Fancy, Patricia Polacco (New York: Bantam, 1990).

The Keeping Quilt, Patricia Polacco (New York: Simon, 1988).

Kente Colors, Debbie Chocolate (New York: Walker, 1996).

Kenya's Family Reunion, Juwanda G. Ford (New York: Scholastic, 1996).

Laila's Wedding, Kaleel Sakakeeny (Cleveland: Modern Curriculum, 1994).

Latkes and Applesuce: A Hanukkah Story, Fran Manshkin (New York: Scholastic, 1990).

Lee Ann: The Story of a Vietnamese-American Girl, Tricia Brown (New York: Putnam, 1991).

Lift Every Voice And Sing, James Weldon Jonson (New York: Scholastic, 1990).

Lights for Gita, Rachna Gilmore (Gardiner, ME: Tilbury, 1995).

Lights On The River, Jane Resh Thomas (New York: Hyperion, 1994).

Lion Dancer Ernie Wan's Chinese New Year, Katie Waters and Medline Slovenz-Low (New York: Scholastic, 1990).

Luka's Quilt, Georgia Guback (New York: Greenwillow, 1994).

Magid Fasts For Ramadan, Mary Matthews (New York: Clarion, 1996).

Masai And I, Virginia Kroll (New York: Four Winds, 1992).

Mi Compleaños, Esther Torres.

The Morning Chair, Barbara Joosee (New York: Clarion, 1995).

Mother's Day, Ann Consuelo Matiella (Cleveland: Modern Curriculum, 1994).

My Aunt Otilla's Spirits, Richard Garcia (San Francisco: Children's Book, 1987).

My Father, Laura Maye.

My First Kwanzaa Book, Debbie Chocolate (New York, Scholastic, 1992).

Navajo ABC: A Dine Alphabet Book, Luci Tapahonso and Eleanor Schick (New York: Simon, 1995).

One Day We Had To Run, Sybella Wilkes (Brookfield: Millbrook, 1994).

One Nation, Many Tribes: How Kids Live In Milwaukee's Indian Community, Kathleen Krull (New York: Lodestar, 1995).

One Smiling Grandma: A Caribbean Counting Book, Ann Marie Linden (New York: Dial, 1992).

Our People, Angela Shelf Medearis (New York: Atheneum, 1994).

Over The River And Through The Woods. Illustrated by John Steven Gurney. (New York: Cartwheel, 1992).

The Path Of The Quiet Elk: A Native American Alphabet Book, Virginia Stroud (New York: Dial, 1996).

The People Shall Continue, Simon Ortiz (San Francisco: Children's Book, 1993).

Powwow Summer, Marcie R. Rendon (Minneapolis: Carolrhoda, 1996).

A Prairie Alphabet, Jo Bannatyne-Cugnet (Plattsburgh, NY: Tundra, 1992).

Pueblo Boy: Growing Up in Two Worlds, Marcia Keegan (New York: Cobblehill, 1991).

Ramadan, Suhaib Hamid Ghazi (New York: Holiday, 1996).

Ravi's Diwali Surprise, Anisha Kacker (Cleveland: Modern Curriculum, 1994).

Red Bird, Barbara Mitchell (New York: Lothrop, 1996).

A Sense Of Shabbat, Faige Kobre.

Seven Candles For Kwanzaa, Andrea Davis Pickney (New York: Dial, 1993).

Soul Looks Back In Wonder, Tom Feelings (New York: Dial, 1993).

This Land Is My Land, George Littlechild (San Francisco: Children's Book, 1993).

Tiktala, Margaret Shaw-Mackinnon (New York: Holiday, 1996).

Too Many Tamales, Gary Soto (New York: Putnam, 1993).

Treasure Nap, Juanita Havill (Boston: Houghton, 1992).

Trees Of The Dancing Goats, Patricia Polacco (New York: Simon, 1996).

A Trip To A Powwow, Richard Red Hawk (Sacramento: Sierra, 1987).

Two Lands One Heart, Jeremy Schmidt and Ted Wood (New York: Walker, 1995).

Two Pair Of Shoes, Esther Sanderson (Winnipeg, Canada: Pemmican, 1990).

A Visit With Great-Grandma, Sharon Hort Addy (Morton Grove, IL: Whitman, 1989).

When Africa Was Home, Karen Lynn Williams (New York: Orchard, 1991).

Where Did Your Family Come From? Melvin Berger and Gilda Berger (Nashville: Ideals, 1993).

Where Indians Live, Nashone (Sacramento: Sierra, 1989).

White Bead Ceremony, Sherrin Watkins (Tulsa: Council Oaks, 1989).

Who Am I? Aylette Jenness (Cleveland: Modern Curriculum).

Who Belongs Here? Margy Burns Knight (Gardiner, ME: Tilbury, 1993).

Music

Bala-Sinem Choir. *American Indian Songs And Chants* (West Music, 1973).

———. *Walk In Beauty My Children* (West Music).

Be A Friend—The Story Of African American Music (Educational Record Center, 1994).

Big Blues For Kids (Educational Record Center, 1996).

Big Country For Kids (Educational Record Center).

Born Jamericans. *Positively Reggae* (Sony, 1994).

"Where We Comin' From"

Canciones de Mi Isla (West Music).

Chinese Folk Songs (West Music, 1984).

Favorite Songs Of Japanese Children (West Music).

Fink, Cathy, and Marcy Marxer. *Nobody Else Like Me* (A&M, 1994).

"A Little Like You And A Little Like Me"

Hinojosa, Tish. *Cada Niño/Every Child* (Rounder, 1996).

"Hasta Los Muertos Salen a Bailar/Even the Dead Are Rising Up to Dance"

———. *Mi Casa Es Su Casa* (Educational Record Center).

Honor The Earth Powwow: Songs of the Great Lakes Indians (West Music, 1991).

Marley, Cedella. *Smiling Island of Song* (Educational Record Center, 1992).

Mattox, Cheryl Warren, *Let's Get The Rhythm Of The Band: A Child's Introduction To Music From African-American Culture With Story And Song* (West Music, 1993).

Music For Little People. *Fiesta Musical*, with Emilio Delgado (Music for Little People, 1994).

"Fiesta Musical"

"Tonadas de Quitiplas"

Paz, Suni, *Canciones Para El Recreo/Children's Songs For The Playground* (Smithsonian/Folkways, 1990).

Pirtle, Sarah. *Two Hands Hold The Earth* (Gentle Wind, 1984).

"De Colores"

Reggae For Kids (Educational Record Center, 1992).

Sklera-Zucek, Lois. *Songs About Native Americans* (Westward Horn, 1994).

Songs of Hispanic Americans (West Music).

Sweet Honey In The Rock. *All For Freedom* (Music for Little People, 1989).

"The Little Shekere"

West Indian Songs and Games for Children (West Music).

Visual Displays

African American Images

20th Century Black Personalities Poster

20th Century Hispanic Americans Poster

Black American Achievement Poster

Black Americans Poster

Contemporary Asian Americans Poster

Great Black Americans Poster

North American Indian Personalities Poster

Beckley-Cardy

20th Century American Women Poster

20th Century Black Personalities Poster

20th Century Hispanic Americans Poster

Black Americans Poster

Contemporary Asian Americans Poster

North American Indian Personalities Poster

Constructive Playthings

American Indians Yesterday and Today Teaching Picture Packets

Black America Yesterday and Today Poster

Black Personalities Photo Posters

Spanish Americans Yesterday and Today Teaching Picture Packets

Knowledge Unlimited

Cultural Kaleidoscope Poster: An American Alphabet

Lakeshore

Children of the U.S. Poster Pack

Families Poster Pack

Sandy and Son
My World Poster

Syracuse Cultural Workers
Judith Jamison Poster

Kwanzaa Poster

Videos

Chinese New Year (Kaplan, 1994).

Cinco de Mayo (Kaplan, 1994).

Hanukkah/Passover (Kaplan, 1994).

The Celebration of Kwanzaa (Educational Record Center, 1996).

Computer Software

All-In-One Language Fun, by Syracuse Language Lab, Educational Record Center

Spanish/Español, by Twin Sisters Productions, Educational Record Center

Teaching Kits

Graeme, Jocelyn, and Ruth Fahlman. *Hand In Hand: Multicultural Experiences For Young Children* (Reading, MA: Addison-Wesley, 1990).

Additional Resources

American Indian Art
7314 East Osborn Drive
Scottsdale, AZ 85251
(602) 994-5445

American Legacy
c/o Forbes, Inc.
60 Fifth Avenue
New York, NY 10011

Asian Business
c/o Far East Trade Press Ltd.
Block C, 10/F
Seaview Estate
2-8 Watson Road
North Point, Hong Kong

Black Enterprise
c/o Earl G. Graves Publishing
130 Fifth Avenue
New York, NY 10011
(212) 242-8000

Colors
c/o Four Colors Productions
2608 Blaisdell Avenue South
Minneapolis, MN 55408

Ebony
c/o Johnson Publishing
820 South Michigan Avenue
Chicago, IL 60605

Essence
1500 Broadway
New York, NY 10036

Heart & Soul
c/o Rodale Press
733 Third Avenue, 15th Floor
New York, NY 10017
(212) 697-2040

Hispanic
c/o Hispanic Publishing Corporation
98 San Jacinto Boulevard, Suite 1150
Austin, TX 78701
(800) 251-2688

Indian Artist
P.O. Box 5465
Santa Fe, NM 87505-5465
(505) 982-1600

Latina
1500 Broadway, Suite 600
New York, NY 10036

Moderna
c/o Hispanic Publishing Corporation
98 San Jacinto Boulevard, Suite 1150
Austin, TX 78701
(800) 251-2688

Native Peoples
Media Concepts Group Inc.
5333 North Seventh Street, Suite C-224
Phoenix, AZ 85014
(602) 252-2236

Our Class

"Is today a school day or a stay home day?" "I don't want to stay home. I wanna go to school." "What are we going to do today, Teacher?" "Mrs. McDonald is the boss of everybody, right?" The child care center, Head Start program, preschool, or elementary school becomes a significant part of a young child's life. We can help make children feel at home by touring the center and introducing them to all of the people who work there. We can also help children adjust to school by examining the classroom and materials, setting some ground rules, and getting to know one another.

Through a unit on the class or school, children can discover that they are part of a larger whole, that there is great diversity of choices within the classroom, and that they can work together to make the classroom safe and friendly for all.

UNIT 7:

OUR CLASS

 Look for this symbol
to find activities you
can use for circle time.

WEB

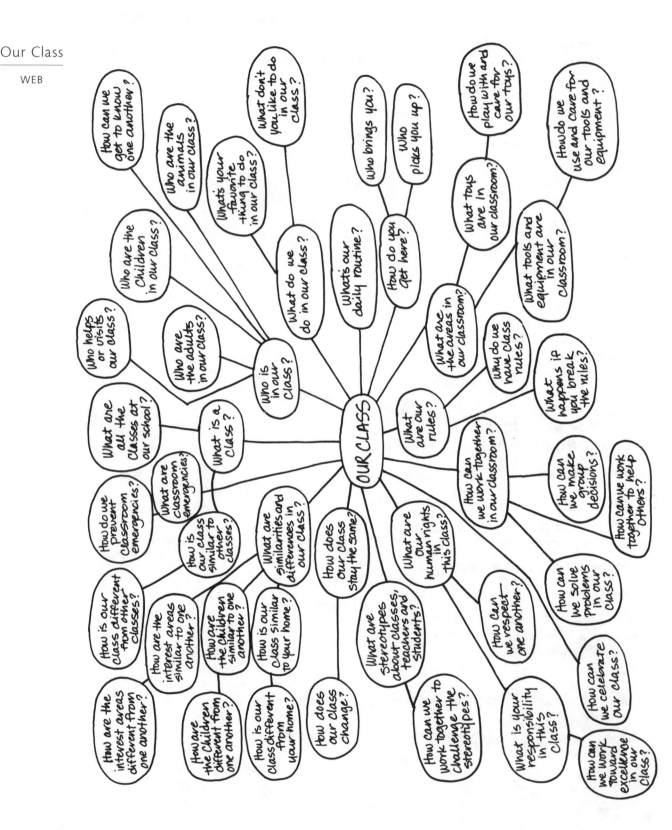

Outline

I. Who is in our class?
   A. Who are the children in our class?
   B. Who are the adults in our class?
   C. Who are the animals in our class?
   D. Who visits or helps our class?
   E. How can we get to know one another?

II. What do we do in our class?
   A. What's your favorite thing to do in our class?
   B. What don't you like to do in our class?
   C. What's our daily routine?
   D. How do you get here?
      1. Who brings you?
      2. Who picks you up?

III. What are the areas in our classroom?
   A. What toys are in our classroom?
   B. How do we play with and care for our toys?
   C. What tools and equipment are in our classroom?
   D. How do we use and care for our tools and equipment?

IV. What are our class rules?
   A. Why do we have class rules?
   B. What happens if you break the rules?

V. What are classroom emergencies?

VI. How do we prevent classroom emergencies?

VII. What is a class?
   A. What are all the classes at our school?
   B. How is our class similar to other classes?
   C. How is our class different from other classes?
   D. How does our class stay the same?
   E. How does our class change?

VIII. What are the similarities and differences in our class?
   A. How is our class similar to your home?
   B. How is our class different from your home?
   C. How are the children similar to one another?
   D. How are the children different from one another?
   E. How are the interest areas similar to one another?
   F. How are the interest areas different from one another?

IX. What are stereotypes about classes, teachers, and students?

X. How can we work together to challenge the stereotypes?

XI. What are our human rights in this class?
   A. How can we respect one another?
   B. What is your responsibility in this class?
   C. How will you work toward excellence in our class?

XII. How can we work together in our classroom?
   A. How can we make group decisions?
   B. How can we solve problems in our class?
   C. How can we work together to help others?

XIII. How can we celebrate our class?

MATERIALS LIST

ART

skin-colored paints, crayons, markers, felt, and craft paper

butcher paper roll

school supply catalogs

rulers

pencils and pencil sharpeners

crayons

scissors

glue

easel paints

BLOCKS

a variety of multicultural people figures, including figures of people with disabilities

pretend school bus

schoolroom play set (miniature desks, chairs, and people figures to create a play school in the block area)

green mats or carpet squares for grass

miniature playground equipment (for example, the Playmobil Playground from *Constructive Playthings*)

aluminum foil for making slides

paper and markers for making signs

DRAMATIC PLAY

classroom: chalkboard and chalk, desks, pencils, paper, empty art containers, dolls, books (see also Pretend and Play School Teacher Set, *Sandy and Son*)

multiethnic preschooler dolls (for example, Friends Dolls, Children with Hearing, Motor, and Visual Impairments Dolls, *People of Every Stripe*; Multi-Ethnic School Dolls, *Lakeshore*; Multi-Ethnic Dolls, *Constructive Playthings*)

LITERACY

children's books: fiction, nonfiction, and bilingual books about school (see resource list at the end of the unit)

cassette player and theme-related storybook cassettes in different languages

blank cassettes

small chalkboards and chalk

school picture cards

children and adult puppets (for example, Children of America Doll Puppets, *Lakeshore*; Classroom Pets Puppets, *Sandy and Son*)

felt people to represent each child and adult in the classroom (see also School Scene Flannel Board Activity Set, *Lakeshore*)

materials to make journals and books

MANIPULATIVES

feely box

school matching, sorting, and board games (for example, The Classroom Behavior Game, The Good Behavior Game, Manners Matter Game, *Childswork/Childsplay*; School Based Activities Social Sequences, *Sandy and Son*)

school-related puzzles (for example, A Day At Pre-School Puzzles, Playtime Puzzle, *Sandy and Son*; Children with Special Needs Puzzles, *Kaplan*; Crossing Guard Puzzle, Multicultural Children Puzzle, *Constructive Playthings*; Great Big Yellow School Bus Floor Puzzle, *Edvantage*; Teacher Puzzle, Multi-Ethnic Kids Floor Puzzle Set, *Lakeshore*)

SCIENCE

thermometer

flannel board set that deals with dressing for the weather

magnifying glasses and a variety of classroom objects

classroom pet

reference books

SENSORY

play school buses

figures of school children

water toys

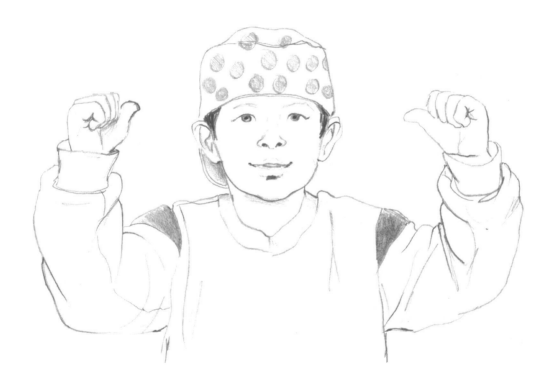

Teaching Through the Interest Areas

Art

Set out school supply catalogs, rulers, pencils and pencil sharpeners, crayons, scissors, glue, and easel paints.

Blocks

Add people figures, a play school bus, and a school play set to encourage school-related play.

Dramatic Play

Add classroom props like a chalkboard and chalk, desks, pencils, paper, empty art containers, dolls, and books to encourage children to play school.

Literacy

Set out a collection of nonfiction, fiction, and bilingual books on school. Add a cassette player and school-related story book cassettes, a collection of children and adult puppets, felt people to represent each child and adult in the classroom, small chalkboards and chalk, a set of school picture cards, and materials to make journals and books.

Manipulatives

Make a feely box by cutting a circle large enough for a child's hand in the side of a small square gift box. Glue a circle of felt over the hole on the inside, and cut slits in the felt from the center of the circle out, like

sun rays (see the diagram below). Cover the box with contact paper, and use it to play a tactile guessing game by putting a small classroom object inside, and having a child reach in and see if he can identify the object by feel. Set out school-related puzzles and classroom object matching games.

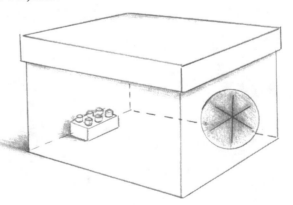

Music

Set out cassettes of children's music with songs that teach basic concepts like numbers, colors, letters, and children's names.

Science

Set out a thermometer, a flannel board set that deals with dressing for the weather, magnifying glasses and a variety of classroom objects, a classroom pet, and reference books.

Sensory

Fill the sensory table with sand, play school buses, and play figures of school children, or fill the table with water and a collection of water toys.

ACTIVITIES:
INVESTIGATING THE THEME

Creative Development

Art Area 101. Introduce children to the basic materials in the art area. Teach them how to use scissors, easel paints, and watercolor paints.

Build a School. Collect a variety of boxes, making sure you have more than enough for each child to have one. Set out the boxes, construction paper, tissue paper, glue, crayons, markers, and scissors. Encourage children to make a child care center or school with the boxes.

Classroom Collage. Set out educational supply catalogs and challenge the children to find pictures of things in the classroom. With the children, draw a simple map or floor plan of the classroom on a large sheet of butcher paper, and label the interest areas. Ask the children to glue the pictures of classroom equipment and materials in the correct interest areas.

Paper Chain. Make a paper chain using skin-colored construction paper. Cut the paper into strips 1 inch wide and 8 inches long. Show the children how to put a paper chain together. Encourage them to use all of the colors and to make a chain that represents all the different kinds of people in the class, school, or community.

Puzzle Me. Invite children to draw a picture or cut out a large picture from a magazine. Have children glue the picture to a piece of poster board or cardboard. (You could cut up cereal boxes for cardboard.) Let the picture dry. Turn the picture over and draw puzzle lines with a marking pen on the back. Help the children cut out the pieces of their puzzles and place them in envelopes with their names on the outside.

Critical Thinking

Choices and Consequences. Introduce the children to the idea of *consequences*. Ask if anyone knows what a consequence is. Tell them a consequence is what happens after you make a choice. Give the children some examples they would understand. For example, if you choose to turn the lights off, the room will be dark. If you choose to go outside on a cold day and not wear your mittens, your hands will get cold. Ask the children to think of some choices and consequences. At a later time, return to this topic and, with the children, make a chart of the choices and consequences that apply to your classroom.

Decisions, Decisions. Teach the children how to make a group decision. Tell the children that sometimes they will all make one choice together. If they wanted to cook, they would need to decide what to make. If they wanted to take a field trip, they would need to decide as a group where to go. If they get tired of the room, they might need to decide on a new way of arranging the furniture. Tell the children that making a decision is like making a choice. You want to use your head and think very carefully when making a decision. You might want to use this step-by-step process to help the children learn how to make a shared decision: (1) What's the situation? (2) What are our choices? (3) What do we like and what don't we like about each choice? (4) Pick one choice.

How Many Kids in the Areas? Help children recognize the need for a way to limit the number of children that can be in an interest area at a time. You could ask them questions like, "What happens when there are too many children in the dramatic play area? What happens when there are too many people in the art area?" As a group, decide how many children can be in each area at a time. You could ask the children, "How many children at a time can play safely and comfortably in each area?" Then you could explore what type of organizing system would help enforce the limits. Ask the children, "What can we do to make sure that there aren't too many children in each of the areas?"

If children have difficulty thinking of an idea, suggest making a planning board for each interest area. Make one planning board for each area out of wood or heavy poster board. Each board should include the name of the interest center and a photo or drawing of the area or what children do there, and pockets or hooks corresponding to the number of children that you decide can be in the area at a time. You will also need name tags or paper dolls or photographs for each child in the group. Children select where they want to play, and put their name tag, photo, or paper doll on that area's planning board. When all the hooks or pockets are full, no more children may play in the area until someone leaves. Display the planning boards just outside each area so that children can see it from the tables or circle area.

You Choose. Children need to learn how to make choices before they can participate in decision making and problem solving. Introduce the concept of choices. Tell the children that they get to make lots of choices at school. Bring out two baskets, each filled with a different snack food. Tell the children that they can make a choice. Ask the children if they know what the choices are (take one food, take the other food, or not take any). Go around the circle and ask each child to make a choice from the baskets. Ask the children to think of other times in the day when they have choices. You may also want to identify the times of the school day when children do not have choices and they need to listen to an adult.

Emotional Development

Classroom Feelings. Ask the children questions like the following ones to generate discussion about common classroom situations and feelings:

> How do you feel when someone asks you to play?
>
> How do you feel when someone says, "Come sit by me"?
>
> How does it feel when someone shares the blocks with you?
>
> How does it feel when someone takes your blocks?
>
> How does it feel when someone says, "No, you can't sit by me"?
>
> How does it feel when someone calls you a name?

I Belong Here. Help children feel a sense of belonging. Take a photograph of each child. Have duplicate prints made of the photographs or duplicate them on a color copier. Make photo name tags for each child's cubby, the back of his chair at the table, and his carpet square for circle time.

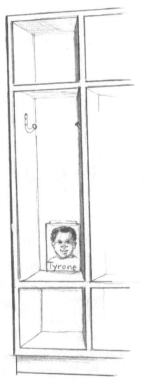

 I Know Many Things. Foster children's self-esteem and confidence. At circle time, ask the children to tell or show the class something they know. Take pictures of the new skills children are learning at school. Display the photos on a bulletin board or in a book to foster conversation among children.

 I'm Responsible. Help children develop responsibility. Set up the classroom so that the children can act independently, and establish the expectation that children will be responsible for themselves and their personal belongings. Help the children identify ways that they can be responsible at school. As a group, make a list of all the responsible things they can do. It might include:

> I can hang my coat in my cubby.
>
> I can put my boots in my cubby.
>
> I can throw away my cup and napkin after snack.
>
> I put away toys when I'm done playing.

You could turn your list into a responsibility pledge and invite each child to take the pledge.

Look at What I'm Learning. Purchase or make a portfolio for each child in your class. Label the portfolios with the children's names and photographs. Invite the children to put samples of their own work in the portfolio. Try to date children's work whenever possible. Store the portfolios in an area of the classroom where children can easily access them. To recognize and celebrate the children's work, periodically bring the portfolios to circle time and look through one or two of them.

Practice Makes Perfect. Help children understand that it takes time and many attempts to learn something new. Some children become frustrated when they can't complete a task. Ask the children what they already know how to do. Children might say things like, "I know how to zip my coat," "I know how to whistle," or "I know how to cut with scissors." Ask children how they learned those skills. Remind children that it takes a lot of practice to learn a new skill. When we want to learn how to do something new, we have to do it over and over. Ask children, "What would you like to learn how to do?" List their answers on a piece of poster board and display on a wall in the classroom. Help the children think of ways they can learn the new skill. Involve parents in helping the children learn the new skills. Check in with the children once a week for four weeks, to monitor their progress and help them master the new skill.

A Safe and Happy Place. Invite each of the children to share their ideas for making the classroom an emotionally safe and happy place. Ask them, "What do you need to feel safe in our classroom? What would help you to feel happy here?"

This Is the Way We Come to School. Many young children have difficulty separating from their parents each day. Help children learn to recognize and manage their feelings during arrival and departure. Ask the following open-ended questions to begin a discussion:

> How does it feel when your mom or dad brings you to school in the morning and leaves you here?
>
> Who feels happy when they're dropped off at school?
>
> How do you show us that you are happy? Do you say hello to all your friends? Do you jump right into an activity? Do you come sit on a teacher's lap?
>
> Who feels sad when they're dropped off at school?
>
> How do you show us that you are sad? Do you cry? Do you pout? Do you sit quietly by yourself?
>
> Who feels mad when you are dropped off at school?
>
> How do you show us that you are mad? Do you scream? Do you throw your coat down and stomp around the room? Do you say to your friends, "Don't look at me. Don't talk to me"?

Have the children role-play ways to manage their feelings when they come to school. Help the children identify appropriate words and actions to express their sad or mad feelings without taking them out on others.

This Is the Way We Go Home. Some young children have difficulty reuniting with their parents each day. Children may cry, run around the room, refuse to clean up, or lose self control and throw toys. Help children recognize that ending the school day and going home makes some children sad, mad, or anxious. Use small people figures to role-play common going home incidents. Role-play a child who cries and is sad, one who runs around the room and out the door or hides because they are feeling anxious and one who isn't ready to go home and knocks over the blocks, throws the toys, and refuses to clean up. Ask the children to help the children in the role-plays think of better ways to end their school day and make a smoother transition to time at home.

Health, Safety, and Nutrition

Healthy Practices. Introduce children to ways they can keep their bodies healthy and safe in the classroom. Teach children how to use the toilets and wash their hands. Teach them about using tissues to blow their noses and covering their mouths when they cough or sneeze. Safety practices include keeping scissors at the art table and using walking feet inside. For younger children, make a chart with line drawings showing the steps to using the toilet, washing hands, and blowing noses. Invite older children to write a chart of classroom health and safety practices.

 It's a Fire Drill! Introduce children to your school's fire drill procedures and rules. Talk with children about why you need to have fire drills. Introduce your rules for fire drills: (1) Stop what you are doing. (2) Stop talking. (3) Listen to adults. (4) Walk to the door. (5) Follow an adult. You may also want to introduce children to the escape route and building exits they are to use in case of a fire. If your school uses an alarm or buzzer, make a tape recording of the sound the alarm makes, and play it for the children so that they can recognize and get used to it. Some young children are terrified and immobilized by the loud sound of alarm systems.

Language Development

Home Language. *Learn the words for* school, teacher, student, *and* classroom *in American Sign Language and the home languages of the children in your class.*

Children at School Picture Cards. Make your own set of children at school teaching pictures by cutting out large magazine pictures of children and teachers and gluing them onto construction paper. Hold up one picture at a time and ask open-ended questions:

> Who can tell me about this picture?
>
> What do you see?
>
> Who is in this picture?
>
> What are the people in this picture doing?
>
> Where are they?
>
> How is this like our school?
>
> How is this different from our school?

Classroom Finger Plays. Use these finger plays about school for circle time, or as conversation starters at other times during the day.

SCHOOL BUS

I go to the bus stop each day *(walk one hand across table)*
Where the bus comes to take us away. *(stop, have other hand wait also)*
We stand single file *(one hand behind the other)*
And walk down the aisle *(step up imaginary steps onto bus)*
When the bus driver talks, we obey.

(*Creative Resources for the Early Childhood Classroom*, second edition, Judy Herr and Libby Yvonne. Albany, NY: Delmar Publishers, 1995; p. 94. Used with permission.)

AT SCHOOL OR CHILD CARE

When everyone is singing,
That's what I like to do. *(pretend to sing)*
And when they're drawing pictures,
I draw pictures, too. *(pretend to draw pictures)*
When it's time to work with toys,
I build a house of blocks.
  (pretend to build with blocks)
When they say, "Put toys away,"
I put them in a box. *(pretend to put toys away)*
When someone asks for help,
I always say, "I will." *(point to self)*

And when it's time for "Quiet, please"
I'm very, very still. *(put index finger to lips)*

(*Busy Fingers Growing Minds: Finger Plays, Verses and Activities for Whole Language Learning*, Rhoda Redleaf. St. Paul: Redleaf Press, 1993; p. 47. Used with permission.)

Classroom Scrapbook. Provide a visual and written record of the year's classroom events and help children remember past events. Use the scrapbook like a diary to capture the celebrations, special events, field trips, visitors, and multicultural activities that go on throughout the year.

 Name That Toy. Collect a variety of classroom toys and tools and bring them to circle time. Hide the objects from the children's view in a bag or box. Give the children clues about one object at a time. Describe its color, shape, size, texture, where it's stored in the room, and what it's used for. Let children guess what it is after each clue, and keep giving clues until the object is named by one of the children. When a child guesses the object, give it to him to hold while you continue to play the game.

Our Class Book. Make a class book with a page for each child and adult in your class. Include the person's name, age, their favorite thing to do in the classroom, what they want to learn at school, and what they will do to be a positive member of the class.

Picture Labels. Invite the children to help make labels for the toys in your classroom. Set out educational supply catalogs, index cards, and crayons or markers. Invite the children to cut out pictures of the toys in your classroom and glue them to the index cards. Help the children write the names of the toys below the picture. Secure the labels to the shelf unit or plastic dish tub that holds each toy.

School Stories. Sit down with a small group of children and some pictures of children in a variety of classroom situations. Ask the children what they see in the pictures. Encourage the children to make up stories about the children in the pictures. If possible, write down the children's stories.

 That's My Name. Make a name card for each child. Show the cards one at a time during circle time. See if the children can recognize their own names and the names of the other children in the class. Make the name cards in English, American Sign Language, and the languages spoken in your classroom.

Math

A Place for All of Us. As a group, count the chairs at the tables and make sure that there is a chair for each person in the class. You may want to make name tags for the chairs. Also check to make sure there is a cubby for each child. Count the cubbies and count the number of children in the class. Do the numbers match? Make photo name tags to label each child's cubby.

 Calendar Time. Display a calendar near the circle time area. Each day during circle time, mark the day on the calendar and count the days of the month, or the number of days until a special event.

Classroom Match. Make a matching game by cutting out duplicate pictures of toys from educational catalogs and magazines, or use a color photocopier to duplicate the photos. Glue the pictures onto index cards. Write the name of the toy on the back of each card. Place the cards in a basket, and invite children to find the matching pairs.

Classroom Sort. Collect a variety of pictures of classroom furniture, equipment, and materials. Glue the pictures to index cards. Write the name of each object on the back of the picture card. Place the pictures in a basket. Invite the children to sort the pictures by interest area. You could also make a floor map of your classroom and have the children place the cards directly on the interest areas.

Daily Attendance. Each day with the children, count how many children are present. You may want to make an attendance chart that allows the children to put their pictures in pockets to show that they are at school that day. As the year progresses, replace the photographs with shapes selected by and unique to each child or a self-portrait by each child. By the end of the year, children could use a written name tag to show that they are at school.

Line Up. Tape butcher paper to a wall or fence. Have the entire class line up side by side with their backs to the paper. Draw around their bodies with a felt-tip pen. When you are finished, encourage the children to look at the mural and see if they can recognize each person's outline. How do they know which outline belongs to which child? Give the children an opportunity to color their body outlines.

Measure It. Give each child a measuring tool. It could be a piece of yarn, a cut out of a foot or hand, a tape measure, or a ruler. Invite the children to find three things in the classroom to measure. You might want to start a list or a chart of the lengths of various classroom objects.

Our Daily Routine. Take a photograph of children during each part of the daily routine. Encourage them to sequence the pictures from the beginning to the end of the day. Extend this activity by drawing a clock face above the photos to help children associate daily activities with time. Help them notice the positions of the big and little hands on the clock at different times.

Where Does This Go? Gather a variety of objects from around the classroom. Put them in a bag, paper sack, or pillow case. Have each child reach in and take out an object. See if he can say which interest area of the classroom the object came from. Then have him go to the area and see if he can find where it goes and put it back.

Music

School Songs. Here are four songs about going to school to sing with the children.

DOWN AT THE CENTER

Tune: *Down by the Station*

Down at the center, early in the morning
See all the children hurry through the door
See the busy parents scurry to and fro
Hug, hug, kiss, kiss, off to work they go
Here at the center, later in the afternoon
See all the parents hurry through the door
See the busy children with so much to show
Hug, hug, kiss, kiss, now it's home we go

(*Busy Fingers Growing Minds: Finger Plays, Verses and Activities for Whole Language Learning*, Rhoda Redleaf. St. Paul: Redleaf Press, 1993; p. 42. Used with permission.)

HELLO SONG

Original lyrics by Paul Fralick

Hello, hello,
We sing in many ways!
Hello, hello,
Let's sing it now today.

(Sing additional verses, inserting "hello" in different languages.)

(*Make It Multicultural—Musical Activities for Early Childhood Education*, Paul Fralick. Hamilton, Ontario, Canada: Mohawk College, 1989; p. 24. Used with permission.)

OH, I WENT TO SCHOOL

Tune: *I Stuck My Head in a Little Skunk's Hole*
by Susan Welhouse

Oh, I went to school
And my teacher said to me,
"There's a lot to do,
There's a lot to see!"
With my eyes, with my ears,
With my hands, with my head
I learn here.

(*The Giant Encyclopedia of Circle Time and Group Activities for Children 3 to 6*, Kathy Charner, editor. Beltsville, MD: Gryphon House, 1996; p. 426. Used with permission.)

THIS LITTLE SMILE OF MINE

Tune: *This Little Light of Mine*

This little smile of mine
I'm going to let it shine!
This little smile of mine
I'm going to let it shine!
Let it shine, let it shine, let it shine!
Hide it under a frown? No!
I'm going to let it shine!
Let it shine, let it shine, let it shine!

Additional verses:
All over our classroom
All over my house
All over (*child's city*)
All over the planet
All over the universe

Physical Development

Classroom Obstacle Course. Arrange the shelf units, chairs, and tables to make a maze that the children can go over, under, through, and around.

Crayon Scribbles. Invite the children to pretend that they are a crayon and the floor is a piece of paper. Encourage the children to "scribble" all over the paper.

Find a Place for Everyone. Play a cooperative version of musical chairs. Arrange the chairs in a circle, and play music. When it stops, challenge the children to get up, change seats, and make sure that everyone has a place to sit. Take a chair away each time you stop the music. By the end, the children will all be piled onto one chair.

Hoops. Give each child a 3-foot-in-diameter plastic hoop. If you don't have hoops, cut lengths of rope. Ask the children to sit down on the floor inside of the hoop. Tell the children that the hoop is a circle that goes all the way around them. The hoop is their personal space. Invite children to look around at everyone else's personal space. Invite children to think of all the different movements they can do inside their hoops.

Name Roll. Help the children learn one another's names by playing a simple game. Ask the children to sit in a circle. Roll a ball to someone in the group, saying, "I roll the ball to (*child's name*)." That child catches the ball and rolls it to someone else, repeating, "I roll the ball to (*child's name*)."

Rock School. This game is adapted from African American culture. One children pretends to be the "teacher" and hides a rock in one of his hands. The rest of the children stand side by side in a line and guess which hand the rock is in. All of the children who guess correctly get to move forward one step. The first child to reach the teacher becomes the teacher for the next round.

Science

Dressing for the Weather. Make a model of a thermometer. Use colors along the side of the thermometer to go along with the temperature. For example, 115° to 80°F is hot (red), 80° to 65°F is warm (pink), 65° to 40°F is cool (blue), and 40°F and below is cold (purple). Use a movable arrow to mark the temperature each day, and help the children associate the daily temperature with dressing appropriately for the weather.

Let's Make Playdough. Playdough is a staple in most early childhood classrooms. Introduce science skills of measuring and mixing and the concept of liquids and solids. Make a simple rebus chart to illustrate the sequence of making playdough. Use a line drawing for each step, and write the words to each step beside or underneath the picture. Arrange the pictures from top to bottom and from left to right to foster prereading skills. Set out the ingredients, measuring cups, measuring spoons, a large mixing bowl, and a mixing spoon, and invite a group of children to make playdough with you.

Magnify It. Set out a variety of magnifying glasses and a variety of classroom objects. Invite the children to look at the objects with their eyes and then with a magnifying glass. Ask the children, "Did you see a difference? What do you think happened? Are there things you can see with the magnifying glass that you can't see with your eyes?" Talk about how the magnifying glass makes objects look bigger, which makes details more visible. Magnifying glasses help us use our eyes to observe and learn about ourselves and the world. Invite the children to find other classroom objects to look at through the magnifying glasses.

What Do Our Classroom Pets Do? Help children learn about the routine behavior of the pets in the classroom. Make charts to record their behavior and activity during the day. The columns can be used to represent the hours and the horizontal lines can mark the days of the week. Check the animals each hour and, with the children's help, record what they are doing. If you have a camera, take pictures of the pets at different times during the day to illustrate the chart.

What's in Our Air? Help children identify if the air in the classroom is clean or dirty. Spread a layer of petroleum jelly over the bottom of a glass pie pan. Leave it out for a day or two and see if anything collects on the surface. Invite children to take out their magnifying glasses to look at the pie pan. Talk about how there is dirt and dust in the air that we might not usually notice. To extend this activity, cover lengths of string with petroleum jelly and hang them around the room. You might want to place them near the interior door, the exterior door, a heater or air conditioning vent, the return air vent, a window, and the bathroom fan. After a day or two, children can compare the amount of dirt and dust particles in different parts of the classroom.

Social Development

Class Banner. Foster a sense of belonging to a group by creating a class banner. Cut a 3-foot-by-4-foot rectangle from a piece of cotton(for example, an old sheet). Collect or mix skin-colored acrylic paints. Ask each child to mix or select a color of paint that matches their skin color. Use a brush to apply the paint to the palm of each child's hand and have them make a print on the fabric. Use a permanent marker or fabric paint to write the children's names below their handprints. You could also add the name of your class, school, or center.

Classmates Paper Dolls. Help children learn to recognize and develop relationships with their classmates. Take a full length picture of each child. Enlarge it on a color photocopier so that it is 10 inches high. Glue the photos to cardboard and cut them out. Make stands for the dolls out of wood molding and set them out in the block area to foster dramatic play.

Classroom Helpers. Introduce the concept of interdependence. Tell the children that in a classroom, we need to work together. There are lots of jobs that need to get done during the day, and we can work together to get them done. Introduce the class jobs and the system you will use for choosing classroom helpers. Or compile a list of jobs with the children, and decide as a group how to choose helpers each day.

Cooperation. Introduce the word *cooperation* to children. Tell the children that cooperation is when we all work together, and when we cooperate, everyone wins. Use dolls to role-play a clean-up incident in which one child is left to clean up a mess made by others. Ask the children the following questions:

> What's wrong with this story?
>
> How does (*doll's name*) feel?
>
> What does (*doll's name*) want and need?

What would happen if all of (*doll's name*) friends cooperated?

What if everyone did their fair share and cleaned up together?

Felt Friends. Gather felt squares in a variety of skin colors. Ask each child to pick out a color that is like the color of their own skin. Have the children use a marker to trace a gingerbread cookie cutter on the felt. Help them cut out their "felt friends." You might want to give them fabric paint to paint faces on the felt friends. Write their names on the back, and set the felt friends out with a flannel board for dramatic play.

Join Hands at Circle Time. Here is a simple chant that children can recite at circle time to promote group identity:

> Hands together,
> Hand together, make a group, *(join hands)*
> Hands together, make a group,
> All together, here we stand, *(hands now joined)*
> This is our group, so lend a hand. *(raise joined hands)*

(*The Peaceful Classroom*, Charles Smith. Beltsville, MD: Gryphon House, 1993; p. 28. Used with permission.)

Learn Our Names. Here's a simple chant to help children learn the names of the children, adults, and even animals in your classroom. "Ann, Ann, look at everyone. Point to Sue, and then you're done." Clap as you chant and repeat faster and faster as children learn the names of their classmates.

Make a Choice. Help children practice making choices and learn responsibility for their decisions. Initiate a planning board system to help children choose what interest area they will go to in the classroom, follow through with their choice, and readily recognize when an interest center is full. This system will be familiar to teachers who are acquainted with the High Scope curriculum.

Make one planning board for each area out of wood or heavy poster board. Each board should include the name of the interest center and a photo or drawing of the area or what children do there and pockets or hooks corresponding to the number of children that you decide can be in the area at a time. You will also need name tags or paper dolls or photographs for each child in the group. Children select where they want to play (usually during circle time or small-group time, just before free-choice time), and put their name tag, photo, or paper doll on that area's planning board. When all the hooks or pockets are full, no more children may play in the area until someone leaves. Display the planning boards just outside each area so that children can see it from the tables or circle area.

Our Class Mobile. Take a photograph of each child. A Polaroid camera is great because children can watch the photographs develop in front of their eyes. Punch a hole at the top of the pictures and write the children's names below the photos. Tie a string to each of the photographs and hang them from a branch or coat hanger. Display the class mobile at the children's eye level. Help the children name everyone and talk about how everyone belongs in the class.

We Can Work It Out. Teach children how to do nonviolent problem solving using a peace table. Decorate a table with a cloth, a picture of people getting along, and the steps for problem solving that you use in the classroom. When children fight or are in conflict with one another, invite them to come to the peace table. Help the children negotiate their conflict. You could use the following five-step method:

1. Find out what happened.
2. Name the problem, our feelings, our wants, and our needs.
3. Think of solutions.
4. Make a choice.
5. Do it!

We Have Rules. Help the children learn the rules of your class. Make a chart with simple drawings to illustrate each of the rules. When setting classroom rules, remember to keep them short, simple, and positive. For example, you might have rules like the following: Treat yourself well. Treat others well. Treat the furniture and toys well. Use your words. Try your best. Listen to adults.

We Missed You. Each day, encourage the children to notice who is at school and who is missing. If a child has missed more than three days, call the family to find out if the child is ill or hospitalized. Invite the children to make a get well card, a mural, or a book of pictures and mail it to the sick child with a note saying, best wishes, we miss you, and hurry back!

Who Is Missing? Help children recall their classmates. Take pictures of each child in the class. Set them all faceup for the children to see. Pick up the pictures, shuffle them, and take one out. Lay the rest down faceup. Ask the children to look at the pictures and guess which one is missing. The child who guesses correctly can shuffle the pictures, pull one out, and lay them out again.

Activities:
Affirming Ourselves
and One Another

Human Rights

Every child has the right to an education and to go to school. Children deserve to go to schools that are safe, healthy, clean, and well-supplied.

Barrier: Some children live in places where there aren't enough schools or there isn't enough money to pay for good schools.

Everyone has the right to be treated fairly at school.

Barrier: Sometimes people are treated unfairly at school because of their skin color, whether they're a boy or girl, because of their learning style, because they have a disability, or because they speak a language other than English.

Discussion Questions: Help children think about what we need to learn and grow at school. Ask them, "What things do children need to learn and grow at school? Why do you think some children don't get what they need? What choices could people make to help children learn and grow? How could we help school children learn and grow?"

Here is a statement of human rights for the classroom. Share it with the children and post it near the circle time area. Consider using it to help your class write their own statement of human rights.

Our Human Rights

I have a right to be happy and to be
treated with compassion in this room;
This means that no one
will laugh at me or
hurt my feelings.

I have a right to be myself in this room;
This means that no one will
treat me unfairly because
of my skin color,
or because I am fat or thin,
tall or short,
a boy or a girl,
or because of the way I look.

I have a right to be safe in this room;
This means that no one will
hit me, kick me, push me, pinch
     me, or hurt me.

I have a right to hear and
     be heard in this room;
This means that no one will
yell, scream, shout or make
     loud noises.

I have a right to learn about
     myself in this room;
This means that I will be free
     to express my feelings
and opinions without being
     interrupted or punished.

I have a right to learn
     according to my own ability;
This means no one will call me names because of the way I learn.

(*Individual Differences, An Experience in Human Relations for Children*, M. Cummings. Madison, WI: Madison Public Schools, 1974; in *"Teacher, They Called Me a ____!"* by Deborah Byrnes. Utah State Office of Education and Anti-Defamation League of B'nai B'rith. New York: Anti-Defamation League, 1987;. pp. 30–31. Used with permission.)

Cultural Identity

I Have a Culture. Introduce and learn the names of the cultures represented in your class. Beforehand, ask parents how they identify themselves culturally. At circle time, ask the children if they know what their cultures are. Tell children your name and your cultural identity. Give each child a name tag that says "My name is (*child's name*) and I am (*child's culture*)."

People Who Came Before Us. Use pictures of famous Americans from different cultures to introduce children to leaders from the cultures represented in your class, community, or in American society who were famous teachers, champions of education, or had to sacrifice to get an education.

Diversity

How Are We Similar and Different? Take photographs of each child in your class. You may want to mount them on oaktag and cover them with clear contact paper. Set them out on a tray. Invite the children to look at the photographs and find ways in which they are similar and different.

How Did You Get to School Today? Give children an opportunity to explore the similar and different ways that we come to school. Ask each child, "How did you come to school today?" Make a chart or graph of all the ways children in the class come to school. Compare the similarities and differences in the ways they come to school. Sing the following song to reinforce that children come to school in many ways. Insert the names of the children in your class and the ways they get to school.

How Did You Get to School Today?

Tune: *Johnny Hammers With One Hammer*
by Glenda Manchanda

Markita rode a yellow bus
yellow bus, yellow bus.
Markita rode a yellow bus
To get to school today.

(*The Giant Encyclopedia of Circle Time and Group Activities for Children 3 to 6*, Kathy Charner, editor. Beltsville, MD: Gryphon House, 1996; p. 455. Used with permission.)

Many Things to Learn and Do. Give children an opportunity to explore all of the different interest areas of the classroom and all of the different things they can do at school. Ask the children the following questions:

> How many different interest areas do we have in our classroom?
>
> How many different things are there to do in our classroom?
>
> Can we count all of the choices?
>
> What if we didn't have any interest areas?
>
> What if we only had tables and chairs and everyone had to do the same thing all of the time? What would that be like?

 What Did You Do? At circle time, help the children review what they did that morning during free-choice play. Ask each child to bring something they made or something that they played with to circle time. Point out that some children were involved in similar activities and some were involved in different activities.

Bias and Stereotypes

Equal Time. You may notice that the girls gather in the dramatic play area and limit the boys' participation there and the boys gather in the block or computer area, and limit the girls' participation in building. Talk with the children about what you've noticed. Tell them that you are concerned because you want everyone to have an equal opportunity and equal time to play in all of the areas. Use a timer to monitor children's play. Or you could set up a "boys' day" in the dramatic play area and "girls' day" in blocks once a week to give all children a chance to develop their skills in all of the curricular areas.

 Everyone Belongs Here. Help children recognize and accept that school is a place where everyone in the community comes together to help children learn and grow. Take a walk through the school or child care center and greet all of the people who are in the building. When you return to the class, ask the children to try to remember all of the people they met in the building. Help them recognize that elders, adults, and children belong at school. Children who are able-bodied and children with disabilities belong at school. Children and adults who have different skin colors and come from different cultures belong at school, and children and adults who speak different languages belong at school.

Nobody's Stupid. Young children may start calling each other names like "stupid" and "dummy." Help children recognize that no one in the class is stupid or dumb and that name-calling is making fun of someone and hurts people's feelings. Ask each child, "What are you good at? What is hard for you?" Make a chart for each child. Help the children to recognize that everyone has things that they are good at and things that are hard for them. Encourage children who are good at certain things to use their skills to help others who are just learning.

Community Service

Book Drive. Collect used books to give to a school for homeless children.

Classroom Clean-Up. As a group, clean or paint your classroom, or repair broken toys and torn books.

Toy Workshop. Make simple toys and games for a child care center in another part of the world that doesn't have any toys.

Social Action Suggestions

Dear Governor. As a group, write a letter to the governor of your state, requesting increased funding or better conditions for schools, or more accessible buildings for students, staff, and parents with disabilities.

ACTIVITIES: OPENING THE DOOR

Classroom Visitors

Invite other members of the center or school community to your classroom to talk about what they do to help the center or school. You could invite the director or principal, the cook, the custodian, bus driver, or the office staff.

If you teach in an elementary school or a school age program, invite students from one of the older classes to visit your classroom and read books to your class.

Field Trips

Take a tour of the center or school. Introduce the children to all of the adults at the school who help their class, such as the cook, bus driver, secretary, custodian, and director.

Parent Involvement

Ask parents and grandparents to assist in the classroom by telling stories about their first experiences of going to school and what they think the children need to do to be successful students. Ask parents and grandparents to write or draw messages of encouragement and inspiration. Put their messages into a book that can be displayed in the book area.

Parent Education

Invite a kindergarten teacher to talk about kindergarten readiness. Plan a parent evening and set up the classroom as you would for the children so that they can experience a day in the life of their children at your center or school. Then lead the parents through a discussion about the kinds of things your curriculum is teaching children and why they're important.

Classroom Resources

Children's Books

Aekyung's Dream, Min Paek (San Francisco: Children's Book, 1988).

Amazing Grace, Mary Hoffman (New York: Dial, 1991).

Angel Child, Dragon Child, Michele Maria Surat (New York: Scholastic, 1983).

Annie…Anya: A Month In Moscow, Irene Trivas (New York: Orchard, 1992).

Born In The Gravy, Denys Cazet (New York: Orchard, 1993).

Busy At Day Care Head To Toe, Patricia Brennan Demuth (New York: Dutton, 1996).

By Myself, David Kherdian (New York: Holt, 1992).

Carl Goes To Day Care, Alexandra Day (New York: Farrar, 1993).

Chatterbox Jamie, Nancy Evans Cooney (New York: Putnam, 1993).

The Classroom Pet, Grace Maccarone (New York: Scholastic, 1995).

Cleversticks, Bernard Ashely (New York: Crown, 1992).

Day Care ABC, Tamara Phillips (Morton Grove, IL: Whitman, 1989).

The Day The Teacher Went Bananas, James Howe (New York: Dutton, 1984).

Eagle Song, Joseph Bruchac (New York: Dial, 1977).

The Lunch Box Surprise, Grace Maccarone (New York: Scholastic, 1995).

Friends At School, Rochelle Bunnett (New York: Star Bright, 1995).

Going To My Nursery School, Susan Kuklin (New York: Bradbury, 1990).

Halmoni And The Picnic, Sook Nyul Choi (Boston: Houghton, 1993).

Hemi's Pet, Jan de Hamel (Boston: Houghton, 1987).

I Need A Lunch Box, Jeanette Caines (New York: Harper, 1988).

Jamaica's Blue Marker, Jaunita Havill (Boston: Houghton, 1995).

Jamal's Busy Day, Wade Hudson (East Orange, NJ: Just Us, 1991).

A Kente Dress for Kenya, Juwanda G. Ford (New York: Scholastic, 1996).

Kindergarten Kids, Ellen Senisi (New York: Cartwheel, 1994).

Listen For The Bus: David's Story, Patricia McMahon (Honesdale, PA: Boyds Mills, 1995).

Marcellus, Lorraine Simeon (New York: Writers and Readers, 1995).

Martin And The Teacher's Pets, Bernice Chardiet and Grace Maccarone (New York: Scholastic, 1991).

The Little Painter Of Saban Grande, Patricia Maloney Marku (New York: Bradbury, 1993).

Mine! Hiawyn Oram and Mary Rees (New York: Barron's, 1992).

My First Day At Preschool, Edwina Riddell (New York: Barron's, 1992).

My Friend Leslie: The Story Of A Handicapped Child, Maxine B. Rosenberg (New York: Lee, 1983).

My New School, Harriet Hains (New York: Dorling Kindersley, 1992).

Next Year I'll Be Special, Patricia Reilly Giff (New York: Doubleday, 1993).

Our Peaceful Classroom, Aline D. Wolf (Altoona, PA: Parent-Child, 1991).

Our Teacher's In A Wheelchair, Mary Ellen Powers (Morton Grove, IL: Whitman, 1986).

Rachel Parker, Kindergarten Show-Off, Ann Matrin (New York: Holiday, 1993).

Recess Mess, Grace Maccarone (New York: Scholastic, 1996).

Ricardo's Day, George Acona (New York: Scholastic, 1994).

Rise And Shine, Mariko-Chan! Chiyoko Tomioka (New York: Scholastic, 1992).

Ruby, The Copycat, Peggy Rathmand (New York: Scholastic, 1991).

School Bus, Donald Crews (New York: Greenwillow, 1984).

School Days, Barbara G. Hennessy (New York: Viking, 1990).

Sharing Time Mess, Grace Maccarone (New York: Scholastic, 1996).

Show And Tell, Robert Munsch (Toronto: Annick, 1991).

Starting School, Janet Ahlberg and Allan Ahlberg (New York: Viking, 1988).

This Is The Way We Go To School, Edith Baer (New York: Scholastic, 1990).

Time To..., Bruce McMillan (New York: Lothrop, 1989).

We Are All Alike...We Are All Different, The Kindergartners at Cheltenham Elementary School (New York: Scholastic, 1991).

We Can Do It! Laura Dwight (New York: Checkerboard, 1992).

What Mary Jo Shared, Janice May Udry (New York: Scholastic, 1996).

What Will Mommy Do When I'm At School? Dolores Johnson (New York: Macmillan, 1990).

When Learning Is Tough: Kids Talking About Learning Disabilities, Cynthia Roby (Morton Grove, IL: Whitman, 1993).

When You Go To Kindergarten, James Howe (New York: Morrow, 1994).

Where Did You Get Your Moccasins? Bernelda Wheeler (Winnipeg, Canada: Peguis, 1986).

Who Belongs Here? Margy Burns Knight (Gardiner, ME: Tilbury, 1993).

Will You Come Back For Me? Ann Tompert (Morton Grove, IL: Whitman, 1988).

Willie's Wonderful Pet, Mel Cebulash (New York: Scholastic, 1993).

Music

Fink, Cathy, and Marcy Marxer. *Nobody Else Like Me* (A&M, 1994).

"Twins"

"Walkin' On My Wheels"

Grammer, Red. *Teaching Peace* (Smilin' Atcha, 1986).

"I Think You're Wonderful"

Hartmann, Jack. *Make a Friend, Be a Friend* (Educational Activities, 1990).

"My Name Is Daniel"

"We Know Your Name"

Lefranc, Barbara. *I Can Be Anything I Want To Be* (Doubar, 1990).

"Name Of The Game"

Marley, Damian, a.k.a. Junior Gong. *Positively Reggae* (Sony, 1994).

"School Controversy"

Music For Little People. *Fiesta Musical,* with Emilio Delgado (Music for Little People, 1994).

"A La Escuela"

Pirtle, Sarah. *Two Hands Hold The Earth* (Gentle Wind, 1984).

"I Am A Person"

Rogers, Sally. *What Can One Little Person Do?* (Round River, 1992).

"No One"

Shaggy. *Positively Reggae* (Sony, 1994).

"No Way Around It"

Shih, Patricia. *Big Ideas!* (Glass, 1990).

"Cooperate"

Slonecki, Catherine. *The Dog Ate My Homework* (Educational Record Center).

Sweet Honey In The Rock. *All For Freedom* (Music for Little People, 1989).

"I'm So Glad I'm Here"

Vitamin L. *Walk A Mile* (Lovable Creature, 1989).

"I Want To Get To Know You"

Worl-A-Girl. *Positively Reggae* (Sony, 1994).

"Back To School"

Visual Displays

ABC School Supply
Good Manners Posters

Constructive Playthings
Friends Together Posters

Environments
Busy Children Photo Poster Kit

Lakeshore
Classroom Courtesies Photo Posters
Learning Center Poster Set

National Association for the Education of Young Children
Posters of Children

National Black Child Development Institute
The Spirit of Excellence Poster

Scholastic
I Can Do Poster Packs

Videos

A Kid's Guide To Getting Along With Your Classmates (Kimbo Educational, 1991).

Computer Software

Jump Start Kindergarten, Constructive Playthings

Jump Start Preschool, Constructive Playthings

Teaching Kits

Families and School Kit, Educational Equity Concepts

Additional Resources

Council for Basic Education
1319 F Street, Suite 900
Washington, DC 20004
(202) 347-4171

PLANET EARTH

Some children live in a world of concrete and asphalt, almost totally disconnected and alienated from the natural world. Other children live in rural and farming areas, so that their daily lives are very much intertwined with nature. Certainly, all children are interested in nature. They love dirt, mud, sand, puddles, rocks, snow, grass, and flowers.

You can introduce children to planet Earth and foster respect and appreciation for nature. This unit will help children see how people are interconnected with the environment and have a responsibility to take care of our planet.

UNIT 8:

Planet Earth
TABLE OF CONTENTS

Planet Earth

Look for this symbol
to find activities you
can use for circle time.

WEB

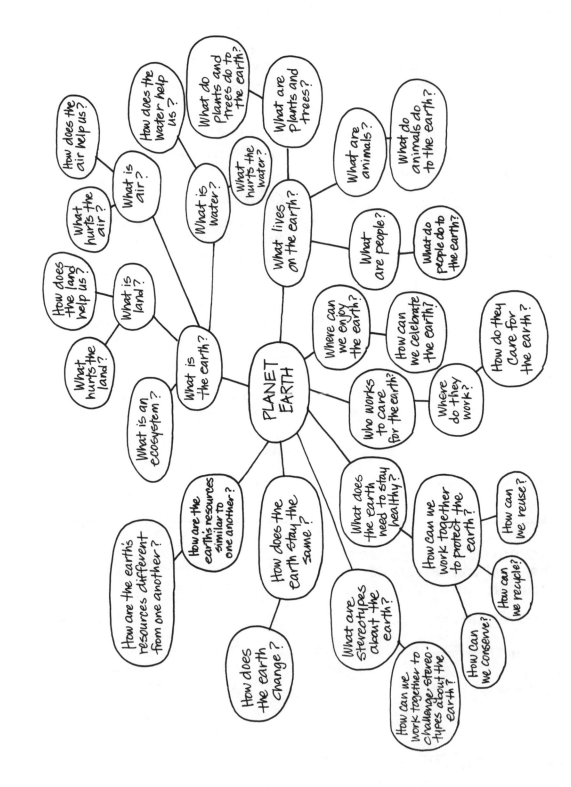

OUTLINE

I. What is the earth?
   A. What is land?
      1. How does the land help us?
      2. What hurts the land?
   B. What is air?
      1. How does the air help us?
      2. What hurts the air?
   C. What is water?
      1. How does the water help us?
      2. What hurts the water?
   D. What is an ecosystem?

II. What lives on the earth?
   A. What are plants and trees?
   B. What do plants and trees do to the earth?
   C. What are animals?
   D. What do animals do to the earth?
   E. What are people?
   F. What do people do to the earth?

III. Where can we enjoy the earth?

IV. How are the earth's resources similar to one another?

V. How are the earth's resources different from one another?

VI. How does the earth stay the same?

VII. How does the earth change?

VIII. What are stereotypes about the earth?

IX. How can we work together to challenge stereotypes about the earth?

X. What does the earth need to stay healthy?

XI. How can we work together to protect the earth?
   A. How can we conserve?
   B. How can we recycle?
   C. How can we reuse?

XII. Who works to care for the earth?

XIII. Where do they work?

XIV. How do they care for the earth?

XV. How can we celebrate the earth?

MATERIALS LIST

ART

skin-colored paints, crayons, markers, felt, and craft paper

butcher paper roll

nature magazines

twigs and branches to use as paint brushes

nature sponges for painting (for example, Giant Leaf Sponges, Rain Forest Sponges, Seashore Sponges, Seasons and Weather Sponges, *Environments*)

BLOCKS

figures of endangered animals (for example, Endangered Animals of the World, *Lakeshore*)

small recycling trucks

paper

felt tip pens

natural materials like palm leaves, coconut branches, corn husks, pine branches, bark, pine needles, stones, and straw

DRAMATIC PLAY

multiethnic preschooler dolls (for example, Friends Dolls, Children with Hearing, Motor, and Visual Impairments Dolls, *People of Every Stripe*; Multi-Ethnic School Dolls, *Lakeshore*; Multi-Ethnic Dolls, *Constructive Playthings*)

camping: campground sign, campground rules sign, freestanding tent and directions for assembly, sleeping bags, flashlights, canteens, mess kits, food containers, empty sunscreen and insect repellent containers, rope, backpacks, firewood

recycling: recycling center sign, recycling bins with labels, empty plastic food containers, empty food cans, newspapers

picnicking: blanket, picnic basket, plates, cups, thermos or water jug, pretend food, map, picnic grounds sign

plant store, gardening center, or gardening: gardening clothes and tools, empty pots, plastic plants

LARGE MOTOR

materials that focus on caring for the earth (for example, Garden Tools Set, *Constructive Playthings* and *Lakeshore*; The Little Gardener, *ABC School Supply*)

LITERACY

children's books: fiction, nonfiction, and bilingual books about the earth (see resource list at the end of the unit)

cassette player and theme-related storybook cassettes in different languages

blank cassettes

flannel board sets about the environment (for example, Endangered and Threatened Animals of North America Flannel Board Set, *Edvantage*)

writing and bookmaking materials

MANIPULATIVES

nature puzzles (for example, "A Counting Garden" Double Puzzle, *Nasco*; Endangered Animals Jumbo Floor Puzzle, *Edvantage*; The Rain Forest Jumbo Floor Puzzle, *Edvantage* and *Sandy and Son*; The Pond Floor Puzzle, *Sandy and Son*; Environmental Awareness Floor Puzzles, *Edvantage* and *Beckley-Cardy*; Seasons/Weather Puzzles, *Beckley-Cardy*; Environmental Floor Puzzles, *Constructive Playthings*; Ocean Puzzle, *Animal Town*; Recycling Puzzle Set, *Environments*) nature board, matching, and sorting games (for example, Beautiful Place Board Game, Nautilus: A Game of Sea Shells, Cinnabar: A Game of Rocks and Minerals, Goldenrod: A Game of Wild Flowers, and Juniper: A Game of Trees, *Animal Town*; Bottles and Bins Recycling Game, *Lakeshore*; Mystery Garden Game, *Sandy and Son*; Nature Memo, *Edvantage*; Take a Hike Game, *Childswork/Childsplay*; The Growing Tree Game, Save the Forest Game, Nature Lotto, *Constructive Playthings*)

other nature-related manipulatives (for example, Nature Sort Picture Blocks, *Constructive Playthings*; Sorting and Counting Shells, *Lakeshore* and *Constructive Playthings*; Math-on-the-Beach Magnetic Board, Seasons and Weather Theme Box, Growing Things Theme Box, Earth and Environment Theme Box, *Lakeshore*; Lacing Leaves, *Sandy and Son* and *ABC School Supply*)

SCIENCE

natural materials: different types of soil, leaves, bark, pinecones, seed pods, rocks

reference books

magnifiers

SENSORY

leaves, pinecones, and seed pods

sand and stones

potting soil, beans, small pots, gardening tools, watering cans

floral, herbal, or wood scents

TEACHING THROUGH THE INTEREST AREAS

Art

Set out nature magazines and use natural materials like twigs and branches as paint brushes.

Blocks

Add small recycling trucks, scrap paper, and a felt tip pen for making signs to the area to encourage role-playing about recycling.

Set out toy endangered animals or rain forest animals and encourage the children to build a rain forest. Add art materials for making trees.

Add natural materials like palm leaves, coconut branches, corn husks, pine branches, bark, pine needles, stones, and straw and encourage the children to create nature settings or natural roofs, houses, and fences.

Dramatic Play

Encourage the children to role-play camping by adding the following equipment to the dramatic play area: a campground sign, campground rules sign, free standing tent and directions, sleeping bags, flashlights, canteens, mess kits, food container, empty sunscreen and insect repellent containers, rope, backpacks, and firewood for a pretend campfire.

To encourage children to role-play recycling in the home living center, add a recycling center sign, recycling bins with labels, empty plastic food containers, empty food cans, and newspapers.

Add a blanket, picnic basket, plates, cups, thermos or water jug, pretend food, map, and a picnic grounds sign to encourage picnic play.

Set out gardening clothes, gardening tools, empty pots, and plastic plants to encourage playing plant store or gardening center.

Literacy

Set out a collection of fiction, nonfiction, and bilingual books on the earth, a cassette player and storybook cassettes in different languages, environment flannel board sets, writing materials, and bookmaking materials.

Manipulatives

Set out puzzles, matching cards, lotto games, and board games that deal with nature.

Music

Set out children's cassettes on the ecology and the environment, nature sounds cassettes and rainsticks.

Science

Set out reference books and different types of soil in baby food jars or small plastic containers and labels.

Set out natural materials such as rocks, different types of plants, live leaves, bark, pinecones, and a reference book on plants.

Sensory

Add leaves, pinecones, and seed pods to the sensory table.

Add potting soil and gardening tools, small pots, watering cans, and bean seeds to encourage the children to plant seeds.

Add floral, wood, or herbal scents to the water in the sensory table.

Add sand and stones to the sensory table.

ACTIVITIES:
INVESTIGATING THE THEME

Creative Development

Clay Play. Set out potter's clay on the art table and encourage the children to pull off and manipulate chunks of clay. Provide the children with rolling pins, butter knives, twigs, acorns, seed pods, and leaves. If they want, the children can roll out the clay and make patterns in it with the natural materials.

Clouds, Lightning, and Rain. Set out construction paper, cotton balls, silver and gold rickrack, and silver Christmas tree icicles. Encourage children to make a stormy picture. They can use the cotton balls for clouds, rickrack for lightning, and the icicles for rain. You could roll the cotton balls in powdered black tempera to make storm clouds.

Earth Collage. Make a group collage by cutting out magazine pictures of the land, earth, and sky and gluing them onto a large piece of butcher paper.

Flower Garden Mural. Lay out a large sheet of butcher paper. Encourage the children to paint flower stems by dipping rug yarn in a tray of green paint and dragging the piece of yarn down the paper. Let the paint dry. Later, set out trays filled with different colors of paint. Invite children to sponge paint or brush flower petals on to the stems.

Flowers, Plants, and Trees Collage. Set out gardening catalogs, gardening magazines, seed catalogs, and empty seed packets. Encourage children to cut out pictures of flowers, plants, and trees and arrange them on a piece of construction paper. Older children can arrange their pictures so they look like a garden.

Handprint Leaves. Encourage the children to paint a picture of the fall leaves. Lay out a large sheet of butcher paper. Invite the children to dip their hands into pans of fall-colored paint (yellow, orange, red, green, and brown) and then press their palms onto the paper in a variety of positions and locations.

Handprint Trees. Invite the children to dip both hands into a pan of green paint (you could even use different shades of green) and then press their palms onto paper in a variety of positions to make the leaves of a tree. When the handprints dry, the children can use a brush to paint a tree trunk and limbs.

Landscape Artists. Take the art supplies along on a field trip to a park or nature center. Invite children to pretend that they are painters who paint landscapes to share the beauty of nature with others. Ask the children if they can paint a picture of what they see.

Landscapes. Take the art materials outside to the playground or to a nearby park, and encourage children to observe their surroundings and draw or paint a picture of the natural world.

Planet Earth Crayon Melt. Cover the bottom of an electric skillet with a sheet of aluminum foil. Turn on the skillet to the lowest setting. Peel the paper off green, blue, and brown crayons. Using the crayons, slowly draw a design on the aluminum foil. The crayons will melt and make puddles. To make a print of the earth-like design, lay a piece of paper over the crayon design, press down, and lift off.

Rain Painting. On a rainy day, use a fine hand-held strainer to sprinkle different colors of powdered tempera paint onto construction paper. Carry the paper outside, being careful to hold it flat. Hold the paper out in the rain for just a minute or two. Let the paper dry and notice the patterns the rain drops created.

Rock Painting. Collect enough smooth round rocks for each child in your class. Wash the rocks with dish-washing detergent and let dry. Set out a variety of tempera paints. Add a little liquid dish-washing detergent to the paint to make sure it adheres to the rocks. Invite children to paint the rocks.

Waxed Paper Leaves. Brush glue that has been diluted with water over a piece of waxed paper. Arrange a variety of leaves on top of the glue and brush with another layer of glue. Lay another piece of waxed paper over the top. Smooth out the wrinkles and then iron the waxed paper. Tape to a window when dry.

Wind Paintings. Dip a straw into thinned tempera paint. Blow through the straw to spread the paint and make designs on easel paper. Ask the children what color they think of when they think of the wind, and give them that color of paint.

Critical Thinking

Reduce Our Waste. Challenge the children to think about reducing waste. At the end of a morning session, bring a classroom trash can to circle time. Dump it out so the children can see the contents. Ask them, "What are ways that we can reduce the amount of trash that we produce?" Encourage them to think of ways they can use less and reuse containers or packaging that they would normally throw away. For example, a large ice cream bucket could become a container for toys, and an empty egg carton could hold scissors.

Emotional Development

Calm and Stormy Feelings. Encourage children to use the weather to describe how they are feeling. For example, a child who is mad might say, "I'm feeling like thunder and lightning," or, "I feel like there's a tornado inside of me." A child who is feeling happy might describe feeling like the warm sunshine or a rainbow.

Nature Sounds. Listen to sounds of nature cassettes, like a thunderstorm, ocean waves, or a stream, and ask the children how it makes them feel. Use open-ended questions like, "How would you feel if you were at the ocean? How would you feel if you were in the woods? How would you feel if you were in a thunderstorm?"

Health, Safety, and Nutrition

Emergency Drills. Introduce children to the safety procedures used in the event of natural disasters. Focus on natural disasters common to your geographic region. You may want to discuss and practice tornado, earthquake, or fire drills.

Poisonous Plants. Introduce children to plants that might be in their homes or yards that are poisonous. You can cut pictures of poisonous plants to show children. Some common plants that are poisonous include bittersweet vines, buttercups, castor bean, lily of the valley, mistletoe, rhubarb leaves, sweet peas, cherry tree, oak tree, rhododendron, wisteria, and yews. Contact your local poison control agency for a list of regional plants that are poisonous.

Tree Snacks. At snack time, serve foods that grow on trees. Select foods that children are familiar with or grow in your geographic region. You might consider apples, oranges, grapefruit, peaches, pears, plums, or nuts such as walnuts, almonds, or pecans.

Language Development

> **Home Language.** *Learn the words for* water, air, sun, land, *and* earth *in American Sign Language and the home languages of the children in your classroom.*

Earth Keepers Picture Stories. Sit down with a small group of children and some pictures of children or adults caring for the earth. Show the children one picture at a time. Ask the children what they see in the pictures. Encourage the children to make up stories about the people in the pictures. If possible, write down the children's stories.

Environment Picture Cards. Use a commercial set of environmental pictures or make your own set by cutting out large magazine pictures of nature scenes and gluing them onto construction paper. Hold up one picture at a time and ask open-ended questions:

> Who can tell me about this picture?
>
> What do you see?
>
> What is it?
>
> Where is it?
>
> What do you like about this place?
>
> How is it like where we live?
>
> How is it different from where we live?

Litterbug Poem. Use this poem to help children remember to pick up their trash and toss it in the waste basket.

> Litterbug, litterbug, that's not
> nice.
> Litterbug, litterbug, you better
> think twice.
> Litterbug, litterbug, don't you care?
> Litterbug, litterbug, let's be fair!

(*The Kindness Curriculum: Introducing Young Children to Loving Values*, Judith Anne Rice. St. Paul: Redleaf Press, 1995; p. 42. Used with permission.)

Name It. Collect a variety of nature pictures (different types of weather, seasons, clouds, the sun, rainbows, plants, trees, flowers, mountains, lakes, rivers, oceans, the desert) and bring them to circle time. Hide the pictures from the children's view. Give the children clues about the scene depicted in one of the pictures. Describe the environment's colors, shapes, and characteristics. Let the children guess after each clue.

When a child answers correctly, give her the picture to hold while you continue to play the game.

Our Planet Earth. Make a class book about the planet Earth. Include sections on the land, the water, the air, and how the children can take care of the planet.

Planet Earth Helps Us. With the children, make a list of all of the ways the land, the plants, and the sky help us.

Planting Finger Plays. Here are three finger plays about growing seeds and plants to provide a language experience that reinforces the science activities. Teach them to children to accompany planting activities.

MY GARDEN

This is my garden *(extend one hand forward, palm up)*
I'll rake it with care *(raking motion with fingers)*
and then some flower seeds *(planting motion)*
I'll plant it right there.
The sun will shine *(make circle with hands)*
And the rain will fall *(let fingers flutter down to lap)*
And my garden will blossom *(cup hands together, extend upward slowly)*
And grow straight and tall.

(*Creative Resources for the Early Childhood Classroom*, second edition, Judy Herr and Libby Yvonne. Albany, NY: Delmar Publishers, 1995; p. 285. Used with permission.)

LITTLE RAINDROP

This is the sun, high up in the sky. *(hold hands in circle above head)*
A dark cloud suddenly comes sailing by. *(slide hands to side)*
These are the raindrops. *(make raining motion with fingers)*
Pitter-patter down.
Watering the flowers. *(pouring motions)*
Growing on the ground. *(hands pat the ground)*

(*Creative Resources for the Early Childhood Classroom*, second edition, Judy Herr and Libby Yvonne. Albany, NY: Delmar Publishers, 1995; p. 461. Used with permission.)

Tiny Seed

Tiny seed planted just right.
Not a breath of air, nor a ray of light. *(cover right fist with left hand)*
Rain falls slowly to and fro,
And now the seed begins to grow. *(remove left hand and slowly uncurl right fist)*
Slowly reaching for the light
With all its energy, all its might. *(right hand makes creeping motion upwards with fingers together)*
The little seed's work is almost done,
To grow up tall and face the sun. *(stretch out fingers of right hand)*

(The Peaceful Classroom, Charles Smith. Beltsville, MD: Gryphon House, 1993; p. 145. Used with permission.)

Math

Earth Sort. Collect pictures of trash, dumps, environmental waste, toxic waste, and nature scenes. Glue the pictures to cards and place the pictures in a basket. Set out the basket and a sorting tray. Invite the children to classify the pictures any way they like.

Environments Sort. Collect pictures of different environments. Glue the pictures to cards and write the name of the environment on the back of each card. Place the pictures in a basket. Set out the basket and a sorting tray. Invite the children to classify the pictures any way they like.

Land, Sea, and Air. Collect pictures of animals that live on the land, in the sea, or fly in the air. Glue the pictures to cards and write the name of the animal on the back of each card. Place the pictures in a basket. Set out the basket and a sorting tray. Invite children to classify the pictures by land, sea, or air.

Leaf Shapes and Colors. Make a set of leaves to match and classify. Cut out four or five different leaf shapes from dark green, light green, yellow, orange, red, and brown construction paper. Put the leaves in a tray and encourage the children to sort the leaves by color, shape, and by both color and shape.

Nature Scenes Match. Make six or more sets of nature scenes matching cards. Find duplicate photos in magazines or old calendars, or use a color photocopier to make duplicates. You could also use picture post cards. Write the name of the scene on the back of each card, such as "lake," "ocean," "mountains," "desert," "canyon." Place the cards in a basket and encourage the children to find the matching sets.

Plant Match. Make six or more sets of plant matching cards. Find duplicate photos of flowers, shrubs, and trees in gardening catalogs and magazines, or use a color photocopier to make duplicates. Write the name of the flower, plant, or shrub on the back of the card. Place the cards in a basket and encourage the children to find the matching sets.

Rocks. Gather a large variety of rocks. Set out a basket of rocks and a sorting tray. Invite children to examine and sort the rocks. Make a list of all the different ways the children sort the rocks. The children could also count the rocks.

Seasons Sort. Collect pictures reflecting the four seasons. Glue the pictures to cards and write the name of the season on the back of each card. Place the pictures in a basket. Set out the basket and a sorting tray. Invite the children to classify the pictures any way they like.

Sprouting Seeds. Plant four different kinds of seeds. You might want to plant beans, radishes, lettuce, and tomatoes. Make a chart to help the children count how many days it takes for the seeds to sprout, and graph the germination rates of the different seeds.

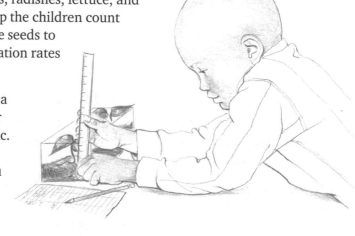

Take Out the Trash. Gather a variety of trash. Include paper goods, metal, glass, and plastic. Invite the children to sort the trash by types of material. You could also ask them to pick out and count how many pieces of trash they could recycle and use again.

Music

Garbage and Recycling Songs. Here are four songs about recycling and garbage to teach the children.

DOWN AT THE DUMP

Tune: *Down by the Station*
by Jean Warren

Down at the dump
Early in the morning,
See all the dump trucks
Standing in a row.
See them dump the garbage
In a great big pile—
Dump, dump, dump, dump,
watch them go.
Pretty soon our dumps
Will all be full,
We had better figure out
Something to do.
We could all recycle
Some of our garbage—Recycle, recycle,
Watch us go.

Out in the garden
We could make a pile
Of all our food scraps,
So they can decay.
See us dump the scraps
In a great big pile—
Dump, dump, dump, dump,
Watch us go.
Then we could send off
All our cans and jars,
So they can be used
To make some new ones.
See us dump the cans and jars
In a great big bag—
Dump, dump, dump, dump,
Watch us go.
Let's all recycle,
Let's all give a hand
'Cause if we recycle
We'll have a nicer land.
See us sorting out
all of our garbage—
Sort, sort, sort, sort,
Watch us go.

(*Learning and Caring About Our World*, Gayle Bittinger. Everett, WA: Warren
Publishing House, 1990; p.31. Used with permission.)

SAVE THE EARTH

Tune: *Row, Row, Row Your Boat*
by Wilma Kaplan

Save, save, save the cans throw them in the bin,
We can help to save the earth if we all pitch in.

Additional verses:
Save, save, save the paper…
Save, save, save the bottles…
Save, save, save the plastics…

(*The Giant Encyclopedia of Circle Time and Group Activities for Children 3 to 6*, Kathy
Charner, editor. Beltsville, MD: Gryphon House, 1996; p. 131. Used with permission.)

LOOK FOR LITTER

Tune: *London Bridge is Falling Down*

Let's look for litter and pick it up,
Pick it up, pick it up.
Let's look for litter and pick it up,
We'll help our earth stay clean.

(*The Kindness Curriculum: Introducing Young Children To Loving Values*, Judith Rice.
St. Paul: Redleaf Press, 1995; p. 42. Used with permission.)

RECYCLING SONG

Tune: *The More We Get Together*

The more we all recycle, recycle, recycle
The more we all recycle
The happier we'll be.
'Cause your world is my world
And my world is your world.
The more we all recycle, the happier we'll be!

(*Science Is Fun! For Families and Classroom Groups*, Carol Oppenheim. St. Louis: Cracom Corporation, 1993; p. 156. Used with permission.)

Green Grass Growing. Sing this familiar folk song to reinforce the interconnectedness of the natural world. Sing as many verses as you have time for (or your children will sing through!).

THE GREEN GRASS GROWS ALL AROUND

Oh in the woods there was a tree,
The prettiest little tree that you
    ever did see.
Now the tree was in the hole
    and the hole was in the
    ground,
And the green grass grew all
    around, all around,
And the green grass grew all
    around.
Now, on that tree, there was a limb,
The prettiest little limb that you ever
    did see.
Now the limb was on the tree and the tree was in the hole,
And the hole was in the ground,
And the green grass grew all around, all around,
And the green grass grew all around.

Additional verses:
Now on that limb, there was a branch…
Now on that branch, there was a twig…
Now on that twig, there was a nest…
Now in that nest, there was an egg…
Now in that egg, there was a bird…
Now on that bird, there was an eyelash…
Now on that eyelash, there was a bug…
Now on that bug, there was a wing…
Now on that wing, there was a germ…

(Lyrics reprinted from *Abiyoyo and Other Story Songs for Children* (1958) in *Make It Multicultural—Musical Activities for Early Childhood Education*, Paul Fralick. Hamilton, Ontario, Canada: Mohawk College, 1989; p. 63. Used with permission.)

Planet Earth

MUSIC

Rain Song. Many children are afraid of thunder. Here's a simple song about rain that may help to calm children's fears.

I'M A LITTLE RAIN CLOUD

Tune: *I'm a Little Teapot*
by Frances Youngblood

I'm a little rain cloud fat and round *(extend arms out and clasp hands)*
When it thunders, I make this sound. *(cover ears with hands)*
Boom! Boom! Boom! Rolling around *(sing loudly, roll arms in front of you)*
Splash! The rain comes tumbling down. *(close hands in front of you, spread fingers, and move fingers down like raindrops)*

(*The Giant Encyclopedia of Circle Time and Group Activities for Children 3 to 6*, Kathy Charner, editor. Beltsville, MD: Gryphon House, 1996; p. 465. Used with permission.)

The Whole World. Sing this well-loved folk song to promote a sense of caring for the earth.

WE'VE GOT THE WHOLE WORLD

Tune: Traditional

We've got the whole world in our hands
We've got the whole world in our hands
We've got the whole world in our hands
We've got the whole world in our hands

Additional verses:
We've got the land and the mountains…
We've got the lakes and the rivers…
We've got the air that we breathe…
We've got the flowers and the trees…
We've got the oceans and fish…
We've got the birds and the animals…
We've got all the earth's people…

Physical Development

Earth Elements. Encourage children to move their bodies like elements of the earth. Ask them if they can run like the wind, flow like a river, roll like the waves, or shine like the sun. Ask the children if they can move like a snowflake or raindrop, or if they can move like thunder and lightning.

Flowing Water. Take the children outside to the sandbox. With the children, dig channels and lakes. Turn the hose on low and let water flow through the channels and into the lakes. Make dams and reservoirs. Try to control the flow of the water. Children may want to sail leaves, sticks, or small plastic boats on the rivers.

Growing Mediums. Set out tubs of soil, potting soil, seed-starting medium, vermiculite, perlite, and peat moss. Invite children to touch, feel, and smell each of the different growing media. Ask them the following questions:

Which is heaviest?

Which is lightest?

What do they smell like?

Which smell do you like the best?

I Am a Storm. Talk with the children about wind, rain, thunder, and lightning, types of weather often associated with a storm. Invite the children to use their bodies to make a thunderstorm. Encourage them to run with their arms outstretched like the wind, then tiptoe lightly like the rain. As the rain begins to fall harder, ask them to jump up and down, and then to jump very loudly like thunder and lightning. Then, as the storm passes, the children can tiptoe lightly again like the rain, and sway back and forth like a gentle breeze, until the air is still.

Mud! Place dry dirt or potting soil in the sensory table. Set out buckets of water and small pitchers or turkey basters. Invite children to add small amounts of water to the soil to make mud. Let the children play with the mud. Encourage the children to talk about how the mud feels. Set out cookie, candy, or sand molds for the children to fill with mud. Set the molds in the sun and see what happens.

Puddle Jumpers. Draw a puddle on the floor for each child with chalk, masking tape, ropes, or plastic hoops. Invite children to jump in and out of the puddle. Then ask them to jump in another puddle. Begin to remove puddles so that more than one child is jumping in the puddle at a time.

 Rock Solid. Help children recognize they are strong. Give each child a rock to explore. Ask children to describe their rocks. Invite the children to take off their shoes and try to stand on their rocks. The rock is solid, strong, and doesn't crumble or fall apart when something heavy is on top of it. Challenge children to use their muscles to make their bodies solid and strong like a rock. Children can sit on the floor and pull their knees up tight against their chests, wrap the arms around their legs, and clasp their hands together. Children can also get on their arms and knees and curl up their bodies tight. Walk around and check the strength and solidness of the "rocks" by gently pushing them. See if the children can resist and hold their position without moving. Affirm the children's strength, their ability to hold their ground, and the use of their muscles to be solid as a rock.

A Walk in the Woods. Invite children to move their bodies to the following poem:

NATURE WALK ACTION RHYME

by Kathryn Sheehan

We're going on a nature walk

To see what we can see.
We might smell some flowers
We might hear some bees. Buzz!

The sun is mighty hot
So let's find a shady tree.
Oh look, there's a perfect one
Hey, come follow me!

Shhh! Whisper!
I see a rabbit eating grass.
So we don't disturb him
Let's tiptoe as we go past.
Now, on to the tree
And there we'll take a rest.
Let's just lie down there
Hey, look up! I see a nest.

Birds are flying over me
As they look for bits of twig
To add to their nest
To make it nice and big.

A squirrel is climbing down the trunk
Let's try not to make a fuss.
If we are very quiet
She might crawl over to us.

Keep still, here *she* comes!
Creeping neater and nearer to you.
Close your eyes. listen for *her*.
Can you feel *her* tickle too?

We fall asleep under the tree
And soon the afternoon is gone.
And as we walk toward home again
We can count as stars turn on.

(*The Giant Encyclopedia of Circle Time and Group Activities for Children 3 to 6*, Kathy
Charner, editor. Beltsville, MD: Gryphon House, 1996; p. 283. Used with permission.)

What's in the Soil? Fill a bucket with dry soil from a garden or yard. Pour the soil into the sensory table. Ask the children what they think is in the soil. Invite the children to sift the soil using colanders, sieves, and strainers. Children may find small rocks, sand, earthworms, grubs, or ants. Encourage the children to look up the insects in resource books. Ask the children to be gentle with the insects and to return them to the outdoors. Children can continue sifting through the soil.

Science

Compost Pile. Nature has a way of renewing itself. Each year leaves fall off the trees. They form a mat on the ground. The leaves help keep the soil from drying out and prevent weeds from growing. Over time they decompose, making the soil rich and crumbly. We can recycle our yard waste and food scraps by composting them. There are many ways to make a compost pile. You could dig a 6-inch hole, make a pile of leaves, or make a bin to hold the waste. Add leaves, grass clippings, plant trimmings, and food waste. The only things that should not go into a compost pile are oily and greasy foods, dairy products, meat, and animal feces. The smaller the pieces of scraps, the quicker they will decompose. Keep the pile wet like a damp sponge and turn it over once a week.

Glycerin Leaves. Prune a small branch with leaves on it from a tree or shrub or find a small branch with leaves on it that has fallen to the ground. Tap the end of the branch with a hammer to crush it. In a jar, mix one part glycerin and two parts water. Set the branch in the jar. The glycerin will keep the leaves from drying out. This is a great activity to do in the fall as a way of preserving the fall colors.

Log Rubbings. Bring in some firewood with bark of varying texture. Invite children look at and feel the texture of the logs, then encourage them to make rubbings. Lay a piece of paper over the log and rub a crayon across the paper to see the pattern.

Nature Imprints. Make plaster molds of things from nature. Collect twigs, rocks, shells, pinecones, branches of leaves, or pine needles. Fill a plastic dish tub with wet sand. Press the objects in the sand and take them out. Fill the print with plaster and let it harden (about 10 minutes). The children can compare the plaster molds with the real objects.

Nature's Water Cleaning. Help children observe how nature works to keep water in rivers and streams clean. Place a large funnel in a gallon glass jug. Fill the funnel a quarter full with gravel. Add a layer of sand to bring it to the half-full point, and then a second layer of gravel to make it three-querters full, leaving space at the top to pour water in. Fill liquid measuring cups with muddy water. Invite children to slowly pour the muddy water into the funnel and watch it move through the layers of gravel and sand. Encourage the children to observe the clean water in the jug. The gravel and sand at the bottom of rivers and streams serve as filters, helping to keep our water clean.

Rock Collections. Give each child an egg carton and let the child decorate it any way she likes. Put each child's name on the top of the carton. Encourage the children to look for rocks. They can glue their favorite rocks into each compartment of the egg carton. The children can compare their collections with one another.

Sunny Reflections. Make cards to reflect the sun rays. Cut aluminum foil into strips, squares, circles, or zigzags. Glue the foil pieces to dark-colored poster board with the shiny side up. Take the cards outside into the sunshine and turn them at different angles to make reflections.

Water Magnifier. Make a tool for looking at objects under water. Cut a big circle out of the bottom of a clean plastic pail. Secure a piece of plastic wrap or dry cleaning plastic to the bucket with a large rubber band or duct tape. Fill the sensory table with water. Place rocks or shells on the bottom. Use the water magnifier to look at the items by placing your hands on the edge of the bucket and gently pushing the bucket down into the water.

What's in Our Soil? Collect a soil sample from the playground or your own yard. Take a cross section of soil at least 6 inches deep. Stir the soil. Spoon some soil into a clear jar with a lid. Add water and shake to thoroughly mix the soil and water. Set the jar on the table. The soil will gradually settle into layers. A layer of sand will be on the top, loam (a mixture of clay, silt, and sand) will be in the middle, and clay will settle to the bottom. Invite the children to use magnifying glasses to examine the layers. Ask them, "Which layer is the largest? Which layer is the smallest? Do we have sandy, loamy, or clay soil?" Repeat the activity with soil samples from other places.

Social Development

Classroom Tree. Make a paper tree by cutting out a large tree trunk and branches from brown butcher or craft paper. To make the leaves for the tree, offer to trace each child's hand onto construction paper. Use construction paper that is skin-colored or in shades of green. Invite the children to cut out the tracings of their hands. Write their names on the paper hands. At circle time, distribute the leaves to each child. Ask the children to hold up their leaves for everyone to see. Talk about how each leaf is important to a tree, just as each child is important and belongs in the class. The tree needs all of its leaves, and the class needs all the paper hands to make leaves on the tree.

Curbside Recycling. Make containers to collect recyclables. In many communities, glass bottles and jars, newspapers, aluminum cans, plastic bottles, magazines, and corrugated cardboard are collected at the curb. With the children, find out what day the recycling truck comes and recycle your classroom's waste.

Earth Workers. Introduce children to people whose work involves caring for the earth and helping others learn about the earth, such as a naturalist from a local nature center, a ranger with the forest service, an educator with the pollution control agency, or a landscaper. Invite them to talk to the children about what they do, what they need to know to do their jobs, what they like about their jobs, and how children can help care for the earth.

Our Garden. Plant seeds in a windowsill, patio, or small garden plot. Plant flowers to help children recognize the beauty of plants and some vegetables to give children an experience with people's interdependence with the environment. Allow the plants to go to seed so that the children can observe the entire life cycle. Help the children take responsibility for preparing the soil, planting the seeds or seedlings, and watering and fertilizing the plants.

Respect. Help children learn to respect the environment. Help children develop sensitivity and respect for the natural world. Take the children on a nature walk. Compare and contrast how many things are done to the classroom pets and garden in order to care for them, but we protect nature and wildlife by leaving it alone.

Responsibility. Help children recognize that they have an individual responsibility to do their part to help take care of the earth. Ask the children, "Whose responsibility is it to take care of the earth? What can we do to take care of the earth?" You may want to make a list of all the ways children can help take care of the earth, or make a classroom helper chart for environmental jobs like taking care of the classroom animals or plants, collecting the trash and recycling, and maintaining the playground.

ACTIVITIES: AFFIRMING OURSELVES AND ONE ANOTHER

Human Rights

Every person needs clean air to breathe, clean water to drink, and clean soil for growing food and plants.

BARRIER: When we don't take care of the earth, the air, water, and soil get polluted.

DISCUSSION QUESTIONS: Help children think about what the earth needs to be healthy. Ask them, "Why do you think that sometimes the earth doesn't get what it needs? What choices could people make to help the earth be healthy? How could we help the earth be healthy?"

Cultural Identity

My Homeland. Set out a globe or a map and locate some of the children's homelands. Show the children picture books of the land, plant life, and weather of the region. Talk about how it is similar to and different from land, weather, and plants in the region where they live now.

Our Region. Set out a globe or map and locate your geographic region. Set out picture books that show the land forms, plant life, and weather of your geographic region. Label your region. For example, you may live in the prairie, the mountains, or the desert. Set out materials in the sensory table so that children can re-create their environment.

Diversity

All Kinds of Weather. To explore the similarities and differences between types of weather, make a weather chart. Depending on the region, you might include sunny, partly sunny, cloudy, rainy, windy, snowy, and foggy. Each day during circle time, ask one child to check the weather. Chart the weather for the month to notice and record the different types of weather. You could also collect a set of pictures that depict various weather forms by cutting pictures from magazines and old weather calendars. Show the pictures to the children and see if they can identify the different types of weather.

Different Seasons. Explore how the earth changes through the seasons. Adopt a tree on your playground or in the neighborhood. Keep a class journal on how the tree changes through the seasons. Take a picture of the tree every month or two. Collect a leaf sample from the tree during each of the seasons and iron it between two sheets of waxed paper. Include the samples in the journal.

Ecosystems. Introduce ecosystems as an example of many different elements of nature coming together to make a healthy whole that is able to sustain itself. Tape a large piece of butcher paper to the wall. Draw a large web on the paper. Tell the children that an ecosystem is like the web of life. The web of life needs all of the elements in order to survive. Invite the children to think of all the things the earth needs to live and all of the things that people need to live on the earth. Invite the children to cut pictures from magazines to add to the web of life.

Many Types of Plants. Explore the similarities and differences between various plant forms. Introduce children to the different forms of plant life. Young children can easily identify trees, shrubs, flowers, grass, fruit trees, and vegetable plants. Take children on a walk around the school and through neighborhood gardens and identify the different plant forms. Take a picture of the plant specimens and make a poster of the different plant forms in your neighborhood.

The Earth Is Full of Differences. Explore the similarities and differences between various land forms. Set out photographs of different terrain, including mountains, seashore, prairie, forests, desert, farmland, plains, and rivers and lakes. Introduce children to the different land forms. Ask the children if they have ever been to a place that looks like the ones in the pictures. Ask them what it would be like if all the land on the earth was the same.

Bias and Stereotypes

Nature Isn't Scary. Many young children who grow up in urban areas find the natural world very frightening. Because of their lack of experience, they think that monsters live in the woods. Take the children on a field trip to a nearby state park or nature center and take a walk on a trail through the woods. Talk about the things you see and the sounds you hear and what might be creating those sounds. Help the children recognize that monsters don't live in the forests and that the woods might be scary to them because they haven't had much experience in them.

Outdoor Women. Children may think that only boys and men spend time in the outdoors. Show children pictures of both women and men actively engaged in outdoor activities such as hiking, rock climbing, kayaking, canoeing, camping, skiing, gardening, and on expeditions. Show the children the pictures and ask them, "Who do you see in this picture? What is this person doing?" Tell the children that the earth is for both boys and girls to enjoy, and that both girls and boys are responsible for taking care of the earth.

Community Service

Hazardous Waste. Contact your local county government to set up a day for collecting household hazardous waste, such as paint, motor oil, oil filters, cleaning solvents, fluorescent lights, and batteries.

Neighborhood Clean-Up. Take a walk through the school yard or neighborhood and pick up all the trash.

Tree Planting. Plant a tree on the playground of your school or center, or participate in a community tree-planting event.

Recyclers. Collect recycling from other classrooms each week and take it to the curb on recycling day, or take it to the local recycling center.

Social Action Suggestions

Dear City Council. Write a letter to your city government asking them to set up a curbside recycling program.

Is Our School an Environmental Hazard? Write a letter to school officials requesting that they test for asbestos or radon in the building, or test the paint and drinking water for lead.

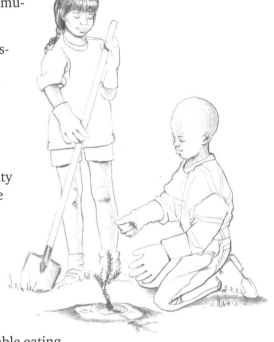

No Disposables. Protest the use of disposable eating utensils, paper plates, and Styrofoam cups at your school or center. Advocate for reusable utensils and dishes.

Pollution Solution. Ask someone from the local environmental protection agency or an environmental group to talk to the children about what they can do if they discover that someone or a local business is polluting the earth.

School Recycling. Set up a recycling program at your school or center.

ACTIVITIES: OPENING THE DOOR

Classroom Visitors

Ask gardeners, park rangers, naturalists, or activists for environmental organizations to come to the classroom and talk about their work and what children can do to care for the environment.

Field Trips

Take a trip to a local nature center, state park, or national forest.

Parent Involvement

Invite parents or grandparents who are gardeners to share their skills with the children. Ask parents or grandparents who are concerned about the environment to share ways that their family recycles, reuses, reduces, or conserves natural resources.

Parent Education

Invite a naturalist to talk about sharing nature with the children. Or invite a home economist or someone from the local pollution control agency to talk about healthy ways to clean homes using natural and nontoxic products.

CLASSROOM RESOURCES

Children's Books

A B Cedar: An Alphabet Of Trees, George Ella Lyon (New York: Orchard, 1989).

Aani And The Tree Huggers, Jeannine Atkins (New York: Lee, 1995).

Alaska's Three Bears, Shannon Cartwright (Homer, AK: Paw IV, 1990).

Alejandro's Gift, Richard E. Alpert.

America: My Land, Your Land, Our Land, W. Nikola-Lisa (New York: Lee, 1997).

America The Beautiful, Katherine Lee Bates.

The Boy Who Loved Morning, Shannon Jacobs (Boston: Little Brown, 1993).

The Cherry Tree, Ruskin Bond (Honesdale, PA: Caroline, 1991).

Counting Wildflowers, Bruce McMillan (New York: Lothrop, 1997).

The Desert Is My Mother, Pat Mora (Houston: Piñata, 1994).

The Desert Mermaid, Alberto Blanco (San Francisco: Children's Book, 1992).

The Dreamer, Cythia Rylant (New York: Blue Sky, 1993).

The Earth And I, Frank Asch (San Diego: Gulliver, 1994).

Earth Dance, Joanne Ryder (New York: Holt, 1996).

Fernando's Gift, Douglas Keister (San Francisco: Sierra, 1995).

Flower Garden, Eve Bunting (San Diego: Harcourt, 1994).

Four Ancestors, Joseph Bruchac (Mahwah, NJ: BridgeWater, 1996).

Giving Thanks: A Native American Good Morning Message, Chief Jake Swamp (New York: Lee, 1995).

The Great Kapok Tree: A Tale Of The Amazon Rain Forest, Lynne Cherry (San Diego: Harcourt, 1990).

Have You Seen Trees? Joanne Oppenheim (New York: Scholastic, 1995).

How Does The Wind Walk? Nancy White Carlstrom (New York: Macmillan, 1993).

How We Came To The Fifth World, Harriet Rohmer and Mary Anchondo (San Francisco: Children's Book, 1988).

I Celebrate Nature, Diane Iverson (Nevada City, CA: Dawn, 1993).

I Love You, Sun—I Love You, Moon, Karen Pandell (New York: Putnam, 1994).

In The Small, Small Pond, Denise Fleming (New York: Holt, 1993).

The Kingdom Of The Singing Birds, Miriam Aroner (Rockville, MD: Kar-Ben, 1993).

Listen To The Desert, Pat Mora (New York: Clarion, 1994).

The Lorax, Dr. Seuss (New York: Random, 1971).

My River, Shari Halpern (New York: Macmillan, 1992).

North Country Spring, Reeve Lindbergh (Boston: Houghton, 1997).

The People Who Hugged The Trees, Deborah Lee Rose (Boulder, CO: Roberts Rinehart, 1990).

Peter's Place, Sally Grindley (San Diego: Harcourt, 1996).

Planting A Rainbow, Lois Ehlert (San Diego: Harcourt, 1988).

Red Leaf, Yellow Leaf, Lois Ehlert (San Diego: Harcourt, 1991).

A River Ran Wild: An Environmental History, Lynne Cherry (San Diego: Harcourt, 1992).

Roses for Gita, Rachna Gilmore (London: Mantra, 1996).

Save My Rain Forest, Monica Zak (Santa Cruz, CA: Volcano, 1992).

The Sky, Ariane Dewey (New York: Simon, 1993).

Someday A Tree, Eve Bunting (New York: Clarion, 1993).

Thirteen Moons On Turtle's Back, Joseph Bruchac and Jonathon London (New York: Philomel, 1997).

This Year's Garden, Cythia Rylant (New York: Bradbury, 1984).

Weather, Seymour Simon (New York: Morrow, 1993).

What Is The Sun? Reeve Lindbergh (Cambridge, MA: Candlewick, 1996).

Why The Sky Is Far Away, Mary-Joan Gerson (San Diego: Harcourt, 1974).

Wind, Ron Bacon.

Windsongs And Rainbows, Burton Albert (New York: Simon, 1993).

A Winter Walk, Lynne Barasch (New York: Ticknor, 1993).

Music

Allen, Lillian. *Nothing But A Hero* (Redwood, 1991).

"I Dream A Redwood"

"Mother Earth"

Bonkrude, Sally. *Celebrating Differences With Sally B* (Musical Imaginings, 1992).

"Snowflakes"

Fink, Cathy, and Marcy Marxer. *Nobody Else Like Me* (A&M, 1994).

"May There Always Be Sunshine"

Gibson, Dan. *Solitudes* (Dan Gibson Productions, 1981).

Hartmann, Jack. *Let's Read Together And Other Songs For Sharing And Caring* (Educational Activities, 1990).

"Save The World"

————. *Make A Friend, Be A Friend* (Educational Activities, 1990).

"Sunshine Sun On Me"

Hinojosa, Tish. *Cada Niño/Every Child* (Rounder, 1996).

"Magnolia"

"Quien/Who"

Hooper, Richard. *Earth, Sea, And Sky* (World Disc/Nature Recordings, 1990).

Hunter, Tom. *Bits And Pieces* (Song Growing, 1990).

"The Rain Is Running Down The Sky"

Music For Little People. *Peace Is The World Smiling* (Music for Little People, 1989).

"Hug The Earth"

"The Whale Gulch Rap"

Pirtle, Sarah. *Two Hands Hold The Earth* (Gentle Wind, 1984).

"My Roots Go Down"

"Two Hands Hold The Earth"

"The Moon's Lullaby"

Raffi. *Baby Beluga* (Troubadour, 1980).

"Thanks A Lot"

————. *Rise and Shine* (Troubadour, 1982).

"He's Got The Whole World"

Rainforest (Ryko, 1990).

Rogers, Sally. *Peace By Peace* (Western, 1988).

"It's A Miracle"

Sounds of Nature Sampler (Special Music, 1990).

Sweet Honey In The Rock. *I Got Shoes* (Music for Little People, 1994).

"Look! Look! The Sun Woke Up!"

Thomas, Marlo, and Friends. *Free To Be...A Family* (A&M, 1988).

"On My Pond"

Tropical Rainforest (Gateway, 1970).

Visual Displays

Beckley-Cardy
Leaves of North America
Rain Forests of the World Poster

Edvantage
Our Environment Discovery Posters Theme Pack

Northern Sun Merchandising
Poster of the Earth

Sandy and Son
Fragile Earth Poster

Videos

Everything Grows, Hullabaloo Videos (Educational Record Center, 1995).

Eyewitness Living Earth Video Series (Educational Record Center, 1996).

Nature Friends, Hullabaloo Videos (Educational Record Center, 1995).

On The Day You Were Born (Educational Record Center, 1996).

Which Way Weather? (Bo Peep Productions).

Computer Software

A World of Plants CD-ROM, Beckley-Cardy

Seasons CD-ROM, Beckley-Cardy

Teaching Kits

Graeme, Jocelyn, and Ruth Fahlman. *Hand In Hand: Multicultural Experiences For Young Children* (Reading, MA: Addison-Wesley, 1990).

Additional Resources

Rain Forest Alliance
65 Bleeker Street
New York, NY 10012
(212) 677-1900
A membership organization that offers school-wide recycling programs.

National Arbor Day Foundation
100 Arbor Avenue
Nebraska City, NE 68410

America the Beautiful Fund
219 Shoreham Building
Washington, DC 20005
(205) 638-1649

U.S. Environmental Protection Agency
Office of Environmental Education
401 M Street SW
Washington, DC 20460
(202) 260-8749

Insect Lore
P.O. Box 1535
Shafter, CA 93263
(800) Live Bug
Offers a wide selection of science materials such as children's books, reference books, science kits, and puppets.

Earth Foundation
5151 Mitchelldale, Suite B-11
Houston, Texas 77092
(800) 5MONKEY
A project to support the efforts of The Nature Conservancy's Adopt an Acre rain forest project, Rescue the Reef campaign, and the ABCs Conservation Project for teaching about nature in early childhood education.

Wee Recyclers Early Childhood Program
Wisconsin Department of Administration
Document Sales
202 South Thornton Avenue
P.O. Box 7840
Madison, WI 53707-7840
Offers a recycling curriculum specifically designed for early childhood education.

RESOURCES
AND REFERENCES

Educational Supply Companies

Early childhood educational supply companies began making multicultural materials in the mid- to late eighties. Today most suppliers carry very similar materials, but there are a few standouts that are worth mentioning.

Lakeshore Learning Materials carries the most complete selection of multicultural teaching materials and seems to put the most effort into the development of new products. Lakeshore recently came out with children puppets that are exceptional, and they are the only major supplier to have developed their own skin-colored art materials. Their people-colors paints, crayons, and papers are the most realistic and include the greatest number of colors. Lakeshore also has decent anatomically correct, multiethnic baby dolls and school dolls. Their block play people figures are by far the best. They are three dimensional, plastic, and include people of all colors, abilities, and ages, all with natural facial expressions. And to top it off, some of the women are wearing pants.

Other companies also offer fine materials and excel in certain areas. Look to Scholastic to produce some of the best photographs in the industry. The bright, clear faces of children are available in posters, children's books, and classroom magazines like *Let's Find Out, Parent and Child*, and *Early Childhood Today*. Constructive Playthings offers the widest array of multiethnic pretend food. Sandy and Son has the best multiethnic puzzles. Kaplan has wonderful puzzles of children with disabilities. Environments carries the best animal figures and environmental teaching materials. They also have some very interesting multicultural clothes that are cultural without being stereotypic. If you are interested in using persona dolls, check out People of Every Stripe. Their cloth dolls are perfect for storytelling, and they'll custom make a doll to fit your specific need. They're also the friendliest folks around.

Resources and
References

EDUCATIONAL
SUPPLY COMPANIES

ABC School Supply Inc.
3312 North Berkeley Lake Road
Duluth, GA 30136-9419
(800) 669-4222
Fax: (800) 933-2987
A good resource for multiethnic people
cutouts, posters, Spanish/English ABC
charts, and posters.

African American Images
1909 West 95th Street, Dept. A-Am
Chicago, IL 60643
(800) 552-1991
A large selection of posters, Kwanzaa
materials, and books on African American
culture for both children and adults.

American Academic Supplies
P.O. Box 339
Cary, IL 60013-0339
(800) 325-9118
Fax: (800) 437-8028
E-mail: amacad@aol.com

American Guidance Service (AGS)
4201 Woodland Road
P.O. Box 99
Circle Pines, MN 55014-1796
(800) 328-2560
Fax: (612) 786-9077
E-mail: ags@skypoint.com
Web site: www.agsnet.com
A great resource for teaching kits that support
social and emotional development.

Animal Town
P.O. Box 757
Greenland, NH 03840
(800) 445-8642
Specializes in games and books on
cooperative family activities.

**Arab World and Islamic Resources and
School Services**
2095 Rose Street, Suite 4
Berkeley, CA 94709
(510) 704-0517
A collection of books, posters, and curriculum
materials that relate to Arabic cultures.

Asian American Curriculum Project
234 Main Street
San Mateo, CA 94401
(800) 874-2242
Fax: (415) 343-5711
E-mail: aacp@best.com
A nice selection of books on Asian American
culture for both adults and children. They
also carry Asian American dolls.

Beckley-Cardy Group
1 East First Street
Duluth, MN 55802
(800) 227-1178
Fax: (888) 454-1417
A general school supply company that offers a
wide selection of science materials, posters,
computer software, Playmobil sets, and the
Dinkytown Day Care kids play set.

Bo Peep Productions
P.O. Box 982
Eureka, MT 59917
(800) 532-0420
A producer and distributor of fine early
childhood educational videos.

Childswork/Childsplay
c/o Genesis Direct, Inc.
100 Plaza Drive
Secaucus, NJ 07094-3613
(800) 962-1141
A distributor of board games, children's
books, posters, and resource materials that
help children manage their feelings, learn
nonviolent problem solving, and improve
their social skills.

Constructive Playthings
1227 East 119th Street
Grandview, MO 64030-1117
(800) 448-4115
Fax: (816) 761-9295
A school supply company that includes a
variety of multicultural materials. They offer
posters, videos, art stencils, paint sponges,
wooden figures of special needs children,
flannel board sets, food sets, puzzles, and
computer software.

Educational Activities Inc.
P.O. Box 87
Baldwin, NY 11510
(800) 645-3739
Fax: (516) 623-9282
A good source for a wide selection of
children's music and videos.

Educational Equity Concepts Inc.
114 East 32 Street, Suite 701
New York, NY 10016
(212) 725-1803
Develops and distributes materials that support nonsexist, gender-fair, and disability-aware curriculum materials.

Educational Record Center
3233 Burnt Mill Drive, Suite 100
Wilmington, NC 28403
(800) 438-1637

Edvantage
5806 West 36th Street
St. Louis Park, MN 55416
(800) 966-1561
A school supply company that carries a wide range of materials, including a set of feelings puppets and flannel board sets.

Environments Inc.
P.O. Box 1348
Beaufort Industrial Park
Beaufort, SC 29901-1348
(800) EI CHILD
Fax: (800) EI Fax Us
The most beautiful school supply catalog. Carries the best collections of animals and environmental teaching materials. Also carries great dress up clothes and fabric banners for the classroom.

Gryphon House Inc.
P.O. Box 207
Beltsville, MD 20704-0207
(800) 638-0928
Fax: (301) 595-0051
E-mail: leah@ghbooks.com
Web site: www.ghbooks.com
A publisher and distributor of children's books and curriculum books for teachers. Staff carefully selects children's books for both diversity and literary value.

J. L. Hammett Company
Hoovers Brothers
2050 Postal Way
Dallas, TX 75212
(800) 333-4600

Kaplan School Supply
Box 609
Lewisville, NC 27023
(800) 334-2014
A school supply catalog that includes a number of multicultural materials, including holiday videos, puzzles, and painting sponges. Great puzzle sets of children with special needs and wooden barns and silos. Some of their multicultural kits tend to be stereotypic.

Kimbo Educational
P.O. Box 477
Long Branch, NJ 07740-0477
(800) 631-2187
Fax: (732) 870-3340
A wide selection of children's music and videos.

Knowledge Unlimited
P.O. Box 52
Madison, WI 53701-0052
(800) 356-2303
Fax: (608) 831-1570
A good source for educational resource materials such as books and posters. They carry an Arabic alphabet poster that I haven't seen anywhere else.

Lakeshore Learning Materials
P.O. Box 6261
2695 East Dominguez Street
Carson, CA 90749
(800) 421-5354
Fax: (310) 537-5403
A school supply catalog that has one of the best collections of multicultural materials available. Actively seeks teachers' ideas and consistently develops new materials. Look for poster packs, anatomically correct baby dolls, multiethnic school dolls, Children of America doll puppets, block play people, multiethnic cooking sets, flannel board sets, and skin-colored art materials.

Lee & Low Books
95 Madison Avenue, Room 606
New York, New York 10016
(212) 779-4400
Fax: (212) 683-1894
A small publisher of outstanding multicultural children's books featuring authors and illustrators of color.

mpi School and Instructional Supplies
P.O. Box 24155/1200 Keystone Avenue
Lansing, MI 48909-4155
(800) 444-1773
Fax: (517) 393-8884
Web site: www.mpi-ts.com

Nasco
901 Janesville Avenue
Fort Atkinson, WI 53538-0901
(800) 558-9595
Fax: (920) 563-8296
E-mail: info@nascofa.com
Web site: www.nascofa.com
A school supply company that carries a wide
assortment of materials. Good science
resources, pretend food for dramatic play,
teaching charts, and career block play people.

**National Association for the Education of
Young Children (NAEYC)**
1509 16th Street NW
Washington, DC 20036-1426
(800) 424-2460, ext. 633
Fax: (202) 328-1846
E-mail: naeychq@naeyc.org
Web site: www.naeyc.org/naeyc
The largest professional organization for
early childhood educators. Their catalog
contains excellent posters, a car safety
teaching kit, and Week of the Young Child
resources. Shipping is slow so order early.

**National Black Child Development
Institute**
1023 15th Street NW, Suite 600
Washington, DC 20005
(800) 556-2234
Fax: (202) 234-1738
E-mail: moreinfo@nbcdi.org
Web site: www.nbcdi.org
A professional organization promoting the
well-being of Black children in America.
Some lovely posters are available through
their catalog.

New Moon
P.O. Box 3620
Duluth, MN 55803-3620
(218) 728-5507
Fax: (218) 728-0314
Web site: www.newmoon.org
A magazine for preadolescent girls started
and published by girls. Also offers colorful
posters for the early childhood classroom.

Northern Sun Merchandising
2916 East Lake Street
Minneapolis, MN 55406-2065
(800) 258-8579
Fax: (612) 729-0149
Web site: www.northernsun.com
A supplier of posters, buttons, and T shirts
that support social causes. They always carry
a few posters and materials for early childhood classrooms.

Northland Poster Collective
P.O. Box 7096
Minneapolis, MN 55407
(800) 627-3082
Web site: www.northlandposter.com
A good source for worker and labor move-
ment posters.

The Olive Press
5727 Dunmore
West Bloomfield, MI 48322
(248) 855-6063
(800) 797-5002
A catalog of wonderful multicultural children's books hand-picked by an early childhood educator.

**Organization for Equal Education of the
Sexes Inc.**
P.O. Box 438
Blue Hill, ME 04614-0438
(207) 374-2489
Fax: (207) 374-5350
Posters and resource materials that promote
nonsexist education.

Parent's Choice
Box 185
Waban, MA 02168
A newsletter that reviews all types of early
childhood materials. A great way to stay
abreast of the newest and brightest in toys,
books, and music.

People of Every Stripe!
P.O. Box 12505
Portland, OR 97212
(800) 282-0612
Fax: (503) 282-0615
E-mail: people@teleport.com
Web site: www.teleport.com/~people
One of my favorite companies. This small, family-owned business makes cloth dolls with hand-painted faces and lifelike hair. The collection includes dolls with visual, hearing, and mobility impairments, as well as dolls representing friends and elders. Send them a photograph of somebody and they'll make a special doll to match the person.

The People's Publishing Group Inc.
230 West Passaic Street
Maywood, NJ 07607
(800) 822-1080
Fax: (201) 712-0045
A resource for multicultural children's books and resource books for teachers.

Pueblo To People
2105 Silber Road, Suite 101-80
Houston, TX 77055
(800) 843-5257
A catalog company that sells crafts, fabric, toys, and clothing made by the indigenous peoples of Central America.

Roots and Wings
P.O. Box 19678
Boulder, CO 80308-2678
(800) 833-1787
Fax: (303) 776-6090
A good catalog of multicultural children's books.

Sandy and Son Educational Supplies
1360 Cambridge Street
Cambridge, MA 02139
(800) 841-7529
Fax: (617) 491-6821
A supply company that carries quality resources that are multicultural and inclusive. They have multicultural growth charts, posters, classroom pet puppets, and wooden puzzle sets.

Scholastic Inc.
P.O. Box 7502
Jefferson City, MO 65102
(800) 724-6527
Fax: (573) 635-5881

Scott Foresman/Addison-Wesley Publishing Company
School Services
One Jacob Way
Reading, MA 01867
(800) 552-2259
Fax: (800) 333-3328
Web site: www.sf.aw.com

SRA
220 East Danieldale Road
Desoto, TX 75115
(888) 772-4543

The Story Teller Inc.
P.O. Box 921
Salem, UT 84653
(800) 801-6860
A producer and distributor of flannel board sets.

Syracuse Cultural Workers
P.O. Box 6367
Syracuse, NY 13217
(315) 474-1132

Time Life Education
P.O. Box 85026
Richmond, VA 23285-5026
(800) 449-2010
Fax: (800) 449-2011
Web site: www.timelifeedu.com

UNICEF
United Nations Children's Fund
P.O. Box 182233
Chattanooga, TN 37422
(800) 553-1200

West Music
P.O. Box 5521
Coralville, IA 52241
(800) 397-9378
Fax: (888) 470-3942
A source for music-related materials. Carries a wide selection of classroom instruments, drums, and recordings of children's music.

Resource Books

* = Multicultural/Anti-Bias Curriculum Books

Adcock, D., and M. Segal. *Play Together, Grow Together: A Cooperative Curriculum for Teachers of Young Children* (White Plains, NY: The Mailman Family, 1983).

Althouse, Rosemary, and Cecil Main. *Science Experiences for Young Children* (New York: Teachers College, 1975).

*Baily, Cindy. *Start-Up Multiculturalism: Integrate the Canadian Cultural Reality in Your Classroom* (Markham, Ontario, Canada: Pembroke, 1991).

*Baker, Gwendolyn C. *Planning and Organizing for Multicultural Instruction* (Reading, MA: Addison-Wesley, 1983).

*Banks, James A. *An Introduction to Multicultural Education* (Boston: Allyn, 1994).

*Banks, James A., and Cherry A. McGee Banks. *Multicultural Education: Issues and Perspectives* (Boston: Allyn, 1989).

*Banks, James A. *Multiethnic Education: Theory and Practice*, 2nd ed. (Boston: Allyn, 1988).

Baratta-Lorton, Mary. *Workjobs* (Reading, MA: Addison-Wesley, 1992).

*Berman, Sheldon, and Phyllis La Farge, eds. *Promising Practices in Teaching for Social Responsibility* (Albany, NY: SUNY Press, 1993).

*Bisson, Julie. *Celebrate! An Anti-Bias Guide to Enjoying Holidays in Early Childhood Programs* (St. Paul: Redleaf, 1997).

Bittinger, Gayle. *Learning and Caring About Our World* (Everett, WA: Totline, 1990).

Brick, Peggy, et al. *Bodies, Birth, and Babies: Sexuality Education in Early Childhood Programs* (Hackensack, NJ: The Center for Family Life Education Planned Parenthood of Bergen County, 1989).

*Byrnes, Deborah A., and Gary Kiger, eds. *Common Bonds: Anti-Bias Teaching in a Diverse Society* (Wheaton, MD: Association for Childhood Education International, 1992).

*Byrnes, Deborah A. "Teacher, They Called Me a _____!" *Prejudice and Discrimination in the Classroom* (New York: Anti-Defamation League of B'nai B'rith, 1987).

Carlson, Laurie. *Kids Create!* (Charlotte, VT: Williamson, 1990).

*Carroll, Jeri A., and Dennis J. Kear. *A Multicultural Guide to Thematic Units for Young Children* (Carthage, IL: Good Apple, 1993).

*Chandler, P. A. *A Place for Me: Including Children with Special Needs in Early Care and Education Settings* (Washington, DC: NAEYC, 1994).

*Chang, Heddy Nai-Lin. *Affirming Children's Roots: Cultural and Linguistic Diversity in Early Care and Education* (San Francisco: California Tomorrow, 1993).

Charlesworth, Rosalind. *Experiences in Math for Young Children*, 3rd ed. (Albany, NY: Delmar, 1996).

Charner, Kathy, ed. *The Giant Encyclopedia of Circle Time and Group Activities for Children 3 to 6* (Beltsville, MD: Gryphon, 1996).

*Chech, Maureen. *Globalchild: Multicultural Resources for Young Children* (Reading, MA: Addison-Wesley, 1991).

*Chud, Gyda, and Ruth Fahlman. *Early Childhood Education for a Multicultural Society* (British Columbia: Pacific Educational, 1985).

Colwell, Lida C. *Jump to Learn: Teaching Motor Skills for Self-Esteem* (San Diego: Pennant, 1975).

*Crawford, Susan Hoy. *Beyond Dolls and Guns: 101 Ways to Help Children Avoid Gender Bias* (Portsmouth, NH: Heinemann, 1996).

Cromwell, Liz, and Dixie Hibner. *Finger Frolics* (Livonia, MI: Partner, 1976).

Curtis, Sandra R. *The Joy of Movement in Early Childhood* (New York: Teachers College, 1982).

Cutting, Beth J., and Ann Lovrien. *Parenting with a Global Perspective* (St. Paul: Vocational Consumer and Family Education Network, Minnesota State Board of Vocational Technical Education, 1986).

*Derman-Sparks, Louise, and the ABC Task Force. *Anti-Bias Curriculum: Tools for Empowering Young Children* (Washington, DC: NAEYC, 1989).

*Derman-Sparks, Louise, and Dorothy Granger. *Deepening Our Understanding of Anti-Bias Education for Children: An Anthology of Readings* (Pasadena: Pacific Oaks College, n.d.).

*Derman-Sparks, Louise. "Reaching Potentials Through Anti-Bias, Multicultural Curriculum." *Reaching Potentials: Appropriate Curriculum and Assessment for Young Children*. Eds. Sue Bredekamp and Teresa Rosegrant, vol. 1. (Washington, DC: NAEYC, 1992).

Edwards, Carolyn Pope. *Social and Moral Development in Young Children* (New York: Teachers College, 1986).

*Fleisher, P. *Changing Our World: A Handbook for Young Activists* (Tucson, AZ: Zephyr, 1992).

*Fralick, Paul. *Make It Multicultural—Musical Activities for Early Childhood Education* (Hamilton, Ontario, Canada: Mohawk College, 1989).

*Froschl, M., et al. *Including All of Us: An Early Childhood Curriculum About Disability* (New York: Educational Equity Concepts, 1984).

*Gaeme, J., and R. Falham. *Hand in Hand: Multicultural Experiences for Young Children* (Reading, MA: Addison-Wesley, 1990).

Gikow, Louise. *For Every Child, A Better World*, by Kermit the Frog, in cooperation with the United Nations, as told to Louise Gikow and Ellen Weiss. (New York: Golden Books, Western Publishing Co., 1993).

*Grant, Carl A., and Christine E. Sleeter. *Turning on Learning: Five Approaches for Multicultural Teaching Plans for Race, Class, Gender, and Disability* (Columbus, OH: Merrill, 1989).

Green, Moira D. *474 Science Activities for Young Children* (Albany, NY: Delmar, 1996).

*Guillean, A., ed. *A World of Difference: A Preschool Activity Guide to Celebrate Diversity and Combat Prejudice* (New York: Anti-Defamation League of B'nai B'rith, 1991).

*Hall, Nadia Saderman, and Valerie Rhomberg. *The Affective Curriculum Teaching: The Anti-Bias Approach to Young Children* (Toronto: Nelson Canada, 1995).

Harrison, Marta. *For the Fun of It! Selected Cooperative Games for Children and Adults* (Philadelphia: Philadelphia Yearly Meeting of the Religious Society of Friends—Peace Committee, 1975).

*Hernández, Hilda. *Multicultural Education: A Teacher's Guide to Content and Process* (Columbus, OH: Merrill, 1989).

Herr, Judy, and Yvonne Libby. *Creative Resources for the Early Childhood Classroom*, 2nd ed. (Albany, NY: Delmar, 1995).

*Hoose, Phillip. *It's Our World Too! Stories of Young People Who Are Making a Difference* (Boston: Little Brown, 1993).

*Hopkins, Susan, and Jeffry Winters. *Discover the World: Empowering Children to Value Themselves, Others and the Earth* (Gabriola Island, Canada: New Society, 1990).

*The Human Rights for Children Committee. *Human Rights for Children: A Curriculum for Teaching Human Rights to Children Ages 3–12* (Alameda, CA: Hunter, 1992).

Janke, Rebecca Ann, and Julie Penshorn Peterson. *Peacemaker's A, B, Cs for Young Children: A Guide for Teaching Conflict Resolution with a Peace Table* (Marine-on-St. Croix, MN: Growing Communities for Peace, 1995).

Jenkins, Peggy. *The Joyful Child: A Sourcebook of Activities and Ideas for Releasing Children's Natural Joy* (Tucson, AZ: Harbinger, 1989).

Judson, Stephanie, ed. *A Manual on Nonviolence and Children* (Gabriola Island, Canada: New Society, 1977).

*Kendall, Frances E. *Diversity in the Classroom* (New York: Teachers College, 1983).

*King, Edith W., Marilyn Chipman, and Marta Cruz-Janzen. *Educating Young Children in a Diverse Society* (Boston: Allyn, 1994).

Kissinger, Katie. *All the Colors We Are* (St. Paul: Redleaf, 1994).

Kohl, MaryAnn, and Cindy Gainer. *Good Earth Art: Environmental Art for Kids* (Bellingham, WA: Bright Ring, 1991).

Kohl, MaryAnn, and Jean Potter. *Science Arts: Discovering Science Through Art Experiences* (Bellingham, WA: Bright Ring, 1993).

Kohl, MaryAnn. *Scribble Cookies* (Bellingham, WA: Bright Ring, 1985).

Koskie, Beth, and Jacqui Schafer. *Anti-Biased Curriculum: Teaching Young Children About Native Americans* (Minneapolis: Greater Minneapolis Day Care Association, 1987).

*Kubat, Patricia, et al. *Teaching Young Children About African-Americans* (Minneapolis: Greater Minneapolis Day Care Association, 1990).

*Lewis, Barbara A. *The Kid's Guide to Service Projects* (Minneapolis: Free Spirit, 1995).

*———. *The Kid's Guide to Social Action* (Minneapolis: Free Spirit, 1991).

*Mallory, Bruce, and Rebecca S. New. *Diversity and Developmentally Appropriate Practices: Challenges for Early Childhood Education* (New York: Teachers College, 1994).

Marotz, Lynn R., et al. *Health, Safety, and Nutrition for Young Children*, 4th ed. (Albany, NY: Delmar, 1997).

*Mattiella, Ana Consuela. *The Multicultural Caterpillar: Children's Activities in Cultural Awareness* (Santa Cruz: Network, 1990).

*———. *Positively Different: Creating a Bias-Free Environment for Young Children* (Santa Cruz: Network, 1991).

*McCaleb, Sudia Paloma. *Building Communities of Learners: A Collaboration Among Teachers, Students, Families, and Community* (New York: St. Martin's, 1994).

*McCracken, Janet Brown, ed. *Helping Children Love Themselves and Others: A Professional Handbook for Family Day Care* (Washington, DC: The Children's Foundation, 1990).

*McCracken, Janet Brown. *Valuing Diversity: The Primary Years* (Washington, DC: NAEYC, 1993).

McGinnis, Kathleen, and Barbara Oehlberg. *Starting Out Right: Nurturing Young Children as Peacemakers* (Oak Park, IL: Meyer Stone, 1988).

Meyer, Carolyn, and Kel Pickens. *Sing and Learn* (Carthage, IL: Good Apple, 1989).

*Miller, Darla Ferris. *First Steps Toward Cultural Difference* (Washington, DC: Child Welfare League of America, 1989).

*Moll, Patricia Buerke. *Children and Books I: African American Story Books and Activities for All Children* (Tampa: Hampton Mae Institute, 1991).

*Neugebauer, Bonnie, ed. *Alike and Different: Exploring Our Humanity with Young Children* (Washington, DC: NAEYC, 1992).

Neuman, Susan B., and Renee P. Panoff. *Exploring Feelings: Activities for Young Children* (Atlanta: Humanics Limited, 1983).

Nichols, Wendy, and Kim Nichols. *Wonderscience: A Developmentally Appropriate Guide to Hands On Science for Young Children* (Albuquerque: Learning Expo, 1990).

Nickelsburg, Janet. *Nature Activities for Early Childhood* (Reading, MA: Addison-Wesley, 1976).

*Nieto, Sonia. *Affirming Diversity: The Sociopolitical Context of Multicultural Education* (New York: Longman, 1992).

Oehlberg, Barbara. *Making It Better: Activities for Children Living in a Stressful World* (St. Paul: Redleaf, 1996).

Oppenheim, Carol. *Science Is Fun! For Families and Classroom Groups* (St. Louis: Cracom, 1993).

Orlick, Terry. *The Cooperative Sports & Games Book* (New York: Pantheon, 1978).

———. *The Second Cooperative Sports & Games Book* (New York: Pantheon, 1982).

Park, Mary Joan. *Peacemaking for Little Friends* (St. Paul: Little Friends For Peace, 1985).

*Parker, Carol Johnson. "Multicultural Awareness Activities." *Dimensions* 10 (1982).

*Perry, Theresa, and James W. Fraser. *Freedom's Plow: Teaching in the Multicultural Classroom* (New York: Routledge, 1993).

*Peterson, Bob. "Columbus in the Elementary Classroom." *Rethinking Columbus: Teaching About the 500th Anniversary of Columbus's Arrival in America* (Milwaukee: Rethinking Schools, 1991).

*Prutzman, Priscilla, et al. *The Friendly Classroom for a Small Planet* (Gabriola Island, Canada: New Society, 1988).

*———. *The Friendly Classroom for a Small Planet: A Handbook on Creative Approaches to Living and Problem Solving for Children* (Gabriola Island, Canada: New Society, 1987).

*Ramsey, Patricia G. "Social Studies That Is Multicultural." *Multicultural Education in Early Childhood Classrooms* (Washington, DC: National Education Association of the United States, 1992).

*————. *Teaching and Learning in a Diverse World* (New York: Teachers College, 1987).

Redleaf, Rhoda. *Busy Finger Growing Minds: Finger Plays, Verses and Activities for Whole Language Learning* (St. Paul: Redleaf, 1993).

Rice, Judith Anne. *The Kindness Curriculum: Introducing Young Children to Loving Values* (St. Paul: Redleaf, 1995).

Rocha, Ruth and Otario Roth. *The Universal Declaration of Human Rights: An Adaptation for Children* (New York: United Nations Publications, 1989).

Rockwell, Robert E., et al. *Everybody Has a Body* (Beltsville, MD: Gryphon, 1992).

*Saracho, Olivia N., and Bernard Spodek. *Understanding the Multicultural Experience in Early Childhood Education* (Washington, DC: NAEYC, 1983).

Slaby, Ronald G., et al. *Early Violence Prevention Tools for Teachers of Young Children* (Washington, DC: NAEYC, 1995).

*Sleeter, Christine E., ed. *Empowerment through Multicultural Education* (Albany: State U of New York, 1991).

*Sleeter, Christine E., and Carl A. Grant. *Making Choices for Multicultural Education: Five Approaches to Race, Class, and Gender* (Columbus, OH: Merrill, 1988).

Smith, Charles A. *The Peaceful Classroom* (Beltsville, MD: Gryphon, 1993).

————. *Promoting the Social Development of Young Children: Strategies and Activities* (Palo Alto, CA: Mayfield, 1982).

*Sprung, B. *Non-Sexist Education for Young Children: A Practical Guide* (New York: Citation, 1975).

Sunal, Cynthia. *Early Childhood Social Studies* (Columbus, OH: Merrill, 1990).

*Turney, Monica. *One World Many Children: A Multicultural Program for Early Childhood Education* (Compton, CA: Santillana/Smithsonian, 1994).

*United Nations Association of Minnesota. *WE: Lessons on Equal Worth and Dignity, the United Nations, and Human Rights.* (Minneapolis: United Nations Association of Minnesota, n.d.).

*Vold, Edwina Battle, ed. *Multicultural Education in Early Childhood Classrooms* (Washington, DC: National Education Association of the United States, 1992).

Wade, Rahima Carol. *Joining Hands: From Personal to Planetary Friendship in the Primary Classroom* (Tucson, AZ: Zephyr, 1991).

Walters, Connie, and Diane Totten. *Sing a Song All Year Long* (Minneapolis: Denison, 1991).

Warren, Jean. *Piggyback Songs for School* (Everett, WA: Warren, 1991).

*Wichert, S. *Keeping the Peace: Practicing Cooperation and Conflict Resolution with Preschoolers* (Gabriola Island, Canada: New Society, 1989).

*Williams, Leslie R., and Yvonne DeGaetano. *ALERTA: A Multicultural, Bilingual Approach to Teaching Young Children* (Reading, MA: Addison-Wesley, 1985).

Williams, Robert A., et al. *Mudpies to Magnets: A Preschool Science Curriculum* (Beltsville, MD: Gryphon, 1987).

*York, Stacey. *Developing Roots and Wings: A Trainer's Guide to Affirming Culture in Early Childhood Programs* (St. Paul: Redleaf, 1992).

*————. *Roots and Wings: Affirming Culture in Early Childhood Programs* (St. Paul: Redleaf, 1991).

Magazines

Early Childhood Today
Scholastic Incorporated
P.O. Box 54813
Boulder, CO 80323-4813
(800) 544-2917

Multicultural Education
Caddo Gap Press
3145 Geary Boulevard, Suite 275
San Francisco, CA 94118
(415) 750-9978

Rethinking Schools
1001 East Keefe Avenue
Milwaukee, WI 53212
(414) 964-9646

Teaching Tolerance
400 Washington Avenue
Montgomery, AL 36104

Young Children
National Association for the Education of
Young Children (NAEYC)
1509 16th Street NW
Washington, DC 20036-1426
(800) 424-2460, ext. 633
Fax: (202) 328-1846
E-mail: naeychq@naeyc.org
Web site: www.naeyc.org/naeyc

Organizations

Anti-Defamation League
823 United Nations Plaza
New York, NY 10017
(212) 490-2525

**Association for Childhood Education
International**
17904 Georgia Avenue, Suite 215
Olney, MD 20832
(800) 423-3563

**Council for Exceptional Children,
Division for Early Childhood**
1920 Association Drive
Reston, VA 22901-1589
(703) 620-3660

**Culturally Relevant/Anti-Bias Education
Leadership Project**
Pacific Oaks College
5 Westmoreland Place
Pasadena, CA 91103

Educational Equity Concepts
114 E. 32nd Street
3rd Floor, Room 306
New York, NY 10016

National Association for Family Day Care
725 15th Street NW, Suite 505
Washington, DC 20005

**National Association for Multicultural
Education (NAME)**
1511 K Street NW, Suite 430
Washington, DC 20005

**National Association for the Education of
Young Children (NAEYC)**
1509 16th Street NW
Washington, DC 20036-1426
(800) 424-2460, ext. 633
Fax: (202) 328-1846
E-mail: naeychq@naeyc.org
Web site: www.naeyc.org/naeyc

**National Black Child Development
Institute**
1023 15th Street NW, Suite 600
Washington, DC 20005
(800) 556-2234
Fax: (202) 234-1738
E-mail: moreinfo@nbcdi.org
Web site: www.nbcdi.org

**National Information Center for Children
and Youth with Disabilities**
1233 20th Street NW
Washington, DC 20036

**Southern Poverty Law Center/Teaching
Tolerance Magazine**
400 Washington Avenue
Montgomery, AL 36104

Women's Action Alliance Inc.
370 Lexington Avenue
New York, NY 10017

Children's Music

Allen, Lillian. *Nothing But A Hero* (Redwood, 1991).

Bonkrude, Sally. *Celebrating Differences With Sally B* (Musical Imaginings, 1992).

The Children of Selma. *Who Will Speak For The Children?* (Rounder, 1987).

Fiesta Musical, with Emilio Delgado (Music For Little People, 1994).

Fink, Cathy, and Marcy Marxer. *Nobody Else Like Me* (A&M, 1994).

Grammer, Red. *Hello World!* (Smilin' Atcha, 1995).

———. *Teaching Peace* (Smilin' Atcha, 1986).

Harley, Bill. *I'm Gonna Let It Shine* (Rounder, 1990).

Hartmann, Jack. *Let's Read Together and Other Songs for Sharing and Caring* (Educational Activities, 1991).

———. *Make a Friend, Be a Friend* (Educational Activities, 1990).

———. *One Voice For Children* (Educational Activities, 1990).

Hunter, Tom. *Bits and Pieces* (Song Growing Company, 1990).

———. *Connections* (Song Growing, 1994).

Lefranc, Barbara. *I Can Be Anything I Want To Be* (Doubar, 1990).

Music For Little People. *Peace Is The World Smiling* (Music for Little People, 1989).

Pirtle, Sarah. *Two Hands Hold The Earth* (Gentle Wind, 1984).

Positively Reggae (Sony, 1994).

Raffi. *Baby Beluga* (Troubadour, 1980).

———. *Corner Grocery Store* (Troubadour, 1979).

———. *Everything Grows* (Troubadour, 1987).

———. *More Singable Songs* (Troubadour, 1977).

———. *One Light, One Sun* (Troubadour, 1983).

———. *Rise and Shine* (Troubadour, 1982).

———. *Singable Songs for the Very Young* (Troubadour, 1976).

Rogers, Sally. *Peace By Peace* (Western, 1988).

Seeger, Pete. *Abiyoyo and Other Story Songs for Children* (Folkways, 1958).

Sweet Honey In The Rock. *All For Freedom* (Music For Little People, 1989).

Sweet Honey In The Rock. *I Got Shoes* (Music For Little People, 1994).

Thomas, Marlo, and Friends. *Free To Be…A Family* (A&M Records, 1988).

Tune Into Kids. *Color the World* (Endeavor Music, 1992).

Turney, Monica. *One World Many Children: A Multicultural Program for Early Childhood Education*. (Santillana/Smithsonian, 1994).

Vitamin L. *Walk A Mile* (Lovable Creature, 1989).

Resources and
References

CHILDREN'S MUSIC

INDEX

BiG as LiFE
The Everyday Inclusive Curriculum
Volume
2

Features 8 units and a section to lead you through the steps of planning your own inclusive curriculum.

Units include:
Animals
Community
Foods
Friends
Heroes and Sheroes
Money
Senses
Work

Call Redleaf Press
800-423-8309

Also From Redleaf Press

All the Colors We Are: The Story of How We Get Our Skin Color - Outstanding full-color photographs showcase the beautiful diversity of human skin color and offers children a simple, accurate explanation of how we are the color we are.

Celebrate! An Anti-Bias Guide to Enjoying Holidays in Early Childhood Programs - Filled with strategies for implementing holidays that are exciting, not biased, and developmentally appropriate.

For the Love of Children: Daily Affirmations for People Who Care for Children - An empowering book filled with quotes, stories, and affirmations for each day of the year.

The Kindness Curriculum - Over 60 imaginative, exuberant activities that create opportunities for kids to practice kindness, empathy, conflict resolution, respect, and more.

Making It Better: Activities for Children Living in a Stressful World - This important book offers bold new information about the physical and emotional effects of stress, trauma, and violence on children today and gives teachers and caregivers the confidence to help children survive, thrive, and learn.

Reflecting Children's Lives: A Handbook for Planning Child-Centered Curriculum - A practical guide to help you put children and childhood at the center of your curriculum. Rethink and refresh your ideas about scheduling, observations, play, materials, space, and emergent themes.

Roots and Wings: Affirming Culture in Early Childhood Programs - A unique approach to multicultural education that helps shape positive attitudes toward cultural differences.

Developing Roots and Wings: A Trainer's Guide to Affirming Culture in Early Childhood Programs - Over 170 high-quality multicultural training activities and more than 50 handouts. Everything you need to offer excellent trainings.

Star Power for Preschoolers: Learning Life Skills Through Physical Play - More than 60 active games and movement activities that develop concentration, relaxation, cooperation, imagination, and self-esteem.

Training Teachers - Original strategies and training tools that bring a new approach to the how of teaching and also supports professional development.

Transition Magician - Over 200 original, fun activities that help you magically turn transition time into calm, smooth activity changes.

800-423-8309

JEROME LIBRARY
CURRICULUM RESOURCE CENTER
BOWLING GREEN STATE UNIVERSITY
BOWLING GREEN, OHIO 43403

DATE DUE			
OhioLINK AUG 1 0 REC'D			
OhioLINK			
NOV 2 7 REC'D			
GAYLORD			PRINTED IN U.S.A.

CURR 371.9 Y63b v.1

York, Stacey, 1957-

Big as life